Especially for

Marcia
···

From

Mom
···

Date

12/25/14
···

Scripture quotations marked KJV are taken from the King James Version of the Bible.

Scripture quotations marked NIV are taken from the Holy Bible, New International Version®. NIV®. Copyright © 1973, 1978, 1984 by International Bible Society. Used by permission of Zondervan. All rights reserved.

Scripture quotations marked NASB are taken from the New American Standard Bible, © 1960, 1962, 1963, 1968, 1971, 1972, 1973, 1975, 1977, 1995 by The Lockman Foundation. Used by permission.

Scripture quotation marked ESV are from The Holy Bible, English Standard Version®, copyright © 2001 by Crossway Bibles, a publishing ministry of Good News Publishers. Used by permission. All rights reserved.

Scripture quotations marked CEV are from the Contemporary English Version, Copyright © 1991, 1992, 1995 by American Bible Society. Used by permission.

Scripture quotations marked NKJV are taken from the New King James Version®. Copyright © 1982 by Thomas Nelson, Inc. Used by permission. All rights reserved.

Scripture quotations marked MSG are from The Message. Copyright © by Eugene H. Peterson 1993, 1994, 1995, 1996, 2000, 2001, 2002. Used by permission of NavPress Publishing Group.

Scripture quotations marked NLT are taken from the Holy Bible, New Living Translation, copyright © 1996, 2004. Used by permission of Tyndale House Publishers, Inc. Wheaton, Illinois 60189, U.S.A. All rights reserved.

Published by Barbour Publishing, Inc., P.O. Box 719, Uhrichsville, Ohio 44683, www.barbourbooks.com

Our mission is to publish and distribute inspirational products offering exceptional value and biblical encouragement to the masses.

 Member of the Evangelical Christian Publishers Association

Printed in China.

Whispers of Encouragement for Women

Devotional
Journal

Whispers of *Encouragement* for *Women*

Devotional Journal

BARBOUR
PUBLISHING

Introduction

You may be in the midst of education, career, marriage, kids, ministry—or all of the above. In a life full of so much responsibility, how will you make time to take your relationship with Father God to the next level?

This collection of devotions and journal space is the perfect way to jump-start your spiritual life. Whether you're in a new place, starting a new life, or rooted firmly in a daily routine, this *Whispers of Encouragement for Women* devotional journal will refresh your spirit every day for the next year.

These 365 whispers of wisdom come to you straight from the Father Himself. Make it a priority to meet Him in His word, through a devotional thought and in prayer and with space to jot down your own thoughts, prayers, and praises. Every day for the next year, dedicate a minute or two to time with God—and He'll bless the rest of your day immeasurably.

The New Has Come!

*Therefore, if anyone is in Christ, he is a new creation;
the old has gone, the new has come!*
2 CORINTHIANS 5:17 NIV

It's a brand-new year! Everyone is discussing their New Year's resolutions: to lose weight; to be more organized; to spend more time with their family; to quit a bad habit; the list goes on. Most people tackle their resolutions with determination and do a great job—for a few weeks—only to end up frustrated and discouraged because they tried so hard and failed.

The problem is that most New Year's resolutions are goals people try to achieve through their own strength. As Christians, we are new in Christ and have the power of the Holy Spirit to help and guide us.

This year, instead of working hard at something with your own strength, spend some time with the Lord, asking Him what He would like you to change or accomplish this year. And then seek Him out each day for the power to do what He has asked you to do. Philippians 4:13 reminds us that we can do all things through Him who gives us strength!

*Heavenly Father, thank You for this brand-new year,
and thank You for making me new on the inside.
Show me what I need to change or work on this year
and give me the strength to get it done. Amen.*

Creative Image-Bearer

So God created man in His own image. . .
male and female He created them.
GENESIS 1:27 NKJV

We are made in God's image.

Is bearing God's image limited to demonstrating character qualities like love, forgiveness, hope, or honesty? Is it doing good deeds and acts of kindness? Does it mean every conversation should be peppered with spiritual language? Or is there a larger sense in which we bear God's image?

In the context of Genesis 1, when we imagine, create, and bring order to our world, we are bearing God's image. To bake a beautiful cake or design a quilt is to reflect God's creativity. To put a budget together in a systematic fashion, write a report, or bring organization to a pile of laundry is to show God's ability to make order and beauty out of chaos.

As we work on projects and do our jobs, we reveal the Creator God to a world that doesn't recognize Him. When we get stuck, when no idea will come to mind, we can ask the One whose imprint we bear. The Creator who made us and loves us puts every good, true, and lovely thought in our minds.

Father, may we bear Your likeness better today than yesterday.
Cause us to remember that You are the source of creativity,
imagination, and organization. Help us do Your will.

Right People—Right Place—Right Time

And so find favor and high esteem in the sight of God and man.
PROVERBS 3:4 NKJV

When God laid out the blueprint for building your life, He scheduled the right people in the right places at precisely the right times for every phase of your life. He provided favor, lined up doors of opportunity, and arranged for perfect connections to help you construct a great life. God's blessings have already been ordered and are placed precisely throughout your journey called life.

But now it's up to you to recognize the opportunities and meet each appointment God has for you. You must walk by faith, listening to His direction and instruction so you can be quick to experience every good and perfect gift He has for you. God wants you to experience every favor and rich blessing He's prepared. By faith, expect blessing to meet you at every turn.

Imagine what your future holds when you become determined to step out to greet it according to God's design. Remain alert and attentive to what God wants to add to your life. Expect the goodness He has planned for you—doors of opportunities are opening for you today!

Lord, thank You for setting favor and blessing in my path and help me to expect it wherever I go and in whatever I do. Amen.

Flexible Plans

In his heart a man plans his course,
but the Lord determines his steps.
PROVERBS 16:9 NIV

Have you watched squirrels in the autumn? Squirrels are planners: They dash here and there, gather acorns, and disappear to quiet hiding places. They store up food for winter, when it will be harder for them to find.

We can learn from squirrels. Planning for the future is a good thing. What type of education do you need to work in your chosen profession? How much should you save each month to be ready to purchase an expensive item? What do you need from the store for meals this week?

The Bible teaches against idleness. God wants His people to work and to plan for the future. We must remember, though, that our best-laid plans should be submitted to God for revision. Jeremiah 29:11 assures us that God knows the plans He has for our lives. His plans are to prosper us—never to bring us harm.

Make plans. Set your course. But trust in the Lord for the final word. He may change the direction that you have started to go. Remain flexible as His child so that you do not miss out on the blessing of being in His perfect will.

Father, I pray that You will take control of my life.
You take the wheel. I will ride in the passenger seat. Amen.

Pliable as Clay

*"Like clay in the hand of the potter,
so are you in my hand, O house of Israel."*
JEREMIAH 18:6 NIV

God has great plans for your life. He is the expert craftsman. He has drawn the blueprints and created the clay—that is, you. He has a design in mind that specifically uses your talents, gifts, interests, strengths, and experiences. His design for your life takes all of these factors into account to form one master plan for a valuable piece.

But He won't shape you by force. You must surrender your clay to be shaped by the Master. You must give up any selfish claims on fashioning your own design. The clay cannot tell the potter what it intends to be.

Evaluate your talents, interests, and strengths. What are the activities you especially enjoy? What skills come naturally to you? Where do you see needs in your home? In your school? At work? At church? In your community? How are you especially gifted to meet those needs?

Open yourself to the possibility of being molded into the best version of yourself. God wants to fashion your character, your heart, your life. Let Him.

Lord, forgive me for selfishly holding back my talents and gifts, whether out of pride or out of insecurity. Reveal to me my strengths, and may I use them to better serve You.

. . . And Proud of It!

Remember how the Lord your God led you through the wilderness for these forty years, humbling you and testing you to prove your character.
DEUTERONOMY 8:2 NLT

It might be because of beauty, education, profession, or wealth, but sometimes pride can creep into our lives. Pride cripples us. It shoves objectivity aside. Pride makes us less likely to listen to suggestions from our peers, no matter how helpful their advice.

Even as slaves the Israelites had developed debilitating pride. They had, after all, not only survived four hundred years of slavery, they "continued to multiply, growing more and more powerful" (Exodus 1:20 NLT). Just prior to leaving Egypt, and then during their exit from bondage, the Israelites saw miracles that no generation before or since witnessed. Look what God had done—for them! As they considered their miraculous deliverance, they became proud of themselves.

God took a long time humbling His people. Forty years of wandering, eating the same food, wearing the same shoes, and living in tents forced them to leave their pride in the desert. Only the passing of an entire generation brought the humility God desired.

God's lessons in humility prove our character, too. Whenever we suspect pride is worming its way into our lives, we need to consider this pointed question: "What do you have that God hasn't given you?" (1 Corinthians 4:7 NLT).

Lord, keep me from pride. Teach me humility. Amen.

....

....

....

....

....

....

....

....

Breathing Room for Our Souls

He's solid rock under my feet, breathing room for my soul.
PSALM 62:2 MSG

In a materialistic, ambitious society like ours, the idea of taking time to rest and play isn't always our highest priority. After all, we're told that to get ahead you have to work longer and harder than everyone else.

But God, in His infinite wisdom and love, formed us with a need for downtime. He who created us longs for us to enjoy recreation regularly. So don't let a fear of falling behind rob you of the joy and necessity of recreation. Our bodies and souls need fun in order to thrive.

Find some way to blow off steam, whether it's with art, music, or sports. What did you like to do as a child? Answering that question can guide you to a hobby that relaxes you and gives you deep, abiding joy. Maybe you would enjoy watching movies, running races, or playing games with friends. The possibilities are endless.

And as believers, we can—and should—invite God into our recreation times. He wants to be a part of every area of our daily lives, whether we're working, resting, or blowing off steam.

After all, He is the place where our souls find their ultimate rest and peace.

Father, I praise You for the way You made me—with a need to work, rest, and play. I invite You to join me while I recreate.

Trembling While Trusting

And straightway the father of the child cried out,
and said with tears, Lord, I believe; help thou mine unbelief.
MARK 9:24 KJV

Stretched out on the X-ray table, the little girl trembled. Just ten days earlier, four-year-old Karyssa had undergone open-heart surgery. An outpatient chest X-ray had been ordered to assess her lung condition. Her parents had assured Karyssa that the X-ray would not hurt, that it was just a picture. Reluctantly, the girl stretched out on her back and held her arms over her head. While she trusted her parents, her body trembled.

When the Lord looks at us, what does He see? Do we trust Him enough to be vulnerable? Are we willing to obey even when we are afraid? Do we believe Him? The Lord wants an intimate relationship with us—a relationship so close that we will trust Him implicitly. He wants us to be obedient regardless of our emotions.

Do not be afraid to follow Him, and do not let your trembling hold you back. Be willing to take a step of faith. If you are scared, God understands and is compassionate and merciful. Fear does not negate His love for you. Your faith will grow as you trust Him. Let's trust even while trembling.

Dear Lord, help my unbelief. Enable me to
trust You even though I may be trembling. Amen.

....
....
....
....
....
....
....
....

The Temptation to Gossip

*At the same time they also learn to be idle, as they go around
from house to house; and not merely idle, but also gossips
and busybodies, talking about things not proper to mention.*
1 TIMOTHY 5:13 NASB

Gossip usually starts innocently enough. We hear some juicy bit of news and share it with just one close friend, starting with the disclaimer that "I really shouldn't tell you this, but. . ." and concluding with, "Now be sure not to tell anyone else." How often does the gossip truly stop there?

When we choose to gossip, we're wasting time. Scripture warns us not to give in to idleness. This doesn't mean that we should never rest; it means we should find constructive uses for the time God has given us.

Instead of talking about others to others, consider taking those concerns to God. Be the one in your circle of friends to stop gossip in its tracks by speaking words of encouragement, gently reminding those who talk about other people that you'd rather discuss something else. Soon you'll find that gossip is no longer your go-to topic of conversation.

*Father, may our conversation be pleasing to You.
May we honor You with each word spoken and unspoken. Amen.*

....
....
....
....
....
....
....
....
....

Planning for Tomorrow

*"So don't worry about tomorrow, for tomorrow will bring
its own worries. Today's trouble is enough for today."*
MATTHEW 6:34 NLT

The feeling of being at a crossroads comes to many of us at various times in life. When facing any major change, it's easy to lose sight of the present and focus on the future. Setting goals can easily turn into constant concern over what is to come.

Where to move, what career path to take, what job to apply for, and even whether or not to attend more schooling are just a few of the constant questions that can lead to a daily sense of worry and stress. But God reminds us that those worries are to be left for tomorrow.

Thinking about the future has its place and setting goals is important, but these things should not become our all-consuming focus in life. Jesus said, "Tomorrow will have its own worries," so we need to learn to be content with today and remind ourselves that God will take care of our needs. If we trust in Him each day, a path will be made known. And those worries for tomorrow will fade.

Dear Lord, remind me that You are in control yesterday, today, and tomorrow. Help me not to worry about the future, but actively seek You each day. Amen.

Rooted in Him

*Let your roots grow down into him, and let your lives be
built on him. Then your faith will grow strong in the truth
you were taught, and you will overflow with thankfulness.*

COLOSSIANS 2:7 NLT

Dana wondered if her hydroponic plants would be a success. It didn't take a master gardener to see that these wimpy plants were in sad shape. Three-tiered towers of cone-shaped containers held fluffy artificial soil. Limp, spindly plants were fed through tubes that delivered fertilized water to the roots. To Dana's delight, as weeks passed, the plants grew sturdy, with roots deep and strong. The continual feeding of nutrients strengthened the scrawny plants. An overflow of plump, red berries resulted.

Like the puny plants, we may be in need of nutrient infusion. An infusion of His Word can strengthen us from within. When we take in truth, our souls become fortified. Our surroundings may seem unsuitable, like the artificial soil, but He is the living water that makes the difference. His presence and influence revitalize us to accomplish the tasks at hand for each day. Our sometimes anemic efforts, weary bodies, or lackluster minds can receive the much-needed boost to heartily meet the day's demands. An overflow of thanksgiving becomes the result.

*Sustaining Lord, nourish my inner being with Your
Word and presence. Prepare me for today's tasks and
may a heart of thanksgiving be the result. Amen.*

....
....
....
....
....
....
....
....

Reflecting the Goodness of God

*For if you listen to the word and don't obey, it is like glancing at your
face in a mirror. You see yourself, walk away, and forget what you look like.*
JAMES 1:23–24 NLT

Are you real? There are many reasons people wear masks and refuse to become completely transparent, even with those they consider their closest friends.

It's so wonderful to find people who can be real with us. We are drawn to them because they are genuine and true—never pretending. Such boldness and confidence comes with knowing who we are in Christ. As we trust Him to help us, we examine our lives and then learn to shape them to reflect the goodness of God.

It is a process. We begin by looking into the mirror to see what we need to remove of the old person we used to be, so that we can take on the character and nature of God.

Too often, we miss the value of sharing our failings. When we share from personal experience—especially failures—we increase empathy, become more approachable, and increase our "relatability" to others. Let your guard down and be all you were created to be.

*Lord, help me to be real with those You have put around me.
I pray that they see You through me and it
draws them closer to You. Amen.*

....
....
....
....
....
....
....
....
....
....

Harmony in Love

Love from the center of who you are; don't fake it.
Run for dear life from evil; hold on for dear life to good.
Be good friends who love deeply; practice playing second fiddle.
ROMANS 12:9–10 MSG

The call to love in Romans 12:9–10 is extremely difficult to put into practice. Sure, it's easy to love friends and family, but how easy is it to love that person at school or at work when you just can't relate to her? Being polite is one thing, but truly loving that person is much harder.

Paul tells us that we should not fake love. God says we sin against Him when we pretend to love others but dislike them. Instead we are called to genuine love.

The Message uses the metaphor, "practice playing second fiddle," to help us understand how we are to honor one another. In a musical ensemble, the first fiddle typically plays the melody and all of the fancy runs. The second fiddle performs the supporting role, harmonizing with the first fiddle, and acting as the musical anchor. We should always take the second part, putting others before ourselves and encouraging them with all our love and devotion. When we love without hypocrisy and honor others above ourselves, we will live in beautiful harmony with one another.

Dear Lord, please help me to love with a genuine heart
and to take second place to those around me. Amen.

Time to Run

Run from anything that stimulates youthful lusts.
Instead, pursue righteous living, faithfulness, love, and peace.
2 TIMOTHY 2:22 NLT

Nick, Karen, and their dog, Webber, left the city to do some wilderness camping. On the second day, they left their campsite. They hiked for more than two hours, exploring the landscape.

When Webber came to an abrupt stop, Nick followed his dog's gaze. Coming at them faster than Nick would have ever believed possible for something of such bulk was a bear. Even crouched down and running on all fours, it was nearly as tall as Nick.

Nick grabbed Karen and gave Webber a command. Neither Karen nor Nick could remember what they were supposed to do when meeting a bear. They just ran. In less than twenty minutes, the threesome covered the same ground they had traversed over the previous two hours. Shaken and breathing hard, they collapsed inside the safety of their van.

When we find ourselves in tempting, compromising situations, the best course of action is to run. We're no more of a match for the temptation of sin than we are for a wild bear. It's time to just get going and get out.

Father, empower me to run away from
the temptations that I can't resist. Amen.

....

....

....

....

....

....

....

....

....

Passing the Buck

And the Lord God said unto the woman, What is this that thou hast done?
And the woman said, The serpent beguiled me, and I did eat.
GENESIS 3:13 KJV

"The devil made me do it!" It's an age-old excuse that holds no weight with God. When He created you, He gave you a choice. You alone are responsible for the decisions you make, whether they are good or bad. That is why you must carefully consider each situation before you. It should always be your desire to please God in everything you do.

It is important to realize, however, that even though no one can make you do right or wrong, the people you choose to associate with do influence you. Be sure that your closest friends are those who will encourage you in your walk with the Lord.

Where you spend your time makes a difference, too. Although it wasn't wrong for Eve to walk near the tree, it did open the door to temptation. There are times you cannot help being near such places. Be sure to ask God for strength to face these situations. Determine to do right, and remember that when you stand before God, you alone will answer for your actions.

Lord, I know I am responsible for my decisions.
Please give me determination to do right.

God Is Our Real Boss

Put God in charge of your work,
then what you've planned will take place.
PROVERBS 16:3 MSG

Jobs come in all shapes and sizes, as do bosses and fellow employees. Bosses can be kind or abrasive. And while we can meet our best friends at our place of employment, many of our coworkers are challenging to be around. Some places to work are fun and fulfilling, and some are simply miserable.

But no matter what kind of workplace, manager, or coworkers we have, we need to remember that God, in His sovereignty, placed us in our jobs for a reason. Maybe we are the only Christian our boss comes in contact with. Perhaps our fellow employees need to see the light of Jesus shining through us.

Whatever our career, as Christians we are called to a standard of God-honoring excellence and professionalism. After all, God is our heavenly boss. It honors Him when we treat our earthly boss and our coworkers with respect and kindness.

Are you stuck in a job in which you feel lonely, overworked, and underappreciated? Take comfort, knowing that God is with you. He sees you and will give you the strength to do His will—even in a difficult situation.

God, help me to treat my boss and fellow workers
with kindness and respect. May the words I
say and the things I do truly represent You.

Chosen Words

May the words of my mouth and the meditation of my heart be pleasing to you, O Lord, my rock and my redeemer.

PSALM 19:14 NLT

Kim couldn't sleep. She was too busy beating herself up over what she said to her sister earlier in the day. Kim had been stewing in anger toward her mom for months, but it wasn't until she put her feelings into words and saw the shocked look on her sister's face that she actually felt guilty about it. Now it was too late to undo the damage from her careless talk.

The children's song says, "Be careful, little mouth, what you say." Guarding our tongues requires more than merely censoring our words. It's impossible to speak the right words if we're not thinking the right thoughts. The things we think about every day will eventually come out in our conversations. Those thoughts will emerge in words that can hurt others or encourage them, words that lift them up or tear them down. Since this process begins in our minds, it is essential for us to filter our thoughts through God's Word so that the words we speak will glorify Him.

Lord, help me to be mindful of the connection between my thoughts and my words. Teach me to meditate on those things that are pleasing to You.

Made of Dust

For he knows how we are formed,
he remembers that we are dust.
PSALM 103:14 NIV

How easy it is to become preoccupied with ourselves. We women, in particular, tend to focus on our flaws. Many feel inadequate about physical appearance. Others suffer "mommy guilt" about how they're raising their children. Still others experience regret over their career paths. Our disappointment in ourselves happens because we are prideful. We expected more from ourselves and for ourselves. Our failures or inadequacies remind us of weaknesses that we don't want to face.

This disappointment can quickly disintegrate into low self-esteem and even self-loathing. At those times we need to remember who God's Word says we are. Our heavenly Father made man from the dust of the earth. He knows how fragile we are, yet we are the crown of His creation. What great compassion is in this verse! He is not looking for accomplishments, performances, or perfection from us. He knows, understands, and loves us just as we are. Psalm 103:13 (NIV) says, "As a father has compassion on his children, so the Lord has compassion on those who fear him."

Heavenly Father, help me to come to You as a child,
the crown of Your creation; but remembering I am made of dust.
Show me what false ideas of perfection I am trying to attain.
Help me live in the light of what Your Word says about me.

Missionary Dating

Don't become partners with those who reject God.
How can you make a partnership out of right and wrong?
That's not partnership; that's war. Is light best friends with dark?
2 CORINTHIANS 6:14 MSG

Imagine standing on a chair while a friend stands on the ground right next to you. You clasp hands and try to pull your friend up onto the chair. Now imagine your friend on the ground, trying to pull you off of the chair. It would be much easier for you to be pulled to the ground than for you to lift your friend to the chair.

In the same way, it's very difficult for a Christian to raise a nonbeliever to a higher level of spirituality by herself. On the other hand, it can be very easy for worldly influences and non-Christian attitudes to affect the convictions and resolve of a Christian's walk.

Of course we should reach outing and sharing the Gospel with unbelievers, but scripture clearly warns against partnering with them. God's perfect plan is for His children to be joined with those who will encourage and support them in their walk with their Savior.

Jesus, thank You for the plan that You have for me.
Please guide my dating choices so that they honor
You and are according to Your will for me. Amen.

....
....
....
....
....
....
....
....

New Every Morning

*Because of the Lord's great love we are
not consumed, for his compassions never fail.
They are new every morning; great is your faithfulness.*
LAMENTATIONS 3:22–23 NIV

What's the first thing you do when you get up in the morning? Hop on the treadmill? Stumble to the kitchen for a mug of fresh-brewed caffeine? Walk blindly to the bathroom, not opening your eyes until a jet of hot water jolts you awake?

God starts out His day offering renewed compassion to His children. No matter what trials, difficulties, and sins yesterday brought, the morning ushers in a fresh experience, a brand-new beginning for believers who seek His forgiveness. All you have to do is accept the gift.

Are you burdened from yesterday's stress? Are the worries of tomorrow keeping you awake at night? Consider the dawning of the day as an opportunity to begin anew with our heavenly Father. Seek Him in the morning through studying His Word and through prayer, embracing His compassion to be a blessing to others throughout your day.

Father, Your promise of never-ending compassion for me is amazing! I never want to take for granted the grace You offer every day. I'm so undeserving, but still You give and give and give. Please help me to show mercy to others the same way You do to me. Amen.

Rejoice! Rejoice!

Rejoice in the Lord always. I will say it again: Rejoice!
PHILIPPIANS 4:4 NIV

Paul must have really wanted the Philippians to know he was serious about this idea of rejoicing. He says it not once, but twice. Perhaps Paul wanted to emphasize the double impact of what the Lord has done for them—and us. We have new life because Jesus died on the cross for our sins!

Paul was also aware that our actions as Christians cannot be self-absorbed. We must be constantly focused on our brothers and sisters and on those outside the faith.

Paul's command to rejoice affects others as well as ourselves. Smiles are contagious, and true joy spreads easily. When we rejoice, we encourage others and remind them of our blessings in Christ. Those who do not know the peace of Christ see our great joy and want to know what is different about us. By constantly rejoicing in the Lord, we are able to spread the Word of God and tell others about the love of Christ.

Dear Lord, thank You for Your love. Teach me to continually rejoice, and may my joy spread to those around me. Amen.

Get Real

The Lord says: "These people come near to me with their mouth
and honor me with their lips, but their hearts are far from me.
Their worship of me is made up only of rules taught by men."
ISAIAH 29:13 NIV

The world is full of hypocrites. To be honest, sometimes the church is, too—hypocrites who profess to know and honor God, but when it comes right down to it, they are only going through the motions of religion. Their hearts are far from Him.

Do you know someone like this? Maybe you struggle with hypocrisy yourself. You go to church and say all the right things to impress family, friends, neighbors, and coworkers, but you aren't really sure what church and God are all about or how faith applies to your life.

Take the time to find out who God is, what He has done for you, and why He is worthy of your devotion. Following God is not about a bunch of man-made rules. He loves you; He sent His Son to die for you; and He longs to have a deep, personal relationship with you. Get real with God and get real with yourself!

Dear God, reveal Yourself to me. Show me who You are and show me how to live so that I honor You not only with my lips, but with my heart as well. Amen.

Facing Grace and Truth

And the Word became flesh and dwelt among us, and we beheld His glory,
the glory as of the only begotten of the Father, full of grace and truth.
JOHN 1:14 NKJV

In the life of Jesus, we behold the glory of the Father. The Word became flesh so that we could know God intimately. We see in Jesus what the Father is like. The Incarnation shows us that God is full of grace and truth.

When we belong to Christ and are in Him, we are surrounded by grace and truth. Grace is unmerited favor and approval. Truth is an absolute standard, a definitive answer, or a measuring rule. Grace is the cleansing, rushing water of a river. Truth, the banks holding fast, gives the water its power and force.

What does that mean for us in our daily lives? Truth tests thoughts, ideas, and things we hear and see. It helps us evaluate our culture, face our past, and acknowledge and confess our sins. Facing the truth is necessary for repentance.

We must stop denying and rationalizing, and admit our problem before we can truly turn in a new direction. Having faced the truth, we turn in repentance, and what we find before us is grace. Grace forgives us, saves us, loves us, and accepts us unconditionally. Experiencing this grace frees us to forgive, love, accept, and choose others regardless of their performance.

Father, thank You for giving us the Son,
all of Your grace and truth.

Cheering You On!

If God is for us, who is against us?
ROMANS 8:31 NASB

When others believe in you, they encourage you. You know they're going to lift you up, and it helps you to reach higher for your goals and stand stronger against your opposition. It helps to know that they are cheering you on.

Think about a little boy on a baseball team. It's his first year, but his coach lets him know he's nothing special. The boy knows his coach doesn't believe in him, and he doesn't have a single good game all year.

The next year he has a new coach who sees potential in all his players. The coach treats the boy like a star. With encouragement from him, the boy performs like the winner his coach sees him to be.

Consider your own support network. Who do you rely on to help you up when you're down or to inspire you? The Lord is your number one fan. He sees you at your fullest potential, and He's always ready to hold you up. The Bible is a great place to find His encouraging words and instruction. No matter what you're facing, He's cheering you on right now.

Lord, help me to see myself as You see me. I know that You believe in me. I am determined to reach higher and stand stronger knowing You are on my side. Amen.

Speaking Truth

My mouth speaks what is true, for my lips detest wickedness.
PROVERBS 8:7 NIV

Mary sighed as she hung up the phone. It was her mom—for the third time that day.

"Your sister says I'm too involved in your lives," her mother announced. "You don't think that's true, do you?"

Mary hesitated. Her sister was right, but Mary couldn't bear to tell her mother what she actually thought. Instead she said, "Mom, I think you just care very much about us, that's all."

As the words left her mouth, Mary felt her face redden. Once again she had copped out and missed an opportunity to have an honest conversation with her mom. The truth was, her mother's constant meddling was really starting to take its toll on their relationship.

Telling the truth is often accompanied by consequences. When we are truthful with others, it can sometimes mean hurting their feelings or changing the relationship. But the Bible is clear—when we fail to speak the truth in love, we are failing to live authentic lives and ultimately can do real damage to ourselves and others.

Is there someone in your life you are having difficulty telling the truth? What steps can you take today to be more truthful?

Lord, teach me how to speak truth in love,
even when I am unsure of the outcome. Amen.

....

....

....

....

....

....

....

....

A Personal Counselor

*"But the Counselor, the Holy Spirit, whom the Father will send in my name,
will teach you all things and will remind you of everything I have said to you."*
JOHN 14:26 NIV

Isn't it amazing how the Spirit will sometimes guide you right to a Bible verse, a sermon, a song, or a book containing the very message you need to hear? In a bookstore, you aimlessly meander, flip through books, and unintentionally find one—complete with scriptures to chew on—that addresses issues you've been quietly wrestling with.

While it's not always so blatant, the Spirit moves and flows in our hearts when we open ourselves to Him. Truths that we have stored in our minds are retrieved later by the Spirit, maybe for encouraging a friend or for pulling us through tough times. He connects scriptural principles with life situations to keep us from harm's way, to guide our paths, and comfort our hearts.

*Holy Spirit, thank You for being my counselor.
Bring truths to my mind, words to my mouth, and guide
my paths that I might honor You in all walks of life. Amen.*

Works of Darkness

And have no fellowship with the unfruitful
works of darkness, but rather reprove them.
EPHESIANS 5:11 KJV

Have you ever known Christians who adopt worldly standards to attract friends? Popularity and fitting in rank higher on their list of priorities than bringing people to the Savior. Some try to combine questionable or blatantly sinful activities with some form of religion, with the excuse that it's their way of reaching people for Christ. They may even do it in the name of Christianity in order to make themselves and others comfortable in sin. This hinders their witness, and the unsaved still don't trust Christ.

Paul calls this "fellowship with the unfruitful works of darkness." He says we must have no part of it. Making people comfortable in their sin is nothing more than facilitating their rejection of Christ. No favors are done by encouraging any sinful lifestyles. All that does is to make people comfortable on the way to eternity separated from God.

There just is no fellowship between godliness and worldliness. God calls us to avoid the darkness in the world. Jesus asks us to reach out to others in His name through prayer and God's Word—not by lowering our standards.

Father, help me to base my standards on Your
Word and not let the world infiltrate my life.

Healthy Living

Do you not know that your body is a temple of the Holy Spirit,
who is in you, whom you have received from God?
1 CORINTHIANS 6:19 NIV

As Christians, we've got a big responsibility—to nurture our spirits, our minds, and our bodies. God's Word tells us that our bodies are temples of the Holy Spirit, and a temple of God should not be defiled. That's exactly what many of us do, however, when choosing not to take care of our physical body.

In the midst of all our commitments, it is easy to let the idea of our bodies as a temple fall by the wayside. Grabbing fast food and avoiding exercise are certainly easier than carving out time to work out or to cook healthful foods.

The truth is that taking steps toward healthy living can be as easy as adding a few positive habits to your daily life. Choose stairs instead of an elevator, walk to your destination whenever possible, and select a nutritious side instead of fries at lunch.

Healthy living must be a daily effort, but it can certainly pay off in the long run—and be an act of worship.

Dear heavenly Father, help me to make time for taking care of both my spiritual and my physical well-being. Remind me each day that my body is a temple of Your Holy Spirit. Amen.

God's Wisdom vs. Man's Wisdom

For the foolishness of God is wiser than man's wisdom,
and the weakness of God is stronger than man's strength.
1 CORINTHIANS 1:25 NIV

We humans think we are so wise. Earning a college degree or living a long life qualifies us as wisdom experts to the world. But we all know individuals that have a lot of head knowledge but lack wisdom. Similarly, age and wisdom do not always go hand in hand. So what is the true source of wisdom?

God is the source of all wisdom. Man's thoughts are limited and finite. God's thoughts and ways are infinitely higher. Man discovers nothing that is new to God. God existed prior to creation. He invented the laws of physics. He fashioned the inner workings of the human body. The universe is held together by His power. Man can only uncover what God has already established. Scientists discover much, yet still fall short of complete understanding. Man's mind cannot grasp God's ways.

Human knowledge puffs up. It may prevent us from obtaining true wisdom. Only by realizing our own foolishness can we gain godly wisdom. We must admit that apart from God, we are nothing. This compels us to humbly seek God as our only recourse. Let's admit we are limited and glean wisdom from the Lord.

Dear Lord, my thoughts are so finite.
May I seek Your infinite wisdom each day. Amen.

Priceless Peace

Better the little that the righteous have than the wealth of many wicked.
PSALM 37:16 NIV

She sits serenely in the dark, stripped, most basic of homes. A thin, tired mattress; an empty fridge; and a plastic chair are not comforts for healing after hip surgery, but they are all she has. Her mother, frailer than she, sits with her through the long, slow Jamaican days. Her meager, scanty surroundings could indicate a miserable, bitter heart, worn and weary from life's hard battles. Yet nothing could be further from the truth.

Paulette lives a life far richer than the wealthiest of the world. She has what no amount of money can buy—peace. Her gentle smile reveals a soul at peace with God. A settled, contented soul, patient and waiting on God. A soul whose hope in God is very evident. She knows her earthly days of suffering are numbered, but her days of heavenly delight are forever! The sweet aroma of the knowledge of Christ radiates through her warm and gracious character, and her serenity reflects the intimacy she has with God.

A visiting American friend, upon seeing her stark environment, asks Paulette, "What can I get to help you and make your healing more comfortable?"

Paulette sweetly smiles back, "I have everything I need."

God, I am convicted of my lack of contentment in You. You provide all I need. Help me to daily rest in You, accepting Your arrangement of my life, looking forward to what lies ahead, walking in You. Amen.

Light

"You are my lamp, O Lord; the Lord turns my darkness into light."
2 SAMUEL 22:29 NIV

The Bible begins with light. Genesis 1:3 (NIV) says, "And God said, 'Let there be light,' and there was light." It also ends with light. Revelation 22:5 (NIV) says, "There will be no more night. They will not need the light of a lamp or the light of the sun, for the Lord God will give them light."

Unfortunately, there's a lot of darkness in between. War. Murder. Pain. Loss.

Scripture certainly doesn't candy-coat the difficulties of life, but even in the midst of the darkness there are glorious glimpses of His marvelous light. David's sin is forgiven, and he becomes a man after God's own heart. Paul is transformed from a murderer of Christians to a passionate evangelist. Peter denies Christ but later defends Christ to the death. God has the amazing ability to turn even our darkest situations into personal and spiritual victories.

Perhaps you are facing a dark situation right now. When it seems that you're surrounded by darkness, remember that light is both your foundation and your future. Release the situation to His marvelous light and know that He is able to transform it into something more than you could ever dream.

God, You are Light. In You there is no darkness at all.
Thank You that Your light illumines even my blackest night.

Commands and Reminders

Make allowance for each other's faults, and forgive anyone who offends you.
Remember, the Lord forgave you, so you must forgive others.
COLOSSIANS 3:13 NLT

Paul gives the Colossians a pretty difficult command: Forgive others and bear with each other's faults. Why do we have such a hard time forgiving people? When other people offend or hurt us, it is hard for us not to want to get even or to hurt them back. We want them to suffer as we have suffered and to feel the consequences of their hurtfulness.

Paul wisely includes more than the command to forgive and make allowances, though. He also offers a reminder. The command to forgive would probably be rather ineffective by itself. It's such a difficult one to follow that we might be tempted to give it up as impossible. But Paul's reminder, "the Lord forgave you," is enough to stop us in our tracks. Time after time we hurt God with our flagrant sins. We have caused Him pain with our indifference or downright disobedience—yet He still forgives our sins. Surely we can forgive others for their offenses when God has forgiven us so much more.

Dear Lord, please teach me to forgive, and give me the strength to love others. Thank You for Your forgiveness for my sins. Amen.

Equipped to Do God's Will

May the God of peace. . .equip you with everything good for doing his will,
and may he work in us what is pleasing to him, through Jesus Christ,
to whom be glory for ever and ever. Amen.
HEBREWS 13:20–21 NIV

Proper equipment is necessary for sports and hobbies, such as football, snow skiing, scrapbooking, and cooking.

Equipment is also necessary for our spiritual journey. Are you using all that God has given you to do His will? He has given you the Bible to teach you and the Holy Spirit to guide and comfort. He puts people in your life to offer godly counsel. He provides a church where you can worship, serve, and grow with others. He converses with you when you come to Him in prayer.

Hebrews says God will work in us what is pleasing to Him. When He is at work in you, you may be stretched mentally, emotionally, physically, and spiritually to new places. The good news is that He provides you with everything you need. Like a good football coach wants his team to succeed, God wants His children to receive the blessing of living in His perfect will. You are equipped for the ride!

Father, I ask that You equip me to do Your will in my life.

Procrastination

Work willingly at whatever you do, as though you
were working for the Lord rather than for people.
COLOSSIANS 3:23 NLT

Some people pride themselves in being procrastinators. Maybe they enjoy the rush of adrenaline when deadlines loom and the sense of accomplishment when a project is completed at the last minute. Sometimes laziness lies at the root of procrastination—laziness that God says is a sin.

What if Jesus had been a procrastinator? Miraculous healing, earth-rocking teaching, and servant leadership could have taken a backseat to the distractions of the day. Instead of avoiding the unpleasant parts of His ministry, Jesus took the initiative to live each day to the fullest by completing the plans the Father had for Him.

Today, focus on the tasks at hand. Whether it's in your career, family, at home, at church, or at school, give your all. After all, Jesus didn't put off the job; He came to earth to complete His Father's will by dying on the cross for our sins. He deserves our very best, not tomorrow—today.

Jesus, please forgive me when I don't always do my best.
Help me to always remember Your example of hard
work and follow-through during Your earthly ministry.
In this way—and many others—I want to be like You. Amen.

A Heavenly Escort

"Behold, I am with you and will keep you wherever you go."
GENESIS 28:15 NKJV

The journey of life is marked with milestones: the beginning of a career, the beginning of a family, the beginning of a new chapter. It can be scary to face so many decisions and so many unknowns. It's difficult to put one foot in front of the other on such a winding path, with no way to see what lies at the end.

A young woman once moved across the country to follow a career opportunity. Steeped in fear, she stared out the window of the plane as it began its descent. Silently she begged God for an answer to her most pressing question, "Will I feel Your presence here?" Over the next few years that were full of successes, failures, joys, and disappointments, she realized that He was there, in that foreign land, because she was there.

On our journey, there are two things that we, as children of God, can claim for ourselves: God's presence and His perfect preservation. He will be with us no matter where life takes us, and He will keep us securely in the palm of His hand.

Heavenly Father, please escort me on my journey.
Guide my path and reveal Your will to
me every step of the way. Amen.

Money, Money, Money

For the love of money is a root of all kinds of evil. Some people, eager for money, have wandered from the faith and pierced themselves with many griefs.

1 TIMOTHY 6:10 NIV

Wealth management. Asset allocation. Financial planning. What is God's perspective on money? Many heroes of the faith were financially independent. Abraham was a wealthy landowner. Joseph was Pharaoh's right-hand man. David lived in an elegant palace. Why, then, did Jesus say it was easier for a camel to go through the eye of a needle than for a rich man to enter the kingdom of God?

Money is not the issue. It's our attitude toward money that Jesus warns about. When we love money, it becomes an idol that dominates our thoughts and actions. We are driven to accumulate more. Compromises are made. Corners are cut. People are trampled. Greed tempts us to make poor business decisions. Hoping to hit that financial home run, we may take foolish risks and lose it all. Loving money also prevents generosity. We become miserly when we cling tightly to our assets, unwilling to let go.

Perhaps these heroes of the faith were blessed financially because they had the ability to put money in its proper perspective. They loved the Lord above anything else. Money never hindered their relationship with Him. Let's strive to follow their example.

Dear Lord, may I have Your perspective regarding money and may I love You foremost. Amen.

....

....

....

....

....

....

....

....

....

Listen to His Voice

Now choose life, so that you and your children may live and that you
may love the Lord your God, listen to his voice, and hold fast to him.
DEUTERONOMY 30:19–20 NIV

Can you hear the voice of God? Cell phones ringing, MP3 players blasting, high-definition TVs blaring. . .how do we hear God in the middle of all this? Our loud and fast-paced society makes it difficult.

God's voice becomes clear when we quiet our lives and pour ourselves into His Word. Take the time to be alone with God and listen to His voice. What does it sound like? It's unlikely that you will hear a burning bush speak to you, as Moses did in Bible times, or an audible, booming voice come out of nowhere. Instead, you will hear Him speak to you through His timeless, authoritative Word.

Memorize His Word so that it will play back in your mind when you need it. That is how God speaks today.

It's important to note that God speaks to those who are listening. In John 10:27, Jesus says for us to listen to His voice. Spending time in God's Word and taking time to listen—this is how we can know Him and follow His leading.

Dear God, I truly want to hear Your voice. Please show me how to quiet my life so that I can know what Your voice sounds like. Help me to hold fast to You and listen for the whispers of Your word. Amen.

....
....
....
....
....
....
....
....

Our Bodies—God's Temple

*Our bodies. . .were made for the Lord,
and the Lord cares about our bodies.*
1 CORINTHIANS 6:13 NLT

Late nights. Early mornings. Caffeine. Stress. Overeating.

All of us have a tendency to burn the candle at both ends. Today's fast-paced society makes taking good care of ourselves seem like a luxury.

However, God's Word tells us that if we belong to the Lord, our bodies are not our own. He lives in us, and we are, in fact, a temple of the Most High God! He cares about how we take care of—or neglect—ourselves.

With that in mind, we need to consider how our daily choices affect our temple. Are you stressed? Take deep breaths and discover things that reduce your anxiety level. Do your food choices leave much to be desired? Meet with a nutritionist and discover how good food can taste—and how good it can make you feel. Is your only exercise jogging to the fridge for a late-night snack? Do some stretches or go for a walk.

This week, be aware of how you rest, work, eat, move, and play. As you move and breathe more mindfully, you'll begin to sense what things are beneficial to your overall health and to the maintenance of your body—God's temple.

*God, thank You for the gift of my body.
Help me be a good steward of that gift.*

Fightin' Mad

Fools vent their anger, but the wise quietly hold it back.
PROVERBS 29:11 NLT

Can you trace the end of a friendship back to something you said in anger before thinking? Has a hasty reaction to a neighbor's or coworker's action stilted subsequent contacts with that person? Have you ever put yourself or others at risk because you gave in to your anger?

It's hard to think before acting or speaking when we're wronged. Most of us struggle to obey the Lord's teaching to "never take revenge. Leave that to the righteous anger of God" (Romans 12:19 NLT). Peter wrote that Jesus shows us it can be done. "He did not retaliate when he was insulted. . . . He left his case in the hands of God (1 Peter 2:23 NLT).

As hard as it is to follow, Christ's example is our lead. Working out our salvation in daily, personal discipline may keep us from saying hurtful things that can never be unsaid—or making costly decisions in anger.

*Lord, help me to think before lashing out in anger.
Even when my anger is justified. Amen.*

Behind the Scenes

*Now faith is being sure of what we
hope for and certain of what we do not see.*
HEBREWS 11:1 NIV

Movies, theater, and sports productions all require people working behind the scenes. The audience very seldom sees what it takes to bring the final product together. Hours of preparation, planning, and technical assimilation come together before an audience sees a single performance—the outcome of the production company's hard work.

In the same way, your faith works behind the scenes of your life to produce a God-inspired outcome to situations you face. What you see is not what you get when you walk by faith.

Be encouraged today that no matter what takes place in the natural—what you see with your eyes—it doesn't have to be the final outcome of your situation. If you've asked God for something, then you can trust that He is working out all the details behind the scenes.

What you see right now, how you feel, is not a picture of what your faith is producing. Your faith is active, and God is busy working to make all things come together and benefit you.

*Heavenly Father, what I see today is not what
I'm going to get. Thank You for working behind the
scenes to bring about the very best for my life. Amen.*

Becoming Wise

*"Choose my instruction instead of silver, knowledge rather
than choice gold, for wisdom is more precious than rubies,
and nothing you desire can compare with her."*
PROVERBS 8:10–11 NIV

Ann felt as if she were about to take the bungee jump of her life—blindfolded. Quitting her secure job to go back to school to become a social worker seemed the right thing to do, but doubt nagged her.

What if I can't make it financially? What if I'm wrong and social work isn't the career for me? Ann had more questions than answers. And yet, her heart wouldn't let go of the dream of one day opening a home for unwed mothers.

One morning, after a sleepless night of praying for wisdom, the answers seemed clear. She wasn't jumping blindly. She knew she was suited for this line of work. She'd asked for advice from trusted friends. And most importantly, she believed God had prompted her to make this decision.

Wisdom helps us make good decisions and keeps us from dangerous situations. And yet at times it seems so difficult to obtain. How do we really know when we're acting wisely? The key is consistency—faithfully seeking God's will through His Word and through prayer. Asking others for advice. Praying some more. Trusting. Gradually the wise choice becomes clear. God imparts wisdom. It's yours for the asking.

*Heavenly Father, help me to be passionate
about seeking Your wisdom. Amen.*

Food, Glorious Food

As one who is in the Lord Jesus, I am fully convinced that no food is unclean in itself.
But if anyone regards something as unclean, then for him it is unclean.
ROMANS 14:14 NIV

A wise sage once said that you couldn't spell "diet" without "die." That's pretty much how many people feel about eating healthy foods.

Paul writes in Romans that no food in itself is unclean, but if anyone regards something as unclean, he or she should not eat it. At the time, Paul was probably talking about food sacrificed to idols, but today it could just as easily refer to fast food and trans fats. We know those foods aren't good for us, but many of us still eat them.

Good food is better for God's temple—our bodies—and it doesn't have to be unpleasant. And eating right sets a good example for others.

Start small. Stock the fridge with fruit, low-fat yogurt, and other healthy snacks. Avoid the temptation to stop at a fast-food chain for lunch. Instead, bring your own lunch. If fast food is your only option, choose a salad instead of a burger and skip the fries. Your body will thank you later.

Dear Lord, help me to choose healthy food to put into my body.
Let this be an act of worship to You. Amen.

Beautiful for the King

*Before each young woman was taken to the [king]. . .she was given the
prescribed twelve months of beauty treatments—six months with oil of
myrrh, followed by six months with special perfumes and ointments.*
ESTHER 2:12 NLT

Esther was just one of many women who had to take her turn at a full year of beauty treatments before being taken to the king. What a regimen!

Sometimes just one morning at the cosmetics counter in a department store can seem like forever, browsing through all of the choices of creams, colors, and scents. Although it is enjoyable to peruse the products, purchasing some necessities—and maybe even a luxury or two—it's important to not focus more on our outward appearance than we should.

Our King does expect us to take care of our bodies. After all, He created us and desires that we maintain optimal health. However, He doesn't expect us to be supermodels. Despite unrealistic beauty images on television and in magazines and movies impossible to live up to, we are beautiful in the eyes of the One who created the whole earth.

Aren't you thankful that the King of kings doesn't require that you endure year-long beauty treatments or be camera-ready for Him? He truly loves you just as you are—created in His image and loved beyond measure.

*Lord, help me not to place too much emphasis on
my outward appearance. Thank You for creating
me and for loving me just the way I am. Amen.*

....
....
....
....
....
....
....

Finding the Godly

And I will make thee swear by the Lord, the God of heaven,
and the God of the earth, that thou shalt not take a wife unto
my son of the daughters of the Canaanites, among whom I dwell.
GENESIS 24:3 KJV

It wasn't an easy task that Abraham put upon his servant's shoulders. He was to find a wife for Abraham's son, but it couldn't just be one of the nice neighbor girls—she had to be someone who knew and trusted God as Isaac did. She had to have similar convictions.

Girls like that didn't live in Canaan. The servant would have to go out of his way to find this woman. He wasn't exactly sure how to go about it, but he made an important move. He prayed and asked God to give him guidance, and God blessed his faith.

Finding godly friends can sometimes be a great challenge. This world is full of both nice and not-so-nice people, but there aren't a lot of truly godly individuals. Still, God expects you to choose people who love and fear Him to have as your closest friends. You might need to go out of your way to find them, and it might not happen overnight, but if you seek God's guidance and live a godly life yourself, your efforts will be fruitful. You will be blessed.

O God, finding friends who glorify You can be difficult.
Help me to please You and find other godly people, too.

You Are Never Alone

Above all else, guard your heart, for it is the wellspring of life.
PROVERBS 4:23 NIV

Happy Valentine's Day! Romance is in the air, boyfriends and husbands are rushing to the supermarket to purchase one of the last cards on the shelf, the price of roses increases to an astronomical amount, and you are either enjoying the festivities, or you just might be a little lonely or simply indifferent to the holiday.

Whatever your thoughts, plans, and emotions concerning Valentine's Day are, remember this: On this day to celebrate love, God is love. We wouldn't know what love is without Him and His example. The book of 1 John says, "We know and rely on the love God has for us. God is love" (4:16 NIV). And a few verses later, "We love because he first loved us" (4:19 NIV).

No matter what your circumstances and relationships might be right now, choose to celebrate love this day; choose to celebrate God, and know that you are never alone. Jesus promises never to leave us or forsake us! (Hebrews 13:5).

So take a bubble bath, make some valentines for your friends and family, enjoy some chocolate, and spend some time with the true love of your life who gave His life for you!

Dear Jesus, thank You for loving me and giving Your life for me. Thank You that I am never alone. Amen.

Stillness Strengthens

Be still, and know that I am God: I will be exalted
among the heathen, I will be exalted in the earth.
PSALM 46:10 KJV

The radio plays in the car. The TV blares in the house. Phones ring in both places. The computer delivers e-mail and instant messages. Text messages beep on a handheld device. Our modern world rarely allows quiet. Our society rushes from one thing to the next. For many people stillness and quiet don't happen until they fall asleep.

Yet God says He is known in stillness. In Isaiah 30:15 (KJV) we read, "In returning and rest shall ye be saved; in quietness and in confidence shall be your strength." God says stillness is good for us. It is how we come to know Him and gain our strength from Him.

He is the Creator of the universe. He makes each twenty-four-hour day. He rules the sun and the moon, the day and the night. He knows every sparrow that falls to the ground. He never slumbers nor sleeps. We can trust Him with the moments of our lives. We can make time for solitude and trust Him to order our day. We can trust Him to meet us in the pause. He is God, so we can be still.

Father, help me today to be still before You.
Enable me to trust You with the cares of my life.

Pleasant Boundaries

Lord, you have assigned me my portion and my cup; you have made my lot secure. The boundary lines have fallen for me in pleasant places; surely I have a delightful inheritance.

PSALM 16:5–6 NIV

When the angel of God told Lot and his family to leave Sodom, He wasn't kidding. The instructions were clear: Pack up; leave; don't look back. But Lot's wife couldn't do it. The temptation to look back on all she had left behind was too great. She paid for her disobedience with her life.

Obeying God's commands is difficult when we focus on what we're giving up. His guidelines for living a holy life might seem restrictive at times, but the truth is, He put them into place because He has our best interest in mind. For example, sex creates intense emotional attachments. God knows that emotional attachment without commitment equals heartache, so He has reserved sex for marriage.

When we only look at what we're missing out on, it's difficult to see what lies ahead. But you can trust your heavenly Father. His boundaries provide security and protection, and your future holds great promise and reward.

Father, thank You for the boundaries You have placed around my life. Help me to focus on what I'm gaining rather than what I'm leaving behind when I choose to obey You.

Purpose in Creation

*"The Spirit of God has made me,
and the breath of the Almighty gives me life."*
JOB 33:4 NASB

Life can often be difficult to understand. When we're hurting or when we've experienced loss, we find it easy to question our existence and purpose.

Job easily might have questioned his reason for living; he experienced a number of hardships in a short span of time. By the thirty-third chapter of the book of Job, he has lost his livestock, his farmhands, his shepherds, his servants, his sons and daughters, and he is suffering from terrible boils all over his body. His three friends and his wife have suggested that he curse God and die, but Job refuses to do so. Instead, he remembers with praise the God who created him.

When we question our existence on this earth, we question God's most treasured creation. Trials and tribulations are certain to come our way—Jesus has promised us that. But we are also promised faithfulness, and we know that even amid our greatest challenges, God will strengthen us.

When life becomes difficult and we wonder what we are doing, let's remember that God created us and that He breathed life into us. We were made on purpose, with a purpose, and no matter how challenging our life becomes, God is there to comfort and sustain us.

Dear Lord, You have given me life. Let me use this gift to praise Your name and further Your kingdom. Amen.

Flee!

Run from sexual sin! No other sin so clearly affects the body as this one does.
For sexual immorality is a sin against your own body.

1 CORINTHIANS 6:18 NLT

Joseph was young and handsome. Potiphar's wife was sensuous and conniving. When tempted to give in to his desire, Joseph turned and ran for his life. He knew the pleasures of sin were short-lived and not worth the price he would ultimately pay.

Joseph's dilemma took place more than 2,000 years ago. Is today's world so much different?

The cultural revolution of the 1960s has influenced today's sexual moral attitudes. Birth control and abortion options have deceived modern women into believing that sex outside of marriage has no consequences. Contrary to God's design, sex has become casual, recreational entertainment. The world has made a mockery of God's intent. Sex within the marriage bed is beautiful and blessed by God. Sex outside the context of lifelong commitment destroys lives.

Don't buy into the world's philosophy. You are a woman of God, loved and esteemed by Him. God's intent is not to withhold pleasure from you but to prevent your self-destruction. Trust that He knows best. Believe that your body is to be honored and protected. Flee like Joseph did.

Dear Lord, it is difficult to follow Your ways in today's world. Help me to truly believe that Your ways are best. Help me flee from sexual sin. Amen.

....

....

....

....

....

....

....

God's Light for Our Path

So the cloud of the Lord was over the tabernacle by day,
and fire was in the cloud by night, in the sight of
all the house of Israel during all their travels.
EXODUS 40:38 NIV

Have you ever been forced to choose between "good" and "best"? When life presents us with more than one great opportunity, it can be hard to decide what to do.

How do we determine God's will? It's an age-old question and not always easy. First, we must pray for God's guidance. He promises to give us wisdom when we ask for it. Second, we need to search His Word and make sure our potential decision lines up with scripture. Third, we should ask for counsel from godly advisers. And fourth, we must search our hearts to see if the opportunity fits well with the personality, talents, and priorities God has given us.

Rest assured, God will shine His light on the right path, just as He led the Israelites with a cloud by day and a fire by night. And when it comes, His guidance will be accompanied with peace, joy, and a certainty that we have followed One who has our (and His) best interests at heart.

Faithful Father, I praise You for Your compassion
and concern for me. Guide me with Your holy
light as I seek Your will for my life.

Lover of My Soul

*Jesus said to them, "Why are you bothering this woman? She has done
a beautiful thing to me. . . . When she poured this perfume
on my body, she did it to prepare me for burial."*
MATTHEW 26:10, 12 NIV

She understood who Jesus was and what was about to happen. To her, no gift was too lavish. No words were adequate to express her gratitude for what He was about to relinquish—His life!

The beauty of it all? Jesus knew her very soul! He knew her heart longed to give more. He knew her message, beyond any words, was a pale reflection of her gratitude. He knew her soul so wholly, so intimately, so deeply. What a connectedness they shared. That is why He said, "What she has done will always be remembered."

This intimate, loving Lord is the same Lord today. He knows the depths of our hearts. He sees our intentions. Take comfort in His level of understanding and in the intimate relationship He wants with us. Its depth is beyond any earthy relationship. It is a spiritual melding of souls, an amazing truth of a perfect loving Bridegroom becoming one with His bride by laying down His life for her.

Oh, Lover of my soul, You know my every thought. As my soul thirsts for You, so You desire realness and oneness with me. Remove all that hinders that intimacy. May my heart be solely Yours. Amen.

In Focus

So they called to the blind man,
"Cheer up! On your feet! He's calling you."
MARK 10:49 NIV

Teddy opens doors. He removes the socks of his owner, Sandra. He helps her lift her legs, and he fetches dropped items. Teddy, Sandra's faithful companion, has made her life with multiple sclerosis a little easier.

Teddy isn't Sandra's son or husband, but her assistance dog. And it's not just assistance that Teddy offers Sandra.

"Teddy's an ice-breaker," Sandra says from her motorized scooter. "People used to avoid eye contact with me when I'd go out in public. Now they look at me differently. Teddy makes me more approachable."

When blind Bartimaeus heard Jesus was walking nearby, he started shouting. The Bible tells us that "many rebuked him and told him to be quiet, but he shouted all the more" to get the Lord's attention (Mark 10:48 NIV). By calling Bartimaeus to Himself, Jesus made the blind man more approachable. Jesus not only opened Bartimaeus's eyes, He opened the eyes of others to see the one they were blind to.

Christ works similarly in our lives today. Sometimes we look at others without really seeing them. Jesus gives us eyes to see people as He sees them. Once we share the Lord's vision, we never see the world—especially those in it—the same way again.

Open my eyes, Lord, to see people as You see them. Amen.

Introducing Jesus

He first found his own brother Simon, and said to him,
"We have found the Messiah" (which is translated, the Christ).
JOHN 1:41 NKJV

We have found. . ." These are loaded words. The speaker implies that he has been looking for something. Andrew's words indicate a prior sense of expectation, longing, and watchfulness. There is triumph in his voice, and the first person he tells his good news to is his own brother, Simon. The Bible does not tell us Andrew worried about Simon's reaction. He simply talks about whom he has found. He introduces his brother to Jesus. Beyond that point, Christ takes the initiative. He immediately calls Simon to Himself and changes his name to Peter.

We often make evangelism much more complicated than it has to be. Witnessing is as simple as what Andrew said to Simon Peter, "We have found. . ." How often do we lose sight of what we have found while focusing on another's problem? Jesus is not merely one part of our lives. He is the Messiah, the Christ, and our Savior. We simply need to say "I found Him"—the simplest way to introduce Him to others. And like He did with Simon Peter, Jesus will take over from there.

Lord Jesus, help me remember the thrill of meeting You and convey that to others. Show me the things that have lured me away. Draw me back to the joy of my salvation, and use that to draw others to You.

A Perfect Fit

You were bought at a price.
1 CORINTHIANS 6:20 NIV

Sometimes life can feel like a huge puzzle, and we're constantly trying to figure out how our piece of life fits into the big picture. We all have a desire to belong to something special—someone important. Surprisingly, we can overlook the most important connection we have: We belong to God.

No matter where you've been or what you've done, God has accepted you. He is all about your future, and that includes spending eternity with Him. He shaped you to the perfect size to fit into His purpose and plan. And no matter what road you take, He has made a place for you. He purchased you with the price of His own Son's life. And He gave you everything you need to be accepted as a joint heir with Jesus.

When it seems others do not want you on their team or you find you're having a hard time fitting in, remember you are part of God's family—born of the household of faith. He created you and formed you to be a perfect fit.

Heavenly Father, thank You for paying the ultimate price for me to be a part of Your family. When I'm tempted to feel rejected or unwanted, remind me that I don't have to look far to find my perfect place in You. Amen.

Working Together

For we are labourers together with God:
ye are God's husbandry, ye are God's building.
1 Corinthians 3:9 kjv

Isn't it amazing that God allows us to work with Him to accomplish great things for His kingdom? In reality God could have called on His angels to do the jobs He assigns to us. He could have chosen a method to fulfill His work that would have required less dealing with stubbornness and excuses; but God chose to use us—His human creation. What a wonderful privilege we have!

Not only does God choose to use us in His work, He also continues to work in our lives to mold us into the masterpieces He has planned. The more we allow Him to do in us, the more He will be able to do through us.

It is important to realize that God wants to work in and through us all our lives. We are not complete until we reach heaven, when we will see Christ as He is. If we become satisfied with who we are while yet on earth, it is pride—the beginning of our downfall. The more content we are with our spiritual maturity, the less God can use us. We must strive daily to be more like Christ if we desire to be useful to God.

O great God, it is an honor to serve You. I ask You
to work in my life that I might be useful to Your work.

Budget

"No one can serve two masters. Either he will hate the one and love the other, or he will be devoted to the one and despise the other. You cannot serve both God and Money."
MATTHEW 6:24 NIV

A dinner out here, a latte there—a new pair of shoes just because. Payday is more than a week away, and the checking account is sadly lacking. Sound familiar? Where did all that money go? And what does God say about how we handle our hard-earned cash?

Jesus says in Matthew that our love of money gets in the way of our love for the Father. Our obsession with new possessions focuses our thoughts on the money we have—or don't have—to spend on such things.

Taking control of your finances isn't always easy, but it is pretty simple. Write down your monthly income, then subtract your monthly expenses, including tithe, groceries, utilities, and rent or mortgage. Then take a look at the amount of money you have left and allot a modest amount for things like entertainment, meals out, or clothes. Finally, commit to saving—even just a few dollars—every month.

Budgeting is a great way to take away the distractions of money, so you can put your whole heart into the most important relationship in your life—between you and God.

Father, help me to squelch my love affair with money and fall more deeply in love with You. Amen.

Working 9 to 5

For we hear that some among you are leading an undisciplined life,
doing no work at all, but acting like busybodies.
2 THESSALONIANS 3:11 NASB

Kris hated her job. It was her first office gig after college, and it wasn't exactly the glamorous career she'd had in mind. She struggled with what to do between 9:00 a.m. and 5:00 p.m. Should she actually do all the mundane things her boss wanted her to accomplish, or should she spend a more pleasant day chatting on the phone, reading magazines, and texting her friends?

It may be difficult to stay on task at a job that's less than rewarding, but God's Word tells us about the importance of living a disciplined life and working hard. Even if you hate your job, ask God to change your attitude about work in general. Instead of considering your work torture, see it as an opportunity to serve the Lord. Work hard and let your actions serve as an example for others. Be cheerful in adversity.

Most of all, try to see your office as a mission field. Instead of chatting on the phone, show the love of Christ to someone at work who needs Him. The most difficult office situation can be turned into an opportunity with a little prayer and dedication.

Father, it's not always easy to stay focused at my job.
Help me to remember that what I'm doing at work
is all part of my service to You. Amen.

Juggling It All

God will make you fit for what he's called you to be,
pray that he'll fill your good ideas and acts of faith with
his own energy so that it all amounts to something.
2 THESSALONIANS 1:11–12 MSG

Do you feel like your life is a nonstop juggling routine? Maybe some days feel more like a juggling act on an ever-swaying, sometimes-lunging cruise ship. Now that takes a special set of skills!

Most of the time our busy schedules aren't as enjoyable as a juggling routine: maintaining a well-ordered home, endless laundry, career, school, kids, grocery shopping, and don't forget small-group Bible study for fellowship and church to feed the soul. To top it all off, maybe there's a nagging sense of failure you feel that each area is done with less than your best effort.

Know that God will make you fit for each task He's called you to do, giving you the energy you need. What doesn't get done lies in His hands. He'll provide the creativity and resources you need through the times of ever-swaying circumstances.

God, anchor of my soul, steady me through these unpredictable
times. Help me to balance all You want me to do.
I trust You with the rest. Amen.

God Knows Your Name

But now, this is what the Lord says—he who created you, O Jacob,
he who formed you, O Israel: "Fear not, for I have redeemed you;
I have summoned you by name; you are mine."
ISAIAH 43:1 NIV

Do you remember the first day of school? The teacher called the roll, and you waited for your name to be announced. When it was, you knew that you were a part of that class—you belonged there.

We wait for our names to be called a lot in life: when captains pick teams, while sitting in a doctor's waiting room, or to be called in for a job interview. There is comfort in hearing our own names, in being recognized.

God knows your name. He created you and redeemed you from sin through His Son, Jesus, if you have accepted Him as your personal Savior. He knows you. He put together your personality and topped off His masterpiece by giving you all sorts of likes and dislikes, dreams and desires, passions and preferences. You are His unique design, His daughter, His beloved one.

No matter if you feel don't belong, you belong to God. He takes great joy in you. You are His treasure. He sent Jesus to die on the cross to give you an abundant life. He wants to spend eternity with you! He calls you by name, and your name is music to your Father's ears.

Lord, I thank You for knowing my name
and loving me unconditionally. Amen.

I Think I Can

"Do not be afraid; only believe."
MARK 5:36 NKJV

A children's story from the 1930s, "The Little Engine That Could", tells of a small switch engine that is asked to pull a long train up over a high mountain after many larger engines refused the job. Someone had to do it, and the optimistic little engine succeeds by repeating to himself, "I think I can! I think I can!"

Our society is filled with people who tell us we can't do this or that. Maybe you were told not to get your hopes up, yet those who defy the odds become heroes as we see their amazing stories on the news. They refused to be stopped by something that only looked impossible.

Take a trip through the Bible and you'll see that those God asked to do the impossible were ordinary people of their day, yet they demonstrated that they believed God saw something in them that they didn't see. He took ordinary men and women and used them to do extraordinary things.

When you believe you can do something, your faith goes to work. You rise to the challenge, which enables you to go further than before, to do more than you thought possible. Consider trying something new—if you think you can, you can!

God, I want to have high expectations. I want to do more than most think I can do. Help me to reach higher and do more as You lead me. Amen.

....
....
....
....
....
....
....

Owning Your Faith

But the Helper, the Holy Spirit, whom the Father will send
in My name, He will teach you all things, and bring to
your remembrance all things that I said to you.
JOHN 14:26 NKJV

Is your faith deeper and stronger than when you first accepted Jesus? Or are you stuck back in the early, childlike days of your faith?

We each must make our own personal choice to continue to build our faith. Rather than just taking things at face value, we need to wrestle with issues so that we can own God's truths and share them with others. No longer a simple, "Because the Bible says so," it now becomes a matter of, "Where does the Bible say it and why?" Instead of expecting others to lead us, we each need to nurture a personal desire for deepening our relationship with God.

While we are responsible for choosing to grow in faith, we can't do it on our own. Jesus promises that the Holy Spirit will teach and guide us if we allow Him to. He will help us remember the spiritual truths we've learned over the years. Fellowship with other Christians also helps us to mature as we share our passions and are encouraged.

God wants you to own your faith. Make it real with words and actions.

Jesus, I want to know You intimately. Help me to
mature in my walk with You daily. Guide my steps
as I seek You through Your Word. Amen.

Run the Race

*Therefore, since we are surrounded by such a great cloud of witnesses,
let us throw off everything that hinders and the sin that so easily entangles,
and let us run with perseverance the race marked out for us.*

HEBREWS 12:1 NIV

Running a marathon isn't for sissies. Months of rigorous training are required in order to run 26.2 miles. Even stellar athletes can succumb to dehydration, muscle cramps, or sheer exhaustion. Runners dress lightly so they are unencumbered. Cheering spectators encourage them throughout the course. Runners are also spurred on by one another. Running a marathon requires training, discipline, and determination. The cost is great, but the reward is well worth it.

A Christian's journey is much like a marathon. The road isn't always easy. Spiritual training is required to keep going and finish the race. Train by reading and obeying God's Word. Discipline yourself to keep your eyes on Jesus at all times. Be determined to spend time in prayer.

The writer of Hebrews reminds us that others are watching. Let their cheers bring encouragement. Let their presence inspire and motivate. Be quick to confess sin in order to run the race unhindered. Persevere. Jesus waits at the finish line. The reward will be well worth it!

*Dear Lord, help me run this Christian
race with perseverance. Amen.*

My Rights

Don't be concerned for your own good but for the good of others.
1 CORINTHIANS 10:24 NLT

Everyone is concerned with their own rights these days: women's rights, animal rights, workers rights. . .the list goes on. Society tells us to be our own advocates. "If you don't fight for yourself, nobody will" is a common philosophy.

While taking care of yourself is necessary and good, it's easy to get carried away. Through God's power, we need to reprogram our minds to think of others first—before we insist on what is best for ourselves. The Bible tells us not to even be concerned about ourselves. Why? Because God promises to take care of us, and He will never leave us or forsake us.

So what rights do you have as a daughter of the King? You have the right to approach God's throne with confidence (Hebrews 4:16) because of what Jesus did for us on the cross. Trust Him to take care of you, and ask Him to help you focus less on yourself and your rights in society and more on those who are hurting, lonely, and poor who may cross your path each day.

Father, help me to get my mind off myself and my own rights. I thank You that I can come to You with confidence, knowing that You will take care of all of my needs. Amen.

Ahhh. . .Refreshment!

For in six days the Lord made the heavens and the earth. . .
but he rested on the seventh day. Therefore the Lord
blessed the Sabbath day and made it holy.
EXODUS 20:11 NIV

Wendy looked forward to four days alone at the beach. No house, work, church, or community responsibilities. Her plans included sleeping in and sitting by the surf soothed by its ebb and flow, admiring God's creation.

Until Wendy stopped for this breather, she was unaware of her deep need for stillness. Month after month, she had pushed herself, filling every day with activity, shutting out God's voice. Even Sundays had become a chance to get caught up. What she really needed was to stop and rest.

God knew we'd run ourselves ragged. He commands us to rest—for our own good! The truth is that it's difficult to be still and focus on God. There are so many other things competing for our attention. But connecting with Him in spirit is essential for a fruitful life that honors Him. We can't hear Him if there's always a TV, radio, computer screen, or just busyness in the way. He is worthy of our time. Resting and communing with Him is the best way to spend a Sunday.

Father, help me to rest on Sunday, quieting myself and being freed from the need to always be doing something. Still me that I might experience Your presence and be refreshed by our time together. Amen.

Balancing Act

"The seed cast in the weeds represents the ones who hear the kingdom news but are overwhelmed with worries about all the things they have to do and all the things they want to get. The stress strangles what they heard, and nothing comes of it."
MARK 4:18–19 MSG

There are twenty-four hours in a day, but for most women, those hours are completely full of "stuff." School, work, family, relationships, church, and other activities make you feel there isn't enough time to fit everything in.

Life is a balancing act. And finding that balance can cause stress and worry—both of which can cause us to become ineffective Christians.

Instead of letting the pursuit of balance rule your life, start by working on small things. Buy a planner or use your cell phone or tablet to keep track of daily activities. Make a list of what has to be done that day and don't add other items unless absolutely necessary. Wake up five minutes earlier so you don't rush while getting ready for the day.

Most importantly, learn to draw a line between work and home. Don't allow work to creep into your home life. You can get everything done during the typical workday. And if not, remind yourself that the world will not end if work has to wait until tomorrow.

Lord, help me to take small steps toward finding balance in my life. Help me not to allow the stresses of life and daily tasks to interfere with my witness for You. Amen.

Ask for Joy

Rejoice the soul of your servant, for to You, O Lord, I lift up my soul.
PSALM 86:4 NKJV

In this verse, the psalmist showed us the source of joy. All we have to do is ask, then look to God to "rejoice our soul."

So often we get stuck in frustration, depression, ingratitude, or anger. We go about our days feeling defeated, without the hope and joy the scriptures promise us. But have we asked our Lord for joy? Have we lifted our soul to Him?

Psalm 16:11 (NKJV) tells us, "In Your presence is fullness of joy." When we draw near to God, confessing our sin and our need of Him, we are met by His mercy, His forgiveness, His perfect love. In the presence of that love, our joy is found, regardless of our circumstances.

Just as we want our children to come to us when they hurt, our heavenly Father longs to hear your voice crying out to Him. He already knows your need; but He also knows there is benefit for each of us in the confession. When we hear ourselves verbally lifting our souls to Him, we are reminded of our need of Him. Confession is good for the soul.

Father, help me to lift my soul to You, the source of joy.
Forgive my pride that keeps me from confessing my sins.
Draw me into Your loving presence where there is fullness of joy.

Defining Moments

For our Lord Jesus Christ has shown me
that I must soon leave this earthly life.
2 Peter 1:14 NLT

Vicky was a new nurse working in a hospital where deliveries of premature infants left the staff floundering, unable to provide the best care for such patients. When the neonatal transport team came from the referral center to stabilize an infant and transfer him to their NICU, Vicky watched in amazement. The nurse inserted the smallest needle she had ever seen into a tiny vein in the infant's hand.

Right then Vicky knew the kind of nursing career she wanted. She went on to become a certified nurse practitioner who specializes in the care of newborns. Today Vicky works at that referral center, performing intricate procedures with expertise and tenderness on some of the world's smallest infants.

The apostle Peter had his defining moment, too. It wasn't the night he denied the Lord Jesus Christ three times over. For him it came when Christ reaffirmed his apostleship and told Peter he would die for Him (John 21:15–22).

After Peter wrote about his impending martyrdom in 2 Peter 1, he wrote these words. "So I will work hard to make sure you always remember these things after I am gone" (2 Peter 1:15 NLT).

If you experience a defining moment, make the best of it. Vicky has. Peter did. So can you.

Lord, use my defining moments to give me determination
in pursuit of my goals and dreams. Amen.

....

....

....

....

....

....

What's in Your Heart?

Delight thyself also in the Lord:
and he shall give thee the desires of thine heart.
PSALM 37:4 KJV

What is it that you most desire? Is it a successful career or large bank account? Do you wish for someone with whom you can share romantic dinners or scenic bike rides? It really doesn't matter. What does matter is that you are fully committed to God. When that is the case, the desires in your heart will be the ones He places there. He will grant them because they honor Him.

Too many times we look at God's promises as some sort of magic formula. We fail to realize that His promises have more to do with our own relationship with Him. It begins with a heart's desire to live your life in a way that pleases God. Only then will fulfillment of His promises take place.

The promise in Psalm 37:4 isn't intended for personal gain—although that is sometimes a side benefit. It is meant to glorify God. God wants to give you the desires of your heart when they line up with His perfect plan. As you delight in Him, His desires will become your desires, and you will be greatly blessed.

Lord, I know You want to give me the desires of my heart.
Help me live in a way that makes this possible.

....

....

....

....

....

....

....

....

....

No Fear

"When you pass through the waters, I will be with you; and when you pass through the rivers, they will not sweep over you. When you walk through the fire, you will not be burned; the flames will not set you ablaze."

ISAIAH 43:2 NIV

Scripture tells us over and over again of God's mighty acts. He parted the Red Sea so thousands of Israelites could cross on dry land. Daniel spent the night in the company of hungry lions and emerged without a scratch. Three of his friends were unscathed after hours in a blazing furnace.

These are more than Sunday school stories. They are real miracles performed by your God. These miracles were not included in scripture merely for dramatic effect, because God's power wasn't just for the Israelites, Daniel, and Shadrach, Meshach, and Abednego. One of the reasons God recorded His mighty acts was so we would have the assurance His power is available to us as well. When you are facing what seems to be impossible odds, return to scripture. Recount His marvelous deeds. Then remember that this promise in Isaiah is yours.

Heavenly Father, when I am facing an impossible task, help me to remember all the miracles You have performed. Thank You for the promise that this same power is available to me whenever I need it.

....

....

....

....

....

....

....

....

Learning as We Grow

*"But I am only a little child and do not
know how to carry out my duties."*
1 KINGS 3:7 NIV

When babies are born, they cannot do anything for themselves; they cannot walk or talk or feed themselves. As children grow, they slowly begin to learn new skills, like sitting up, crawling, and walking. Later, children will be expected to put their toys away, make their beds, dry the dishes, or walk the dog. But children do not innately know how to perform these duties—they must be learned.

When King David died, Solomon became the king of Israel. Just like a child who does not yet know how to put away his toys, Solomon confesses that he does not know how to carry out his duties as king of Israel. Instead of sitting down on his throne in despair, though, Solomon calls on the name of the Lord for help.

As Christians, we are sometimes like little children. We know what our duties as Christians are, but we do not know how to carry them out. Just like Solomon, we can ask God for help and guidance in the completion of our responsibilities. God hears our prayers and is faithful in teaching us our duties, just as He was faithful to Solomon in teaching him his.

Dear Lord, thank You for being willing to teach me my Christian responsibilities. Help me to learn willingly and eagerly. Amen.

Equipped for the Task

[May God] equip you with everything good for doing his will,
and may he work in us what is pleasing to him.
HEBREWS 13:21 NIV

God knew Paul the apostle would face hard times in his life. This distinguished, well-educated Pharisee went through an intensive training period for more than seven years, living obscurely in his hometown. God equipped Paul because He knew the price he would pay for following Christ: lashed five times, beaten three times with rods, stoned once, shipwrecked three times, adrift alone in the sea a night and day, robbed, rejected by his own countrymen, hungry, cold, naked, and resigned to a relentless thorn in his flesh. Through it all, many Gentiles came to know Jesus.

Hopefully, we aren't being equipped for a rigorous life like Paul's. But whatever He's called us to do, He will give what we need to accomplish it. You may not feel you are equipped, but God keeps His word. Scripture plainly states He's given you everything good for carrying out His work. When you are discouraged in ministry and you want to quit, remember He promises to work in you what pleases Him. The Spirit empowers us, making us competent for our tasks.

Lord, help me to draw on Your resources that I might be fully equipped for accomplishing Your tasks. Work in and through me to touch the lives of others as only You can do. Amen.

God Is Our Rescuer

"The Lord is my rock, my fortress and my deliverer;
my God is my rock, in whom I take refuge."
2 SAMUEL 22:2–3 NIV

Patricia worked long hours in a stressful job, and she treasured the quiet of her commute home. One rainy night, however, she relaxed too much. Before she knew it, her car hydroplaned and she drove into a ditch.

When Patricia came to a stop, she breathed a prayer of thanks that she hadn't hit another car. Then she realized that while she was physically okay, she was still in a precarious situation. Her car was stuck in the mud in a dangerous area of town, and traffic was sparse. Worse yet, she had left her cell phone at home that morning.

But Patricia knew she couldn't stay where she was, so she carefully exited her vehicle, climbed back up on the road, and looked around her. "God is my refuge and strength," she said out loud, reminding herself that she wasn't alone.

After just a couple of minutes, a truck pulled over and stopped. Her heart pounded, and she breathed another prayer. But as the window rolled down, she laughed.

The driver was her neighbor and fellow church member, Wade. "Need a ride?" he asked.

"I sure do," she said. *God, You are amazing,* she prayed.

Lord, thank You for Your protection and constant care for me.
Help me to trust in Your rescue when I am afraid.

All You Need

For your Maker is your husband—the Lord Almighty is his name—
the Holy One of Israel is your Redeemer; he is called the God of all the earth.
ISAIAH 54:5 NIV

Do you find yourself longing for a certain relationship in your life? Maybe you never knew your earthly father and there is a void in your heart for a daddy. Perhaps you are single and longing for a mate, or married, but your mate seems absent even though he is there with you. Do you wish for a child? Is your relationship with your mother or sister or friend constantly draining you?

God is the great "I Am." He is all things that we need. He is our maker. He is our husband. He is the Lord Almighty, the Holy One, the Redeemer, the God of all the earth—and these are just the names found in one verse of scripture.

God is the Good Shepherd, your Provider, your Protector, your Comforter, your Defender, your Friend.

He is not a god made of stone or metal. He is near, as close as you will let Him be, and He will meet your needs as no earthly relationship can. Seek the fullness of God in your life. He is all that you need—at all times—in all ways.

Oh, Father, be close to me. Fill the empty spots in my heart.
Be my husband, my redeemer, and my best friend. Amen.

A Clear Focus

Hope deferred makes the heart sick, but a longing fulfilled is a tree of life.
PROVERBS 13:12 NIV

We all have dreams and a desire to pursue them. But then life gets busy, and we become distracted with the choices we have to make on a daily basis. Do you go right or left, choose this way or that? Too much too fast is overwhelming, and looking for balance can leave us lost, not knowing which way to turn. The best way to gain your balance is to stop moving and refocus.

Jesus is your hope! He stands a short distance away bidding you to take a walk on water—a step of faith toward Him. Disregarding the distractions can be hard, but the rough waters can become silent as you turn your eyes, your thoughts, and your emotions on Him.

You can tackle the tough things as you maintain your focus on Jesus. Let Him direct you over the rough waters of life, overcoming each obstacle one at a time. Don't look at the big picture in the midst of the storm, but focus on the one thing you can do at the moment to help your immediate situation—one step at a time.

Lord, help me not to concentrate on the distractions, but to keep my focus on which step to take next in order to reach You. Amen.

Follow the Leader

Lead me, O Lord, in your righteousness because of my enemies—
make straight your way before me.
PSALM 5:8 NIV

Modern culture is full of enemies of righteousness. We seek instant gratification instead of practicing patience. Rudeness is seen as strength; while gentleness is devalued as weakness. Indulgence is promoted, but self-control is not. Greed and deceit are excused as part of competition. Image seems more important than honesty. Rationalization has become an accepted form of making excuses for bad behavior.

Yet the psalmist offers us hope for learning to live as a Christian in an environment that does little to help us. He reminds us to ask the Lord to lead us in righteousness. Too often we believe in Him for our eternal salvation, but go about trying to live our daily lives as if being righteous is something we have to figure out on our own. Christ is the righteousness of God embodied for us. In Him, we have been accepted by the Father and given the Spirit, who enables us to live in right relationship to God and others. Daily and hourly, we can pray for Christ's leading, asking Him to keep us focused on Him and mindful that we are following Him. He has a path that He desires to walk with each of us, guiding us each step of the way.

Lord, help me remember to ask for Your leading. Show me the path
You have designed for my life and give me clear direction.

God's Goal for Women

For the grace of God that brings salvation has appeared to all men.
It teaches us to say "No" to ungodliness and worldly passions,
and to live self-controlled, upright and godly lives in this present age.
TITUS 2:11–12 NIV

Temptations abound. Sometimes it even feels as though there is no way out of a circumstance without sacrificing a bit of righteousness for the sake of the bigger picture. Maybe it's a white lie in the workplace or poor choices made during a night out on the town. Or maybe you're tempted to spend money you don't have.

God doesn't want us to live as hypocrites who profess to know Him but deny Him with our actions. Through His grace, He wants us to say "No" to the ungodly temptations of the world and live with self-control as an example of Him. He will help us do that. There is no temptation or situation that He can't help us through.

Not sure if your daily decisions are pleasing to God? Ask yourself if you would act any differently if Jesus were in the room. If there is anything that would have to change because of His presence, ask Him to help you change it now.

Jesus, thank You for giving me the grace I need to withstand temptations. Help me to recognize the lies of the enemy so that I can avoid being ensnared in sin. Give me strength to live a self-controlled, godly life that honors You. Amen.

....

....

....

....

....

....

....

The Purpose of My Life

I long for your salvation, O Lord, and your law is my delight.
Let me live that I may praise you, and may your laws sustain me.
PSALM 119:174–175 NIV

We each have so many plans and goals and dreams for our lives, but our main mission should be to live each day to please God. Our purpose here on earth is to worship the God who created us and calls us His children.

Praise and worship isn't just about singing songs to God every Sunday morning. Praise and worship should be an everyday activity. Praise is about putting God first in our lives. It's about doing our daily tasks in a way that honors Him.

Can you really do laundry to please God? Can you really go to work to please God? Can you really pay the bills and make dinner to please God? The answer is a resounding yes! Doing all the mundane tasks of everyday life with gratitude and praise in your heart for all that He has done for you is living a life of praise. As you worship God through your day-to-day life, He makes clear His plans, goals, and dreams for you.

Dear Father, let me live my life to praise You.
Let that be my desire each day. Amen.

No Matter What

Be thankful in all circumstances, for this is
God's will for you who belong to Christ Jesus.
1 THESSALONIANS 5:18 NLT

Sometimes being thankful seems almost impossible. How can I be thankful when I'm working as hard as I can and I'm still unable to pay off all my debt? How can I be thankful when my car dies, my water pump breaks, or my wallet is stolen? How can I be thankful when my parents split up or my boyfriend breaks my heart or my children refuse to behave?

Living in today's world is difficult, and we often experience hardships that make being thankful extremely difficult. When Paul wrote this verse, however, you can bet that he did not write it lightly. He knew what it was to experience hardships and suffering. But Paul also knew the wonderful power and blessing that comes from having a relationship with Christ.

Jesus enables us to be thankful, and Jesus is the cause of our thankfulness. No matter what happens, we know that Jesus has given up His life to save ours. He has sacrificed Himself on the cross so that we may live life to the fullest. And while "to the fullest" means that we will experience pain as well as joy, we must always be thankful—regardless of our circumstances—for the love that we experience in Christ Jesus.

Dear Lord, thank You for Your love. Please let
me be thankful, even in the midst of hardships.
You have blessed me beyond measure. Amen.

Abide in the Vine

*"I am the vine; you are the branches. If a man remains in me and I in him,
he will bear much fruit; apart from me you can do nothing."*
JOHN 15:5 NIV

Fruit is the tangible evidence of life. Only live plants can produce fruit. Nourishment travels from the roots to the branches, sustaining the fruit. Jesus refers to Himself as the vine and to us as branches. Unless we are attached to the vine, we are not receiving spiritual nourishment. We become grafted into the vine by faith in Jesus Christ as Lord and Savior. His power then flows through us, producing spiritual fruit.

The fruit we bear is consistent with His character. Just as apple trees bear apples, we bear spiritual fruit that reflects Him. Spiritual fruit consists of God's qualities: love, joy, peace, patience, kindness, goodness, faithfulness, gentleness, and self-control. The fruit of the Spirit cannot be grown by our own efforts. We must remain in the vine.

How do we abide in Him? We acknowledge that our spiritual sustenance comes from the Lord. We spend time with Him. We seek His will and wisdom. We are obedient and follow where He leads. When we remain attached to Him, spiritual fruit will be the evidence of His life within us. Abide in the vine and be fruitful!

*Dear Lord, help me abide in You so that I may produce
fruit as a witness to Your life within me. Amen.*

Finding Mr. Right

*Keep yourselves from sexual promiscuity. Learn to appreciate
and give dignity to your body, not abusing it, as is so
common among those who know nothing of God.*
1 THESSALONIANS 4:3–5 MSG

She'd dated them all. She had played the field with all types, from athletes and academics to businessmen and artists. But they were all missing one thing—the love of God.

Finding the right person to marry can be a difficult task, but it all starts with dating godly men. The Bible reminds us that we, as women, need to think about purity. We must stay away from sexual promiscuity and treat our bodies as a temple of God. Although the temptation is always there, it is less tempting to stray from these ideals if you and your date share the same faith.

When you start dating someone new, be sure to ask the tough questions at the beginning to save heartache and temptation in the end. Does he share the same values as you? Does he allow Jesus to be the ruler of his life? Where do his priorities lie?

Consider all your relationships prayerfully. With God's help, finding Mr. Right is possible.

*Dear heavenly Father, I know that I must choose a godly
man to date and ultimately marry. Help me to prayerfully
consider my relationships and make them glorifying to You.*

God Cares for You

"Consider how the lilies grow. They do not labor or spin. Yet I tell you,
not even Solomon in all his splendor was dressed like one of these. If that
is how God clothes the grass of the field, which is here today, and tomorrow is
thrown into the fire, how much more will he clothe you, O you of little faith!"
LUKE 12:27–28 NIV

Take a look at God's creation. He has created this world with such intricate detail. He designed every tree, the majestic mountains, a glorious sun, and a mysterious moon. Each animal has been given unique markings, parts, and sounds. Consider the long-necked giraffe, the massive elephant, the graceful swan, and the perfectly striped zebra!

If God makes the flowers, each type unique and beautiful, and if He sends the rain and sun to meet their needs, will He not care for you as well?

He made you. What the Father makes, He loves. And that which He loves, He cares for. We were made in His image. Humans are dearer to God than any of His other creations. Rest in Him. Trust Him. Just as He cares for the birds of the air and the flowers of the meadows, God is in the business of taking care of His sons and daughters. Let Him take care of you.

Father, I am amazed by Your creation. Remind me that I am Your treasured child. Take care of me today as only You can do. Amen.

....

....

....

....

....

....

....

....

A Pillar of Strength

On the day I called, You answered me;
You made me bold with strength in my soul.
PSALM 138:3 NASB

Ella struggled during a very difficult time in her life. One day she opened the mailbox to find a letter from a close friend.

Dearest Ella,

I am writing to tell you I love you. You have filled me with courage to move forward in the difficult times in my life. Now, I want to be a pillar of strength for you.

No one can really understand the path you've had to travel. Even if we've had similar experiences, I still can't put myself completely in your shoes, but I am here for you. I don't have to understand anything in order to love you.

God loves you even more than I do, so I know that He wants to see you whole again. He is the repairer of the breach and the restorer of your soul. The picture He has of your destiny probably doesn't look like the one you had. Let Him paint a new picture on your heart.

All my love,
Anna

Maybe you feel like Ella. In your own time you'll be able to let all the pain go and live a life of fulfillment. Look to friends that God has given you and allow them to be your pillar of strength.

Lord, I know I don't have to go through this alone.
Help me to allow others to help me through this situation. Amen.

Seek Him

One thing I ask of the Lord, this is what I seek: that I may
dwell in the house of the Lord all the days of my life, to gaze
upon the beauty of the Lord and to seek him in his temple.

PSALM 27:4 NIV

David understood what it takes to dwell with God. He continually gazed at His beauty. At the time he composed this psalm, David was living on the run, not in the lavish palace of a king. He was finding beauty and richness in the starkest of environments, stripped of amenities.

Do we seek God's beauty in our environment, which is not quite so bleak? Isn't His beauty reflected in the smiling toddler in the grocery store line? What about the elderly married couple's hand-holding throughout the service? Don't these reflect our Creator?

When we bite into an apple—crisp, sweet, and naturally packaged for freshness—or observe the grace and agility of a dancer or listen to the intoxicating notes of a flute, don't they reveal more about God? Where did it all originate? Whose power and creativity is behind it all? Life reveals glimpses of His power and awesomeness. These everyday things draw us into His presence where we can praise Him, enjoying His beauty and greatness all the days of our life.

Magnificent Creator, Your greatness and beauty surround me.
May my eyes gaze at You, seeking You, that I might
dwell in Your presence continually. Amen.

Caution, Danger Ahead

If someone is caught in a sin, you who are spiritual should restore him gently.
But watch yourself, or you also may be tempted.
GALATIANS 6:1 NIV

Grace and Sara had been close friends for years.. So when Sara learned Grace was using her company credit card for personal expenses, she didn't hesitate to confront her. At first Grace was defensive, but then she burst into tears and told Sara how hard things had been for her financially. Sara was shocked.

A few weeks later Grace overheard Sara on the phone telling intimate details of Grace's ordeal, cloaking it in the context of a prayer request. Now it was Grace's turn to be shocked and then angered as she realized Sara had betrayed her confidence.

At times it's appropriate and necessary to confront sin in the lives of another Christian. However, the Bible warns of the need to do this prayerfully and in love. In Galatians, Paul issues another warning: The person doing the confronting needs to be careful not to use the other person's actions as an excuse to sin. Perhaps we are more vulnerable to sin when we see it in the lives of others. It is wise to be on guard.

Father, it is never easy to confront sin in the life of a sister or brother. When the time comes, help me to do so gently and in love.

What's Your Motive?

*Every man's work shall be made manifest: for the day
shall declare it, because it shall be revealed by fire;
and the fire shall try every man's work of what sort it is.*
1 CORINTHIANS 3:13 KJV

Churches offer many places for God's children to serve. There are areas in children's ministries—nurseries, classrooms, music programs, or vacation Bible school—that are often strapped for willing workers. Maybe volunteering to clean the building or help with upkeep is more your style. Does your church have a nursing home ministry or food pantry ministry? Are you involved?

Do you genuinely wish to help in some of these areas to bring glory to God? If you get involved, you will be blessed beyond measure. We are all called to be useful for Christ. When we do so willingly and with a servant's heart, the joy that fills us will be indescribable and lasting.

On the other hand, if our service is merely to receive praise and recognition from our peers, we'll receive our reward, but it won't be the blessing of God that it could have been. God knows our hearts. He recognizes our motives and rewards us accordingly.

*Lord, I want to serve You with a pure heart.
Let all I do bring glory to You.*

Justice and Mercy

"We know that we don't deserve a hearing from you.
Our appeal is to your compassion."
DANIEL 9:18 MSG

Being merciful is not as popular as being just. There are plenty of commercials and billboards for law firms saying they'll "get you what you deserve." Sometimes we have a good idea of what we deserve, but most of the time we think we deserve more than we actually do.

As Christians, we must resist the temptation to think and talk about the ways in which our lives are not fair. Instead, we should remember the words of Daniel and humble ourselves before the God of creation. The world tries to tell us that we deserve to be treated well; we deserve money, success, and possessions; we deserve happiness and an easy life. But Daniel knew the world's sense of justice was not God's justice.

We do not deserve help from God. We don't deserve anything from God. But our God is merciful and loving, and He delights in us. God helps us, listens to us, and loves us because He is merciful. Praise Him for His mercy today!

Dear Lord, thank You for Your mercy. Thank You for Your love. Teach me to humble myself before You and look for Your mercy rather than for the world's justice. Amen.

More Than an E-mail

*You are a letter from Christ.... This "letter" is written not with
pen and ink, but with the Spirit of the living God. It is
carved not on tablets of stone, but on human hearts.*
2 CORINTHIANS 3:3 NLT

Most of us can't go a day or even a few hours without checking our e-mail. It's fast, it's free, and it's practical. But don't you just love it when you go to the mailbox, and stuck between a bunch of bills is a letter from a good friend or loved one? Doesn't that just make your day? A real letter is special because you know the other person took the time to think about you and went to the trouble to purchase a stamp and handwrite a precious note just for you. That beats an e-mail any day!

We've all heard it said that sometimes we are the only Bible a person will ever read. We are a letter from Christ. When you are sharing your faith, or even in your everyday relationships, always try to go the extra mile with people. Go beyond "fast, free, and practical." Be more than an e-mail: Be a precious letter from Christ and take the time to let them know how loved and treasured they are by you and by the Lord!

Father, help me to make the people in my life feel loved and cherished. Help me to remember that I am a letter from You as I interact with others. Amen.

Setting Priorities

*Cause me to hear Your lovingkindness in the morning, for in You do I trust;
cause me to know the way in which I should walk, for I lift up my soul to You.*
PSALM 143:8 NKJV

We twenty-first-century women have more choices than any other generation before us about what we do with our time. How easy it is to overcommit ourselves, become stressed, and let our lives get out of balance. We have work, sleep, relationships, recreation, and responsibilities of every sort vying for our time.

Twenty-four hours. That's what we all get in a day. Though we often think we don't have time for all we want to do, our Creator deemed twenty-four-hour days sufficient. How do we decide what to devote ourselves to? The wisdom of the psalmist tells us to begin the day by asking to hear the loving voice of the One who made us. We can lay our choices, problems, and conflicts before Him in prayer. He will show us which way to go. Psalm 118:7 (NIV) says, "The Lord is with me; he is my helper." Hold up that full plate of your life to Him, and allow Him to decide what to keep and what to let go.

*Lord, make me willing to surrender my choices and activities to You.
Cause me to desire the things You want me to do.*

Hair's a Thought. . .

"You didn't offer me water to wash the dust from my feet, but she has washed them with her tears and wiped them with her hair."
LUKE 7:44 NLT

Marlene owns and operates a hair salon. Two years ago she was approached by a woman who worked for the American Cancer Society. The representative asked Marlene if she would be willing to style wigs for cancer patients. Marlene agreed and performed this service for free. She generated donations of human hair for organizations like Locks of Love and Wigs for Kids.

Michelle heard of the need for human hair for Wigs for Kids. When she decided to get her tresses trimmed, she donated her twelve-inch ponytail. She, too, wanted to make a positive contribution to help someone else. Neither Marlene nor Michelle made a big deal of their service or gifts to others. Their little-known actions stemmed from their compassion.

Today we can't wash our Savior's feet with our tears or dry His feet with our hair. We may not be able to provide genuine hair or even wig styling for someone who needs it. But the Lord focuses on the attitudes that drive acts of repentance, compassion, or kindness. Whatever we do—at work or in private—we're reminded that it all begins at heart level. None of these three women have to tell anyone why they've done their individual acts of love. It simply shows.

Lord, help me to demonstrate real concern for others in real ways. Amen.

....
....
....
....
....
....
....

Be Still

Thou wilt keep him in perfect peace, whose mind
is stayed on thee: because he trusteth in thee.
ISAIAH 26:3 KJV

If you watch the news on a regular basis, you'll find that our world is full of chaos and despair. And while most newscasts only focus on bad news, there's no denying that much of the world is in turmoil. Hurricanes, terrorism, school shootings—it's enough to make hibernation an attractive option.

During the prophet Isaiah's time, the Israelites faced their own reasons for discouragement and fear. They had been taken from their homes, forced into captivity, and persecuted for their faith. And although much of their suffering stemmed from their disobedience to God, He had compassion on them. Longing for His children to know His peace, God sent prophets like Isaiah to stir up faith, repentance, and comfort in the hearts of the "chosen people."

God's message is just as applicable today as it was back then. By keeping our minds fixed on Him, we can have perfect, abiding peace even in the midst of a crazy world. The path to peace is not easy, but it is simple: Focus on God. As we meditate on His promises and His faithfulness, He gets bigger, while our problems get smaller.

God, when I focus on the world, my mind and heart feel anxious. Help me to keep my mind on You, so that I can have hope and peace.

Comfort in Sadness

*You've kept track of my every toss and turn through the sleepless nights,
each tear entered in your ledger, each ache written in your book.*

PSALM 56:8 MSG

In heaven there will be no more sadness. Tears will be a thing of the past. For now, we live in a fallen world. There are heartaches and disappointments.

Call out to God when you find yourself tossing and turning at night, or when tears drench your pillow. He is a God who sees, a God who knows. He is your Abba Father, your daddy.

It hurts the Father's heart when you cry, but He sees the big picture. God knows that gut-wrenching trials create perseverance in His beloved daughter and that perseverance results in strong character.

Do you ever wonder if God has forgotten you and left you to fend for yourself? Rest assured that He has not left you even for one moment. He is your Good Shepherd, and you are His lamb. When you go astray, He spends every day and every night calling after you. If you are a believer, then you know your Good Shepherd's voice.

Shhhh. . .listen. . .He is whispering a message of comfort even now.

*Father, remind me that You are a God who sees my pain. Jesus,
I thank You that You gave up Your life for me. Holy Spirit,
comfort me in my times of deep sadness. Amen.*

Learning Humility

Do nothing out of selfish ambition or vain conceit, but in humility consider others better than yourselves. Each of you should look not only to your own interests, but also to the interests of others.

PHILIPPIANS 2:3–4 NIV

Society tells us that we must be self-confident and proud of ourselves, that we must be self-promoting and bold. But these are lies. Humility and gentleness are not qualities of the weak. The all-powerful Creator of the universe embodied these very traits when He took the form of a human.

In a society that equates humility with weakness and low self-esteem, setting aside our own interests and looking out for another's seems like an impossible command to carry out. If we ignore our own needs, who will take care of them? Shouldn't we all look out for ourselves first?

Christians, however, are called to a higher code of conduct. We are instructed to look out for each other's needs before we examine and meet our own. Imagine a body of believers that truly followed this command. Every need would be met, because every member would be looked after by the others.

Realize that yours is only a small part of the story, just as important as everyone else's.

Lord, forgive my vanity and pride. May I place my confidence in You, not myself. Teach me to look outside of my own interests and to serve others first. Use me to meet the needs of this world.

Standards of Success

"Worship and serve him with your whole heart and a willing mind.
For the Lord sees every heart and knows every plan and thought.
If you seek him, you will find him."

1 CHRONICLES 28:9 NLT

God's view of success is vastly different than the world's.. We find our success in earnestly seeking after God and following His commands.

On the other hand, the world says that we must have a good job, make lots of money, buy the newest toys, and focus on making ourselves happy. The world does not care how we accomplish these things. If we have to tell a lie here or there, no problem. If we have to pretend to be something we are not, who cares?

God cares. God sees our hearts and knows our motives—good or bad. The world's mind-set looks to the tangible elements of success—a good car, a nice job, and big house. On the other hand, God's focus is on our journey. We may not live in the biggest house on the block, and we may not even own a car, but those things are not important to God. Instead, worshipping and serving God with our whole hearts, being genuine and sincere, and willingly seeking God are the aspects of success in God's eyes.

Dear Lord, teach me to seek after You willingly, with sincere motives. Please help me focus on pleasing You rather than seeking success by worldly standards. Amen.

....
....
....
....
....
....
....
....

Living Sacrifices

Therefore, I urge you, brothers, in view of God's mercy, to offer your bodies as living sacrifices, holy and pleasing to God—this is your spiritual act of worship.
ROMANS 12:1 NIV

Mirror, mirror, on the wall, who's the fairest of them all? Full lips. Wrinkle-free faces. Size 4 bodies. Our culture worships the physically attractive. God created our bodies. What should our attitude be toward them? Do we adopt the world's view or God's design?

Society worships the body and neglects the spirit. We may be equally guilty of spending much time, money, and energy trying to perfect our bodies. Man looks at the outward appearance, but God looks at the heart. What are we doing to assure that our hearts are acceptable to Him? God created the body as a temple for our spirit. Like an oyster protecting a pearl, so our bodies are merely physical shells, protecting the real jewel, our eternal souls.

God created our bodies so that we could worship Him in spirit. As we offer our bodies as living sacrifices, we are worshipping our Creator. Sacrifice means putting aside our own needs for the sake of another. Our physical bodies are de-emphasized so our spiritual worth can take precedence. May the Lord teach us to put our bodies in proper perspective so they may be used for God's glory, not solely for man's appreciation.

Dear Lord, help me to desire to offer my body to You in spiritual worship. Amen.

Feeling Pressed?

By his divine power, God has given us
everything we need for living a godly life.
2 PETER 1:3 NLT

People need you—your family, your friends. Adding their needs to your commitments at school or work can sometimes be too much. Maybe your boss demands extra hours on a project, or your sister needs you to help her with a family birthday party.

People pulling you here and there can have you going in circles. Somehow you keep pushing forward, not always sure where the strength comes from, but thankful in the end that you made it through the day.

In those situations you're not just stretching your physical body to the limit, but your mind and emotions as well. Stress can make you feel like a grape in a winepress. But there is good news. God has given you everything you need, but you must choose to use the wisdom He has provided. Don't be afraid to say no when you feel you just can't add one more thing to your to-do list. Limit your commitments, ask someone to take notes for you in a meeting you can't make, or carpool with someone who shares your child's extracurricular activity.

Alleviate the pressure where you can and then know that His power will make up for the rest.

Lord, help me to do, what I can do; and I'll trust
You to do for me those things that I can't do. Amen.

Wisdom from Doing

The fear of the Lord is the beginning of wisdom; all who follow his precepts have good understanding. To him belongs eternal praise.
PSALM 111:10 NIV

Living in the information age, we are easily duped into thinking that knowledge is the answer to all our problems. If we educate ourselves well on a given subject, we believe we can master it. If we identify all facets of a problem, we can solve it. But the truth is, knowing doesn't necessarily lead to doing. If it did, we would all be eating healthy foods and exercising regularly. Knowledge and obedience are not synonymous. Somewhere between the two is our will.

Scripture teaches us fearing the Lord—not gaining information—is the source of wisdom. It is in hearing and obeying, James 1:22 tells us, that we gain clear understanding. To be a hearer of the Word only is to be deceived. To be a doer of the Word removes the spiritual blind spots and keeps our vision clear. This is the difficult part, for doing the Word often involves repentance or giving up our own agendas. Fearing the Lord is living in reverent submission to Him, seeking His will and way in our lives. That is the starting point for a life of wisdom and understanding.

Lord, help me not to be deceived by trusting in knowledge alone. Show me the areas where I have heard and not done, and help me to obey. Give me a reverent fear of You.

Why Not Me?

God gave Paul the power to perform unusual miracles.
When handkerchiefs or aprons that had merely touched
his skin were placed on sick people, they were healed.
ACTS 19:11–12 NLT

It's probably safe to say none of your clothing has ever resulted in an amazing healing. Maybe we have witnessed some unexplainable cures. We prayed, and God healed a friend of cancer. Perhaps God spared a loved one in an accident that claimed the lives of others. Most of the time, however, these kinds of miracles don't happen.

When his fellow missionary, Trophimus, fell sick, Paul was given no miracle to help him. When Timothy complained of frequent stomach problems, Paul had no miracle-working handkerchief for Timothy's misery. Paul himself suffered from an incurable ailment (2 Corinthians 12:7), yet he was willing to leave it with God. We, too, may be clueless as to why God miraculously heals others, but not us or our best friend.

Like Paul, we must trust God when there's no miracle. Can we be as resilient as Job who said, "Though he slay me, yet will I trust in him" (Job 13:15 KJV)? We can—waiting for the day when health problems and bad accidents and death cease forever (Revelation 21:4).

When healing doesn't come, Lord Jesus,
give us grace to trust You more. Amen.

....

....

....

....

....

....

....

....

Family Ties

*But if she has children or grandchildren, their first responsibility
is to show godliness at home and repay their parents by taking
care of them. This is something that pleases God.*

1 TIMOTHY 5:4 NLT

Jessie lives about seven hours away from her family in the town where she went to college. Plenty of her friends live there as well. Her friends have become a surrogate family.

Jessie loves her family but has grown apart from them since she moved away. She struggles to remember to call home and visit.

It's a difficult task to stay in touch with loved ones if you live far away from them. However, distance doesn't mean you have to leave behind family ties. Taking care of your family also does not necessarily mean that you have to be there in person (though if you are, take advantage of the time you have together). Pick up the phone and call your relatives. Maintain a relationship with your parents and grandparents by making time each week for a quick phone call or to send a short note. Not only will you be honoring your elders, but you will also be honoring God.

*Lord, help me to show Your love to my family
by keeping in touch, even when I am away.
Help me make time for my family whenever possible.*

God Goes with Us

"Be strong and courageous! Do not be afraid and do not panic before them. For the Lord your God will personally go ahead of you. He will neither fail you nor abandon you."
DEUTERONOMY 31:6 NLT

Marcia leaned against the airport chair, listening to the loudspeaker. "Flight 529 has been delayed." Groans filled the concourse, but Marcia shrugged. Though she was exhausted from a mission trip, she felt peaceful as she waited for the last leg of her flight to begin.

Lord, she prayed silently, I know I asked You to help my flight be on time. But it's okay. You've answered every other prayer I've prayed about this trip in such amazing ways!

Pictures of poor but happy children, uplifting music, inconveniences turned to blessings, and dozens of other God-incidences filled Marcia's mind as the images of the past few days flitted through her head.

Suddenly, the loudspeaker came back to life. "Ladies and gentlemen, we have a change to announce. Flight 529 will take off as scheduled. Preboarding will begin at this time." Marcia laughed out loud and smiled as people around her looked at her strangely.

"God, You are just too good to me," Marcia said as she got up from her seat.

Lord, You work everything out when we serve You— and no prayer request is too small. Thank You for Your presence and Your faithfulness.

Hard Times

He comes alongside us when we go through hard times, and before you know it, he brings us alongside someone else who is going through hard times so that we can be there for that person just as God was there for us.

2 CORINTHIANS 1:4 MSG

Hard times are bound to come. Don't let that discourage you. God says that in this world we will have trouble (John 16:33), but to take heart because He has overcome the world!

If you are in the middle of something rough right now, remember that God is always there to comfort you. You may feel that you are at the end of your ability to cope, but that is where God likes to meet us. He is close to the brokenhearted. If you have just experienced something difficult, reflect on what God wants to teach you from that.

Try journaling the things that God has taught you so that you can remember all that He has done for and through you. You can share these memories with someone later on. Don't forget that God uses all of our trials for good, to make us more like Christ and to help those around us in their time of need.

Lord, You are the God of comfort. Please help me lean on You during hard times, and help me be a blessing to someone else. Amen.

....
....
....
....
....
....
....
....
....
....

Wearing Baby

He gathers the lambs in his arms and carries them close
to his heart; he gently leads those that have young.
ISAIAH 40:11 NIV

Lisa not only births her children, she "wears" them by holding them or keeping them close in baby carriers, slings, and backpacks. She's convinced that wearing her child for most of the day keeps her more in tune with her infant's needs. At night, her baby sleeps soundly because he has had adequate stimulation during the family's daytime routines.

Some people warn Lisa that she's going to have a mama's boy someday. But that hasn't happened. Her other children are well-adjusted. Lisa has even carried two at once—one in front, one in back. Sometimes Dad gets in on the act, too. He'll wear sixteen-month-old Molly when she wants to be held.

"My kids aren't clingy," Lisa says. "They're attached."

The Lord says in numerous places throughout the Word that He carries us. In Isaiah we have the picture of a shepherd carrying a lamb. In Exodus He carried His people "on eagles' wings" (Exodus 19:4 NIV). He also carries us "as a father carries his son" (Deuteronomy 1:31 NIV). Whether we're unattached or simply feeling detached, it's good to remember the One who attaches us to Himself. He's taken it a step further. He's engraved us on the palms of His nail-scarred hands (Isaiah 49:16 NIV).

I praise You, Lord, that I'm close
and dear to Your heart. Amen.

Gossip or Forgiveness

Hatred stirreth up strifes: but love covereth all sins.
PROVERBS 10:12 KJV

Hate is such an ugly word, yet it seems to be everywhere. The worst part about it is that it is almost as common in Christians as it is in unbelievers. Hate shows up among women in the form of gossip.

Consider Lila. After many years of serving in a particular church ministry, she backed out saying she was tired of dealing with all the gossip and backbiting. Lila failed to realize that she was just as at fault as many of the other ladies. She'd been harboring hatred and bitterness toward several people for so long that it had become her habit to spread venom. The result was extreme discontent in the church.

Justine, on the other hand, attempted to look at each situation through the eyes of Christ. Instead of being angry, she chose to forgive. She positively affected everyone with her bright smile and genuine love for God and people. She was full of infectious joy, and people were thrilled to work beside her.

As Lila became more bitter, she eventually dropped out of church. Justine continued to joyfully serve and was able to be a blessing to many.

Decide today who you will be—Lila or Justine.

Father, there are many reactions I could take to the situations I will face in life. Help me always choose love over hatred.

....
....
....
....
....
....
....
....
....

Good for the Soul

*When I kept silent about my sin, my body
wasted away through my groaning all day long.*
PSALM 32:3 NASB

The shame was too great to bear. Tina could hardly lift her head, let alone face her family. For weeks she was miserable—couldn't eat, couldn't sleep—the burden weighed more heavily on her every day. Finally, she gathered the courage to talk with her mother.

Tina was shocked when her mother received her with open arms. She felt as if a weight had been lifted from her shoulders. She was forgiven, released from the pain of the past.

Shame is a powerful silencer. When we feel guilty and ashamed about our actions, the last thing we want to do is speak of them. However, Psalm 32:3 reminds us of the pain silence can cause. Keeping silent about our sin can literally make us feel as if we were dying.

God does not want His children to live in silent shame. Saying what we've done wrong out loud is the first step to healing. Confession is merely agreeing with God about our actions. While other people may not always forgive us, God promises that if we confess our sins He will forgive us and cleanse us from our unrighteousness.

Grace. A clean slate. It's ours for the asking.

*Father, help me to never be afraid to confess my sins to You.
Thank You for the gift of grace, the promise of
forgiveness, and the healing You provide.*

....

....

....

....

....

....

....

You Are Not Alone

There hath no temptation taken you but such as is common to man: but God is faithful, who will not suffer you to be tempted above that ye are able; but will with the temptation also make a way to escape, that ye may be able to bear it.

1 CORINTHIANS 10:13 KJV

Temptation is a part of life that everyone must face. We can stay away from most temptations simply by avoiding certain places or situations. We live in a world, however, that is full of the filth of sin, and we can't always avoid exposure to temptation.

For instance, have you ever been tempted to cheat or cut corners on a project or to log more hours on your time card than you actually worked? Maybe you've considered stealing something—even something small. What about all those opportunities for gossip and backbiting? When it comes down to it, sin is sin. Maybe you've avoided places that encourage a filthy and promiscuous lifestyle, but temptation abounds everywhere.

The thing is, we don't have to give in. God won't ever let us get into a spot that, with His help, we can't get out of. If we let Him, He will strengthen us. He doesn't want us to try to handle these situations on our own. Let's give our temptations to Him.

Thank You, Lord, that I don't have to face temptation alone. Thank You for providing a way to escape.

Godly Conversation

Let no one look down on your youthfulness, but rather in speech, conduct,
love, faith and purity, show yourself an example of those who believe.
I Timothy 4:12 nasb

God hears the conversations of His children—no matter how young or old. As we spend time together and speak with one another, our Father cares about our conversations and wants them to bless and enrich the lives of those who participate.

Conversations peppered with faith and purity, as directed in 1 Timothy 4, are in stark contrast to the ungodly chatter of the world today. The world is darkened by complaints against God, cynicism, unbelief, and gossip—none of which honor God. His heart aches when we use words to tear others down rather than speak truth that encourages.

He wants us to build each other up with the words we use. True Christ-centered fellowship happens when everyone involved is encouraged and strengthened in their faith. And we must always remember that unbelievers watch and listen, always looking to find Christ in the lives of those of us who profess His name. Let's share God's faithfulness, goodness, and love, because our conversations have an impact in the lives of everyone we reach.

Jesus, please touch my lips and allow nothing dishonorable to
pass through them. Guide me and give me grace and discernment
in my conversations so that they would always be pleasing
to You and give glory to Your name. Amen.

The First 10 Percent

*On the first day of each week, you should each put
aside a portion of the money you have earned.*
1 CORINTHIANS 16:2 NLT

Tamara was finally independent. Armed with a wallet full of plastic and a full-time salary, she was ready to buy the world. And buy she did.

Every Sunday she'd pass the offering plate to the person next to her, never contributing to the collection. *I don't have any kids, so I don't benefit from the expensive children's programs the church offers,* she rationalized. *So why should I give?*

Too many of us have the wrong attitude toward giving. Instead of giving back to God out of thankfulness for our blessings, we think we should give only when we feel He deserves our gifts.

God doesn't need our money. His kingdom will flourish with or without our financial gifts. But He does desire our worship—in praise, service, witnessing to others, and in giving back to Him.

The truth is that everything we have belongs to God. The first 10 percent out of a paycheck may feel like a lot at first, but God promises to bless the gift, the giver, and the remaining 90 percent.

*Dear God, please help me to be faithful in my tithing.
You have done so much for me, and I want my gifts
back to You to be given with a joyful heart! Amen.*

No Further Analysis

I press on toward the goal to win the prize for which
God has called me heavenward in Christ Jesus.
PHILIPPIANS 3:14 NIV

Paula lay awake recounting all the conversations she'd had that day. *Was I too harsh when I made that comment? What if Michael misunderstood what I said? What about the decision to put Janie in preschool? Is she really ready?* Paula's mind raced with questions, overanalyzing the decisions and commitments she made that day.

Suddenly, her husband's words came back to her. "You pray every day for God to help you do the very best you can. Don't you trust Him to complete that work?" Her husband was right, and she was wasting precious time when she could be getting some much-needed sleep. She slipped down beside her bed, knelt, and asked God to help her let go of thoughts that seemed to hold her captive each night.

As women, we often want to cover our bases, assuring ourselves that our decisions are right, but we must not lose ourselves in the analysis. Find your strength in the leadership of the Holy Spirit and then relax and enjoy peaceful sleep.

Lord, help me to trust You in the decisions I make throughout my day. Help me to stop second-guessing myself and trust who You created me to be. Amen.

Giving

"I was hungry and you gave me something to eat, I was thirsty and you gave me something to drink, I was a stranger and you invited me in, I needed clothes and you clothed me, I was sick and you looked after me, I was in prison and you came to visit me."
MATTHEW 25:35–36 NIV

Stephanie wanted to help others—she really did—but she lived in a tiny studio apartment and lived on a meager entry-level salary in an area with a high cost of living. She saw so many worthy causes all around—causes that always needed her money.

Then one day she saw an ad in the paper: Volunteer needed three hours every Tuesday night at the homeless shelter to help residents research housing and job opportunities. After six months of job and apartment hunting herself, Stephanie knew this was God's way of showing her there is more than one way to help others.

No matter what your skills and passions, God places special ministry opportunities in your path. It could mean giving money or things, but maybe it's giving your time and talents. Ask God to show you how He wants you to show His love to others in Jesus' name.

Dear God, You have the perfect plan for me to show Your love to others. Please show me what You want me to do. It's time for me to get to work in Your kingdom! Amen.

....
....
....
....
....
....
....

Career or Calling

But just as he who called you is holy, so be holy in all you do;
for it is written: "Be holy, because I am holy."
1 PETER 1:15–16 NIV

Katie and Jane are roommates, and they both have good jobs. But they both struggle with finding direction in their careers. They wonder if their occupations are really the calling that God had in mind for them.

Calling is a word that's thrown around in Christian circles, touted at Christian colleges and universities, and uttered from the pulpits of churches of all kinds. But what exactly does finding a calling mean? And how can we determine if a career is the divine purpose of our life?

Since we aren't born with explicit instructions from God for the exact career path we should take, the best thing we can do when seeking a career is to pray and read God's Word. By exploring options, praying earnestly, and paying attention to God's leading, we can do our best to find the correct path for our work lives.

Father, whether or not I have found my true calling, I pray that I can be a witness for You in my career. Help me to find the career path that You have planned for me and to be content in my calling.

Christ Is Risen Today!

"He isn't here! He is risen from the dead!"
LUKE 24:6 NLT

Easter is the season when we celebrate the foundation of our faith: Jesus Christ was raised from the dead and is seated at the right hand of the Father in heaven. He is alive and well and at work in our lives today. He fought the fight over sin and death, and the battle has been won! He has saved us from our sins, and we can be with Christ for all eternity.

The power God used to raise Christ from the dead is the same power we have available to us each day to live according to God's will here on earth. What happened on Easter gives us hope for today and for all eternity.

If you haven't accepted Jesus Christ as your personal Savior, take the time right now and start your new life in Christ.

Dear Jesus, thank You for dying on the cross for me and taking away all my sin. You are alive and well, and I praise You today for all You are and all You have done. Amen.

Fences

"If you keep My commandments, you will abide in My love, just as I have kept My Father's commandments and abide in His love."

JOHN 15:10 NKJV

A man who owns horses knows how necessary his fences are. Inside the pasture, his horses are protected from things that can harm them. Wet, boggy ground can cause horses to founder, and certain plants can be poisonous to them. Inside the pasture, they can be fed properly, groomed, and exercised. The fence does not exist to keep the horse from being free; the fence exists so the horse and his owner can enjoy their relationship, and the horse can live to his fullest potential. Most dangers for the horse are outside the fence.

God's commandments are much like the pasture fence. Sin is on the other side. His laws exist to keep us in fellowship with Him and to keep us out of things that are harmful to us that can lead to bondage. We abide in the loving presence of our heavenly Father by staying within the boundaries He has set up for our own good. He has promised to care for us and to do the things needful for us. His love for us is unconditional, even when we jump the fence into sin. But by staying inside the boundaries, we enjoy intimacy with Him.

Father, help me to obey Your commandments that are given for my good. Thank You for Your love for me.

Reconciled to God

Ezra wept, prostrate in front of The Temple of God. As he prayed and confessed,
a huge number of the men, women, and children of Israel gathered around him.
All the people were now weeping as if their hearts would break.

EZRA 10:1 MSG

Sin is not a politically correct topic these days. Yet God talks about sin all throughout His Word. The Bible says God hates sin, and that He sent His Son to die on the cross to save us from the results of sin—our eternal separation from God.

Sins can be "big" (murder, adultery) or "little" (gossip, envy)—but in God's eyes, they're the same. That's why we need His sacrifice, His righteousness. Only through Jesus' death on the cross can we be reconciled to God.

Satan loves to remind us of our sins to make us feel guilty. But God wants us to confess our sins—daily, or hourly if need be!—receive His forgiveness, and move on to live with renewed fervor.

What sins have separated us from God today? Let's draw near the throne of grace, so we can receive His pardon. He will cover us with Jesus' robe of righteousness, so that we don't have to feel guilt or shame anymore.

Lord, forgive me for the sins I've committed today.
Make me ever aware of Your grace and forgiveness,
so that I may share Your love with others.

Big Plans

We humans keep brainstorming options
and plans, but God's purpose prevails.
PROVERBS 19:21 MSG

Abby had a plan. She wanted a North Carolina man to marry, so a small college nestled in a mountain cove was just the place for her. Florida would no longer be her home—just the gorgeous Smoky Mountains. Her man? A wavy- and dark-haired athletic type, business major. She had him pictured.

Well, who says God doesn't have a sense of humor? Abby went to that college, found that man turned out to be hollow inside. God had a plan; it was to meld her heart to a man of strong godly character. A man specially selected for her. He wasn't from the mountains, but a Florida citrus grower she'd known since high school! They did marry and proved that God's plans are best.

We often worry, scheme, and strategize our lives away. And really, there is nothing wrong with planning and thinking ahead. But we must remember that God's ultimate purposes will prevail. We might not like that idea, hanging fiercely to our independence. But a loving God, who has all wisdom and power over all things, genuinely cares for us. His plans will not fail.

Father, You see the bigger picture. Your plan is best for me even though at times I resist it. Help me to trust when things aren't as I think they should be. Your will be done. Amen.

He Has Chosen You

Therefore, as God's chosen people, holy and dearly loved, clothe yourselves with compassion, kindness, humility, gentleness and patience.
COLOSSIANS 3:12 NIV

Four kids stood along the third-base line, kicking dust into the air.

"I'll take Abby," the first team captain said.

"Uhh. . .Simon," the second said.

The final two unclaimed girls glanced up at each other, both fearing they'd be the last one picked for the baseball game.

No matter how athletic, beautiful, popular, or smart you are, you've probably experienced a time when you were chosen last or overlooked entirely. Being left out is a big disappointment of life on earth.

The good news is that this disappointment isn't part of God's kingdom. Even when others forget about us, God doesn't. He has handpicked His beloved children now and forever. And this fact doesn't exclude others who haven't yet accepted Him; the truth is that Jesus died for everyone—every man, woman, and child who has ever and will ever live. The Father chooses us all. All we have to do is grab a glove and join the team.

Father, thanks for choosing me. I don't deserve it, but You call me Your beloved child. Help me to remember others who may feel overlooked or unloved. Let Your love for them shine through me. Amen.

Praying with Confidence

For we do not have a high priest who is unable to sympathize with our weaknesses, but we have one who has been tempted in every way, just as we are—yet was without sin. Let us then approach the throne of grace with confidence, so that we may receive mercy and find grace to help us in our time of need.
HEBREWS 4:15–16 NIV

There is no one like a sister. Whether or not you have a female sibling, you have undoubtedly discovered a sister along life's journey. A sister is someone who gets you. Sometimes a sister understands you even better than a parent, because she is closer to your age and has walked through some of the same things you are experiencing.

Even a sister's love cannot compare to Christ's love. However you're struggling, help is available through Jesus. Our Savior walked on this earth for thirty-three years. He was fully God and fully man. He got dirt under His fingernails. He felt hunger. He knew weakness. He was tempted. He felt tired. He gets it.

Go boldly before the throne of grace as a daughter of God. Pray in Jesus' name for an outpouring of His grace and mercy in your life.

Father, I ask You boldly in the name of Christ to help me. Amen.

....
....
....
....
....
....
....
....
....
....

Harmony of Believers

*May the God who gives endurance and encouragement give you a spirit
of unity among yourselves as you follow Christ Jesus, so that with one heart
and mouth you may glorify the God and Father of our Lord Jesus Christ.*
ROMANS 15:5–6 NIV

Fill 2,900 eggs with candy? Then hide them all? That's next to impossible!

But it wasn't impossible for the energetic teens. With an occasional nibble of candy, they joyfully set about their task. They also tidied and mowed acres of lawn. Others prepared music and a sing along PowerPoint, and others ran the computer and sound system. Adult leaders organized the community Easter egg hunt, advertised, prepared snacks, roped off the hunting areas, and told the Easter story. There were many jobs and many hands.

Until that day, different ministries had been running their own courses, resulting in weary, overloaded believers. But this event was different. There was cooperation and unity among the group. They were energized. Even the rain gave opportunity for a cluster of people of all ages to huddle under a tent to pray that the shower would cease and the little ones would come to hear the gospel and then hunt for eggs. God's people all fulfilled their roles, resulting in a fun, joyful, and fruitful event where He was honored.

*Father, show me what my role is in the body of Christ. Help me
to fulfill that role so the world will see the harmony of believers,
drawing them into fellowship and a relationship with You. Amen.*

....
....
....
....
....
....
....

The Breath of God

*Every part of Scripture is God-breathed and useful one way
or another—showing us truth, exposing our rebellion,
correcting our mistakes, training us to live God's way.*
2 TIMOTHY 3:16 MSG

We have the Word of God available to us every day. Don't take it for granted; it's extremely powerful. Every part of His Word is useful and shows us the truth.

Hebrews 4:12 tells us God's Word is "living and active." When we read the Bible, we aren't just reading a book of fairy tales or historical fiction. We have the Word of God in our hands.

Do you spend time in God's Word each day? Do you let the breath of God wash over you and comfort you? Are you allowing His Word to penetrate your heart and show you where you've been wrong? If not, you are missing out on one of the most important ways that God chooses to communicate with us today. Ask the Lord for the desire to spend more time in His Word. Don't feel you have the time? Consider purchasing the Bible on CD, and listen to God's Word as you drive to work or school.

*Father, Your Word is so important to me. Please give me
the desire to spend more time in the Bible each day. Amen.*

Focus Time

In the morning, O Lord, you hear my voice; in the morning
I lay my requests before you and wait in expectation.

PSALM 5:3 NIV

No team takes the field without first meeting in the locker room for a pregame talk. It would be foolish to build a house without consulting with an architect. For any successful endeavor, preparation is key.

Throughout His earthly ministry, Jesus modeled this principle. He was an incredibly busy man. There were disciples to train, people to heal, and children to bless. No matter what He did or where He traveled, something or someone always needed attention. However, in spite of the many demands placed upon Him, scripture tells us Jesus got up early in the morning and took time to meet His Father in prayer. Jesus was perfect, yet even He knew this discipline was essential to ensure the effectiveness of His ministry.

What is the first thing you do each morning? While it doesn't ensure perfection, setting aside a short time each morning to focus on the Father and the day ahead can help prepare us to live more intentionally. During this time we, like Jesus, gain clarity, so that we can invest our lives in the things that truly matter.

Father, help me to take time each morning to focus on
You and the day ahead. Align my priorities so that
the things I do will be the things You want me to do.

Abiding Peace

He himself is our peace.
EPHESIANS 2:14 NIV

Powerful forces converge as a hurricane develops. Even though turbulent winds swirl uncontrollably, the calm eye, the center of the storm, remains unaffected by its surroundings. Regardless of the hurricane's magnitude, the eye always remains calm.

Have you ever experienced a hurricane—perhaps not a real one, but life circumstances that turned your world upside down? The winds of hardship were fiercely blowing. Your suffering felt like pelting rain. Experiencing havoc all around, you didn't know where to turn. Is peace possible in the midst of such turbulence?

Regardless of life's circumstances, hope and peace are available if Jesus is there. You do not have to succumb to getting buffeted and beaten by the storms of life. Seek refuge in the center of the storm. Run to the arms of Jesus, the Prince of Peace. Let Him wipe your tears and calm your fears. Like the eye of the hurricane, His presence brings peace and calm. Move yourself closer. Desire to be in His presence. For He Himself is your peace. As you abide in His presence, peace will envelop you. The raging around you may not subside, but the churning of your heart will. You will find rest for your soul.

Dear Lord, thank You for being our peace
in the midst of life's fiercest storms. Amen.

Jonah's Prayer

*"In my distress I called to the Lord, and he answered me.
From the depths of the grave I called for help, and you listened to my cry."*
JONAH 2:2 NIV

By the time Jonah uttered this prayer, he was in big trouble. God called Jonah to preach a message to the nonbelievers in Nineveh. Instead of obeying, Jonah fled from God and boarded a ship heading in the opposite direction.

Of course, God knew what Jonah had done, and He caused a storm to rage around the ship. Jonah told the sailors that he was the cause of the storm, and the sailors threw Jonah overboard. Immediately the storm ceased, and all was quiet. Then God sent a large fish to swallow Jonah, and Jonah remained in the belly of the fish for three days and nights. This is where his prayer begins.

Jonah's prayer is distinctive because he's praying from the belly of a large fish—a seemingly hopeless situation. The response you might expect is, "Lord, get me out of here!" Instead, Jonah praises God for listening to and answering him! He prays with gratitude and praise as well as with contrition.

Jonah's example is helpful to Christians today. He teaches us that even in our worst situations we need to approach God with both repentance and thanksgiving. No matter our experiences, we serve a powerful God—One who deserves all honor and praise.

*Dear Lord, thank You for hearing my prayers.
Thank You for having mercy on me. Amen.*

Speak Up!

*It is not only the old who are wise, not only
the aged who understand what is right.*

JOB 32:9 NIV

Five-year-old Yanick was given the responsibility (at twenty-five cents per visit) to accompany her grandmother to the hospital and act as her interpreter. Her grandmother had medical problems and spoke no English. So while Yanick's parents worked, they gave their little girl this very grown-up assignment.

Yanick recalls thinking then that many of the medical professionals purposely used big words that she didn't have the vocabulary to translate. After one such visit, Yanick announced her decision to her parents.

"I'm going to be a doctor when I grow up," said the feisty five-year-old. "I want to help people speak up for themselves when no one else tries to understand." As a practicing pediatrician today who specializes in AIDS treatment for mothers and their babies, Yanick continues to speak up—in plain, everyday English (or French) to her patients and their families.

Sometimes children have more wisdom than their sophisticated, older counterparts. They're not out to impress with their vocabulary. They don't try to baffle others with their knowledge. They just want to help—with or without a twenty-five-cent bonus. That kind of wisdom and tenderness comes from the One whose breath "gives [us] understanding" (Job 32:8 NIV).

*Father, help me to be childlike in my
sensitivity to the needs of others. Amen.*

Confidence

*For I know that my redeemer liveth, and that he shall stand
at the latter day upon the earth: And though after my skin
worms destroy this body, yet in my flesh shall I see God.*

JOB 19:25–26 KJV

What amazing hope we have! We serve a risen Savior.

It is hard to imagine how Job must have felt as he went through such a horrible situation—losing his family, his possessions, and even his health. Yet in all of his misery he said with confidence, "I know that my redeemer liveth." The irony of this is that Christ had not yet been born, much less had He completed His redemptive work. Still, Job's faith did not waver. He knew that one day he would stand before his redeemer in a perfected body.

Although we experience various difficulties throughout life, we can still look forward to the blessed future we have. No matter what our struggles are, our Lord controls everything.

Job had no idea what the purpose of his trial was, but he faced his troubles with confidence, knowing that ultimately he would emerge victorious. Too many times we view our own situations with self-pity rather than considering God's strength and trusting that His plan is perfect. What peace God offers when we finally cast our cares on Him and with great conviction declare, "I know that my redeemer liveth!"

*O great Redeemer, in You I have confidence even when I don't
understand life's trials. Please help me to live victoriously.*

Save Me

God, God, save me! I'm in over my head.
PSALM 69:1 MSG

The bills have piled up almost as high as the laundry. You got a traffic ticket. You lost your keys or dropped your cell phone in the bathtub. People in your life are too busy to listen, and you are too busy to listen to them. It's raining. It's pouring. You stand drenched to the bone and begin to shiver in the cold. Tears start to flow down your cheeks, but no one notices. The tears just mingle with the rain, and maybe everyone else is crying also. We are all too busy, too stressed, too frazzled.

"God, God, save me! I'm in over my head," the psalmist wrote. And in the twenty-first century, we can relate to his plea!

Come, Father, and lift from me these burdens I've created for myself. Help me to shed some extra burdens in order that I might focus again on what's important, which is You, my God. Help me to rest in Your goodness and Your deep love for me.

I am in over my head! I cry out to You. I need You this day, this hour, this moment. I need the One who made me and knit me together in my mother's womb to find me here. I need You to save me—if even from myself.

*Father, there are times I cannot do one more thing. I realize
I have lost You in the shuffle. Find me, I pray. Amen.*

Give Back

*Let them do good, that they be rich in
good works, ready to give, willing to share.*
1 TIMOTHY 6:18 NKJV

Leigh spent a few hours each month picking up trash around her neighborhood with friends. Madison chose to spend one night each week volunteering in a local hospital. Grace enjoyed reading with kids at a nearby school.

We may not be saved through our works, but Christians can show the fruit of our salvation by giving back. Jesus died to give us life. Now we have the opportunity to show His love to others through our works.

In 1 Timothy 6:18, those who are wealthy in this world are told to "do good, that they be rich in good works." The image is one of abundance. Somehow, through giving, we are the ones who are truly blessed.

We don't have to devote a lot of time to do a good work. Spending a few hours a month in volunteer work or even donating items to a local organization can be a big help to those in need. Find an organization—in church or outside—that sparks your interest and get involved. After all, a relationship with God must bear fruit.

*Heavenly Father, thank You for Your love. Remind
me each day to show that love to others through my works.
Help me to bear fruit for Your kingdom by giving to others.*

The Ultimate Thief

And my God shall supply all your need
according to His riches in glory by Christ Jesus.
PHILIPPIANS 4:19 NKJV

One day the wife of a man from the guild of prophets called out to Elisha, "'Your servant my husband is dead. You well know what a good man he was, devoted to God. And now the man to whom he was in debt is on his way to collect by taking my two children as slaves" (2 Kings 4:1 MSG).

Credit companies send credit card offers and buying incentives in the mail, seemingly every day. It's so easy to buy things we want on impulse with the full intention of paying it off in monthly payments. But months become years, and interest owed outweighs the value of the thing we purchased.

Debt can steal your joy in owning something of your own. We must truly count the cost. Is the purchase a wise investment or a long-term debt? God wants you to have the things you want and need. Refuse to become a slave to debt; instead ask God to help you make wise purchases. He will help you find the means to pay for those things you need as well as the things you want if you make a commitment to be wise in your financial commitments.

Lord, show me the difference between wants and needs
and give me the patience to save the money to pay
for the things I really want. Amen.

....
....
....
....
....
....
....
....

Content with Who I Am

So be content with who you are, and don't put on airs.
1 PETER 5:6 MSG

Janette glanced around the gym, noticing the women around her. Several of them were chatting with friends as they ran on treadmills. They haven't even broken a sweat, Janice thought, and I'm drenched like I got caught in a rainstorm. A few other ladies came out of an aerobics class, and Janette realized with dismay that she was—once again—the biggest person in the room.

I exercise and eat right, she grumbled to herself, but I'm still bigger than I want to be. Why can't I look like those celebrities on the cover of fashion magazines? Close to tears, she prayed, *Lord, why did You make me this way?*

Later, Janette shared her thoughts with her mom, who could always lift her spirits. "Janette, you are beautiful—on the inside and the out!" her mother said. "I wouldn't want you to be a waif. God made you the way you are—strong and tall—for a reason."

After Janette hung up the phone, she hung her head. Lord, forgive me for comparing myself to others, she prayed. Help me to be content with who I am.

And then, she stood up, grabbed the latest issue of *Celebrity Weekly,* and threw it in the trash.

Lord, forgive me when I get caught up in the world's idea of beauty. Help me to see myself as You see me—a beloved, beautiful daughter.

....
....
....
....
....
....
....
....
....

Word to the Wise

If any of you lacks wisdom, he should ask God, who gives generously to all without finding fault, and it will be given to him.

JAMES 1:5 NIV

Wisdom should be our request as we seek God's face each day. We all need wisdom for the huge decisions: choosing a mate, which career path to take, or what ministries to pursue. But we also need wisdom for the smaller, day-to-day things as well: what to do in our spare time, how to spend this week's paycheck, or what relationships need attention.

God's Word tells us that He gives wisdom to all who ask—without finding fault. Ask and it will be given to you! However, the verse goes on to say that when you do ask the Lord for wisdom, trust that He will make good on His promise. If you find yourself asking for wisdom but doubting that God will really give it to you, confess that to the Lord and ask Him to change your mind-set. Trust in the Lord and know that He is faithful to hear your prayers and answer according to His will.

Father, forgive me for the times I have doubted You. I ask for wisdom for the big decisions in my life but also for daily wisdom. Help me to trust You more. Amen.

....
....
....
....
....
....
....
....
....
....

Directed by His Word

Direct my steps by Your word,
and let no iniquity have dominion over me.
PSALM 119:133 NKJV

A woman took her trusty yellow Lab out for a walk one day. She did not need a leash. Despite the distractions of playful squirrels, children riding bikes, and even an occasional cat poised on a front porch, her faithful dog walked at her side. When the dog did trot a few steps ahead, a simple click of the tongue, followed by "come back," brought her dog right back to arm's length.

What a pleasure, she thought, to walk with a dog who responds obediently to the sound of my voice. She wondered if her own obedience brought such pleasure to the Lord. She wondered if she was more like the difficult terrier she had left at home, who pulled and tugged at the leash and wanted to chase and bark at every distraction.

God has given us the privilege of having His Word available to us, and His Living Word, Jesus, residing in our hearts. His Word is there speaking to us. Do we listen and respond obediently? Is there pleasure in our walk with God? Or are we allowing sin to reign in our lives? We can pray like the psalmist did that we would be directed by God's Word, and that sin would not distract or dominate us.

Lord, enable me to hear and obey Your Word.
Lead me not into temptation.

....

....

....

....

....

....

....

....

Look Before You Leap

It is not good for a person to be without knowledge,
and he who hurries his footsteps errs.
PROVERBS 19:2 NASB

Janice was furious. Sue was almost thirty minutes late for their meeting and hadn't even called. How typical, Janice thought. Honestly, Sue is one of the most inconsiderate people I've ever met. After checking her watch for the third time, Janice was getting up to leave when Sue rushed in the door, obviously shaken.

"I'm so sorry I'm late," she said. "I just came upon a car accident, and I needed to wait with one of the victims until help arrived." Janice felt like a heel. She sat back down and asked Sue if there was anything she could do.

We've all been guilty of jumping to conclusions before we have all the information. We make judgments and decisions based on what we think might have happened, or what we have seen happen in the past. Assumptions like these can get us into trouble because often there is more to the story. Proverbs 19:2 reminds us that it is wise to avoid making judgments before we have all the information. Ask questions; be patient. It may keep you from having to apologize later.

Lord, help me to wait until I have all the information
before I jump to conclusions and to offer others
grace when they don't meet my expectations.

....
....
....
....
....
....
....
....

Heart and Soul

"But from there you will seek the Lord your God, and you will find Him if you search for Him with all your heart and all your soul."

DEUTERONOMY 4:29 NASB

Have you ever put something aside as a gift to give someone and then when the occasion came, you were unable to find it? You searched through every drawer, rifled through all your closets, checked and rechecked your cabinets, and finally, just as you were ready to give up, you found the gift.

Luckily for us, God has provided us with exact directions on how to seek and find Him. He offers us His Word as His manual for daily Christian living—if we are devoted to study and meditation. God promises that we will find Him if we look for Him with all our heart and soul.

If you had stopped looking after a cursory search for the gift, you would have never found it. It took serious searching to find that gift again, and it took determination and a willingness to not give up. In the same way, reading our Bibles once in a while and saying an offhanded prayer when we think about it is not a satisfactory way to seek God. Only with serious commitment—commitment with all our heart and soul—will we truly find and know God.

Dear Lord, thank You for Your promises. Please teach me to seek You with all of my heart and soul. Amen.

....
....
....
....
....
....
....
....

The True Love

"Love one another, even as I have loved you."
JOHN 13:34 NASB

In a society that has distorted the concept of love, it's reassuring to know that God loves us with a deep, limitless love. He is, in fact, love itself. He gave His Son to die for people who didn't love Him in return. God the Father even had to turn His face from His Son when He died, as He took the sin of mankind upon Himself. What incredible love that is!

We Christians tell Jesus we love Him, and His response is, "I love you more." We cannot comprehend that kind of love, yet we are the recipients of it. And He loves us not because of anything we've done, but because of His goodness. 1 John 4:19 (KJV) says, "We love him, because he first loved us."

Jesus also commands us to love others in the same way that He loves us. We all have unlovable people in our lives. But Jesus doesn't see anyone as unlovable. Look at that difficult-to-love person through new eyes today and love her as God has loved you.

*Heavenly Father, thank You for Your love for me.
Forgive me for not loving others in that same way. Give me
the ability to love others as You have instructed. Amen.*

Bad Company

Do not be misled: "Bad company corrupts good character."
1 CORINTHIANS 15:33 NIV

The young nurse began her career with stars in her eyes. However, her naive bubble quickly burst during her first lunch break. Other nurses gossiped viciously about coworkers and then pretended to be best friends when reunited on the floor. She vowed to avoid the gossip she had just witnessed. But as the weeks passed, she began chiming in during similar conversations. What was happening to her?

We are like sponges, absorbing the contents of our environment. We become like the people we spend time with. Others influence us—for better or for worse. For that reason, we must choose our friends wisely. Decide what kind of person you would like to become. Spend time with people who exhibit those qualities. Good character produces good character. The opposite is also true.

Bad character is contagious. It is subtle. It doesn't happen overnight. Choose to surround yourself with positive role models that foster good character.

*Dear Lord, help me choose my friends wisely
so that I will be positively influenced. Amen.*

The Accepted Time

For he saith, I have heard thee in a time accepted, and in the
day of salvation have I succoured thee: behold, now is the
accepted time; behold, now is the day of salvation.
2 CORINTHIANS 6:2 KJV

There was a flash of light—then a huge crash. Everything went black. When Olivia next awoke she found herself in a quiet, darkened room. She tried to move but found that she was attached to too many machines. Then someone was standing next to her.

"Don't struggle, Livy. You've been through a lot. You need to rest," her mother said calmly.

But Olivia was struggling in her heart. All she could think about was the last sermon she'd heard from her pastor.

"Today is the day!" he said with conviction. "This might be the last opportunity to seek Christ's forgiveness for sins. Won't you bow before Him today? Admit that you're a sinner in need of a savior. Ask Him to cleanse your heart. It's the only way, and it may be the only day."

Olivia wished she'd listened. Now here she was, so near death. Would God still hear her cries?

"O Jesus, I wish I'd accepted You before. Forgive me, Lord. Come into my heart; cleanse me and save me." Sweet peace surrounded her as she once again closed her eyes.

Father, You only guarantee us the moment in which we currently breathe. Help people to understand this and to accept You now.

....
....
....
....
....
....
....

Joyful Perseverance

Create in me a pure heart, O God, and renew a steadfast spirit within me.
Do not cast me from your presence or take your Holy Spirit from me.
Restore to me the joy of your salvation and grant me a willing spirit, to sustain me.
PSALM 51:10–12 NIV

Perseverance. Some days that word sounds so difficult. Maybe you dread Mondays, knowing that a full week of work and errands and demands await you. Maybe mornings in general are tough, each day holding burdens of its own.

Do not grow weary. Strive each day to keep a pure heart. Don't complain or dwell on small annoyances. Recognize your own worth in God's eyes, and recognize the worth of others, as well. Be joyful, even when you are not particularly happy.

This world will do all it can to pull you down, to tell you to give up. When you're tempted to grow discouraged, remember that you stand in the presence of God, and that He has given you the gift of His Spirit for times such as these.

Ask God for the power to press forward when your own spirit grows tired. Turn to other Christian believers for encouragement. Know that you are not alone—that you will never be alone. God craves your devotion. Turn to Him, and persevere.

Lord, forgive me for being shortsighted and feeling overwhelmed by the worries of this world. Remind me of Your grace and salvation. Remind me of Your love for me, so that I might better love others.

A Peaceful Home

My people will live in a peaceful habitation,
and in secure dwellings and in undisturbed resting places.
ISAIAH 32:18 NASB

Home is where you should feel safe and most free to be yourself—a place of refuge from the outside world. Your home should reflect a strength and quiet confidence welcoming to your family, friends, and God.

The atmosphere of your home starts with you. It takes a conscious effort and true discipline to leave the world's cares at the threshold of the front door and stay committed to the pursuit of a peaceful home.

Perhaps you've been running all day and you need to slow down. Take a few moments before you enter your home and find your focus. Let go of the day. Shake off the frustration of work, school, relational, and financial concerns. Make a decision to be proactive and peaceful instead of reactive and defensive.

Then step across the threshold into a place of peace. Put a smile on your face and make a deliberate effort to relax. Speak to your family in a soft, positive, encouraging voice. You set the tone of your home, and you control the pace within it. Make it a place of peace today.

Lord, thank You for reminding me to cast off the cares of the day.
Help me to bring peace, harmony, and unity into my home. Amen.

Get a Life

In him was life, and that life was the light of men.
JOHN 1:4 NIV

Do you have a life?

You've probably been asked that more than once. Having a life usually means you have a busy social calendar, lots of places to go, things to do, and friends to hang out with. The world tells us that those are the things that bring happiness and fulfillment. The Bible defines having a life a bit differently.

In John 14:6, Jesus tells us that He is the way, the truth, and the life. He is our only way to our Father in heaven. Jesus is the light of the world and the only One who can fill us with life. Real life. Deep fulfillment. A life that makes a difference and lasts for eternity.

So, do you have the light of Christ living inside you or do you need to get a life? A place to go, things to do, and people to see don't mean a whole lot at the end of your life here on earth. You will never look back and wish you could have attended one more social event.

Jesus is the only way to eternal life. Make sure you've got a life before you leave!

Dear Jesus, I want You to light up my soul and give me eternal life. Help me to live my life for You. Amen.

Are You a Mary or a Martha?

She had a sister called Mary, who sat at the Lord's feet listening to
what he said. But Martha was distracted by all the preparations that
had to be made. She came to him and asked, "Lord, don't you care that
my sister has left me to do the work by myself? Tell her to help me!"
LUKE 10:39–40 NIV

Are you a Mary or a Martha? Are you sitting at Christ's feet or busying yourself with His work? Aren't both necessary? How do we live and strike a balance between the two?

As you read the rest of this Bible story, you find that Jesus does not tell Mary to help Martha. Instead, He points out that Martha is worried and upset about many things. He is pleased with Mary's choice to sit and listen to Him.

Certainly it is necessary to work. Work must be completed, meals must be made, the house must be kept clean. But beware of becoming so much like Martha that you forget to sit still and listen to your Savior as Mary did. Set aside time in each day to read the Word and pray. You will find Him in a new way as you quiet yourself before Him.

Father, often I seek to please You through my acts of service. I
work hard. Calm my spirit and show me the value of resting in Your
presence. Speak to me as I still myself before You now. Amen.

....
....
....
....
....
....
....
....
....

Enslaved No More

Think of your sufferings as a weaning from that old sinful habit of always expecting to get your own way. Then you'll be able to live out your days free to pursue what God wants instead of being tyrannized by what you want.

1 Peter 4:2 msg

Linda eats even when she's not hungry; it's just habit. She knows she needs to change but can't seem to for more than one day—and her yo-yo dieting produces poor health, fatigue, self-hatred, embarrassment, and guilt, sending her back to food for comfort and perpetuating this dangerous cycle. She feels resigned to being stuck in this sinful pattern.

Isn't that what Satan wants? One more Christian tyrannized, impotent, and unintentionally making a mockery of Christ's power over sin and death?

Spiritual warfare rages every day within believers, but God's Word says we are no longer enslaved to our old habits. They may not die easily; however, we are sustained in our battle by knowing Christ died to conquer sin. Ultimately, Satan is the big loser here, not us. We must daily wag our finger in the master liar's face, claiming Jesus' name and power over all that holds us back from God's perfect will for our life. We are no longer chained. We have soaring freedom in Christ!

Jesus, thank You for Your sacrifice on the cross for my sin and for the victory we have every day in You. Amen.

Laundry List

I can do everything through Christ, who gives me strength.
PHILIPPIANS 4:13 NLT

"Being an adult stinks!" Ava shouted at the giant pile of laundry that awaited her arrival from work. Out on her own for the first time, she had to face the responsibilities of work and home. It wasn't that she didn't know what to do, but at times the tasks of daily life seemed a bit overwhelming.

Whether you've been on your own for a decade, are living with a family of four, or are fresh out of college, the responsibilities can become burdensome. Philippians 4:13 tells us we can do all things thanks to Christ who gives us strength. That includes the little responsibilities of daily life, such as laundry, cooking, dishes, and dusting. Call on God for the strength that He promises His people.

His strength may come in the form of better strategies to tackle your workload. If you're swamped with too many things to do at home, tackle projects one at a time. Spend a few minutes each day cleaning rather than saving the whole house for a weekend project. Make a list of what needs to be done and check it off one at a time. Or, if you've got a spouse or roommate, assign tasks for each of you to complete. More hands make less work for each.

Lord, there are many responsibilities that come with being an adult, and sometimes I get overwhelmed. Remind me that I can do all things, even the small ones, because of Your strength.

For Such a Time as This

*"If you keep quiet at a time like this, deliverance and relief for the Jews
will arise from some other place, but you and your relatives will die.
Who knows if perhaps you were made queen for just such a time as this?"*
ESTHER 4:14 NLT

Esther was between a rock and a hard place. If she approached the king without being invited, she risked losing her life. If she kept silent, she and her family would die. Her wise cousin Mordecai helped put the situation into perspective. He explained that God's plans and purposes would prevail—whether Esther cooperated or not. Esther merely had to choose whether she wanted to experience the joy of participating in God's plan of deliverance for the Jewish people.

Can you imagine the honor of being chosen to help God in this way? God has placed each of us on this earth for a purpose. When we cooperate with Him, we get to experience the blessing of being a part of His plans. If we choose not to participate, there will be consequences. Don't be mistaken—God's purposes will still unfold. But we won't get to be a part of it. Like Esther, the choice is ours. Will we cooperate with God or keep silent and miss out on our place in history?

Heavenly Father, thank You for placing me on earth at this time in history. Thank You for the opportunity to be a part of Your plan. Help me to choose to cooperate with You.

The Perfect Reflection

"Give careful thought to your ways."
HAGGAI 1:7 NIV

You probably know how it feels to have a bad hair day or a huge zit on your face. On days like these, we try to avoid the mirror. The last thing we want is to keep running into a reflection of ourselves when we look less than our best.

Our Christian lives often have a similar feel. Instead of facing our imperfections as followers of Christ, we work hard to avoid any mention of or allusion to them. God's command to give careful thought to our ways may fill us with dread because the reflection can be so unattractive.

As we give careful thought to our ways, we should first look back to where we have come from and reflect on God's work in our lives. We are on a journey. Sometimes the road is difficult; sometimes the road is easy. We must consider where we were when God found us and where we are now through His grace. Even more importantly, we must think about the ways our present actions, habits, and attitude toward God reflect our lives as Christians. Only when we are able honestly to assess our lives in Christ can we call on His name to help perfect our reflection.

Dear Lord, help me to look honestly at the ways
I live and make changes where necessary. Amen.

No Liars Allowed

God is not a man, so he does not lie. He is not human, so he does
not change his mind. Has he ever spoken and failed to act?
Has he ever promised and not carried it through?
NUMBERS 23:19 NLT

Have you ever let someone else down? Or have you experienced disappointment when others didn't follow through with what they said they'd do? As imperfect humans, we've all been on the giving and receiving ends of such circumstances.

But God is different. It's not just that He's upstanding and reliable; instead, God, by His very nature, is incapable of lying, indecision, manipulation, or going back on His Word.

What does this mean for His children? First, it means that we never have to wonder if God is planning to follow through with His promises. It means we can count on Him to do what He says, and He'll never waver or be wishy-washy. God's truth will remain true now and forever.

No matter what frustrations or disappointments are happening in your life, take comfort in the fact that God remains constant. Praise Him for His very nature of stability and support, and thank Him for His everlasting goodness.

I am amazed by You, dear Lord. When I am surrounded by
the sins of the world, still Your awesome perfection shines through.
You are my rock, my redeemer, and ever-faithful friend. Amen.

....

....

....

....

....

....

....

....

His Healing Abundance

Behold, I will bring it health and healing; I will heal them
and reveal to them the abundance of peace and truth.
JEREMIAH 33:6 NKJV

Our health—physical, mental, emotional, and spiritual—is important to God. He longs to see us whole in every area of our lives. As believers in His grace and goodness, we ought to be diligent about seeking health so that we can be good stewards of His gifts.

If we confess our sins to God, He will bring relief to our souls. When we're distressed, we have Jesus, the Prince of Peace, to give us peace. When our emotions threaten to overwhelm us, we can implore Jehovah Rapha—the God Who Heals—to calm our anxious hearts. When we're physically sick, we can cry out to Jesus, our Great Physician. While He may not always heal us in the ways we might like, He will always give us strength, courage, and peace.

So whether our problems affect us physically, spiritually, mentally, or emotionally, we can trust that God will come to us and bring us healing. And beyond our temporal lives, we can look forward with hope to our heavenly lives. There we will be healthy, whole, and alive—forever.

Jehovah Rapha, thank You for healing me. Help me do my part to seek health and the abundance of peace and truth You provide.

....
....
....
....
....
....
....
....
....

Contentment

The Lord is my shepherd, I shall not be in want.
PSALM 23:1 NIV

Probably the most familiar passage in the Bible, the Twenty-third Psalm is a picture of contentment. If the Lord is our shepherd, then we are His sheep. Sheep are fragile animals, easily lost and injured, and in need of constant care. They are vulnerable to predators, especially if separated from the flock, and need to be guarded and led to places of safety.

A shepherd spends all his time with his sheep. Theirs is a close relationship, and He is always guarding them. He is responsible for nourishment, rest, places of safety, and care for the injured. The sheep do not have to seek these things; it is the shepherd's job to know what they need and provide it.

Though it's not very flattering to be thought of as sheep, it does help to describe our relationship with God. Because we are sheep, with Christ as our shepherd, we do not have to worry, strive, want, or lack. We are never alone. As Philippians 4:19 (NKJV) says, "My God shall supply all your need according to His riches in glory by Christ Jesus."

Lord, help me to remember that I am a sheep
and You are my shepherd. In times of loneliness,
anxiety, need, or pain, help me to turn to You.

Count the Cost

"But don't begin until you count the cost."
LUKE 14:28 NLT

What might it have been like to be one of Christ's first followers?

Christ empowered His twelve disciples and sent them out to do miracles (Mark 6:7, 13, 30). When the Lord sent out seventy-two of His closest followers, they returned, exploding with joy and excitement (Luke 10:1–17).When the church began after the Resurrection, the public liked the disciples (Acts 2:47).

But all too soon, the novelty wore off. Persecution began. Christians were hunted, imprisoned, and murdered.

So far, we may not have had to seriously count the cost of following Christ. Yet according to one recent statistic, for more than 2.5 billion people around the world, simply attending a church meeting can mean harassment, arrest, torture, or death. For Christians throughout much of Africa and the Middle East, the cost of their commitment to Christ exacts a high toll. For us in the United States, being a Christ follower might mean being shunned by friends or finding ourselves humiliated. Such persecution may yet take on more serious consequences, as it has in the past. Will you be ready to hold tight to your faith?

The early church counted the cost of following Christ. Today, many of our brothers and sisters worldwide are doing the same. They're ready for whatever comes. We need to be ready, too.

*Lord, don't let me forget that my salvation
doesn't come without cost or sacrifice. Amen.*

....
....
....
....
....
....
....

Daily Choice

"The thief comes only to steal and kill and destroy;
I have come that they may have life, and have it to the full."
JOHN 10:10 NIV

Some days it seems the negative outweighs the positive. People demand so much of our time. Bills demand so much of our money. Feelings of inadequacy surface quickly. It all caves in around us—it's just too much! But when God's words fall on our hearts, those thoughts of defeat are shown for what they really are: lies that delight the enemy who wants to destroy our souls.

But Christ comes to give life! Choosing life is an act of the will blended with faith. We must daily make the decision to take hold of the life Christ offers us. It's this Spirit-infused life that keeps us going; our greatest efforts often come up short. Accepting this gift from Jesus doesn't guarantee a perfect life; it doesn't even guarantee an easy life. But Christ does promise to sustain us, support us, and provide a haven from the storms of life in His loving arms.

Giving Lord, help me daily choose You and the life
You want to give me. Give me eyes of faith to trust that
You will enable me to serve lovingly, as You do.

Forgive Her?

*"If you hold anything against anyone, forgive [her],
so that your Father in heaven may forgive you your sins."*
MARK 11:25 NIV

Good friendships—those few girls you chat with on the phone, go with to the mall, or have a cup of coffee with—are wonderful. At some point, though, one of these close friends may hurt you with her words or actions.

You may have a friend who wounded you deeply. Have you forgiven her? *But she never asked for forgiveness!* you may be thinking. Even so, Jesus tells us to forgive. It may seem impossible to obey His command, but He can help you.

God sent His only Son to die for our sins. If anyone can identify with the pain of being offended, it's He! But He willingly forgave, and we are to follow His example. God tells us in His Word that He will remember our sins "no more" (Hebrews 10:17) when we ask His forgiveness. We may always remember being offended by a friend, but He promises that He will put our offenses out of His mind and never bring them up again. How wonderful to be forgiven—and to forgive!

Lord Jesus, thank You for forgiving me. Please help me to extend that forgiveness to others, even if they don't ask. And help me to do my best to forget the offense. Amen.

The Battle of the Mind

We demolish arguments and every pretension that sets itself
up against the knowledge of God, and we take captive
every thought to make it obedient to Christ.
2 CORINTHIANS 10:5 NIV

What does it mean to take every thought captive to make it obedient to Christ? Prevent the first lie from taking root. Weigh every thought against truth. If a thought is not consistent with God's Word, do not give it credence. Dismiss it from your mind by not dwelling on it.

The battle rages: Who or what will control our minds? We have an enemy who wants to influence our thought life. He masquerades as a friend, whispering deception. But beware! He is no friend. He is the father of lies. We must constantly discern God's truth from Satan's lies. Deception is subtle. Once we buy into one lie, we are quickly led down a path riddled with more. Before we know it, we have drawn false conclusions and made decisions based on wrong information.

We cannot test our thoughts unless we know scripture. Even Satan knows truth. He twists God's Word to accomplish his purposes—our destruction. Saturate your mind with truth by reading the Bible. Meditate on scripture. Learn truth so you can recognize a lie. Then you will be victorious in the battle of your mind.

Dear Lord, help me win the battle of my mind
by taking every thought captive to You. Amen.

....

....

....

....

....

....

....

....

Always Thinking of You

What is man that You are mindful of him,
and the son of man that You visit him?
PSALM 8:4 NKJV

What are you thinking about today? Do you have a list of things you want to get done, people you need to call, or maybe a vacation you want to plan? Your thoughts fill up your days and keep you busy going and doing life.

Have you ever wondered what God thinks about? He thinks about you! You are always on His mind. In all you think and do, He considers you and makes intercession for you. He knows the thoughts and intents of your heart. He understands you like no other person can. He knows your strengths and weaknesses, your darkest fears and highest hopes. He's constantly aware of your feelings and how you interact with or without Him each day.

God is always with you, waiting for you to remember Him—to call on Him for help, for friendship, for anything you need. He wants to be a big part of your life. And if you include Him, He will open the doors to as much goodness, mercy, and love as you'll allow Him to bless you with.

Lord, help me to remember You as I go throughout my day. I want to include You in my life and always be thinking of You. Amen.

I Lift My Eyes

I lift up my eyes to the hills—where does my help come from?
My help comes from the Lord, the Maker of heaven and earth.
PSALM 121:1–2 NIV

Have you ever been told to "keep your eyes on the prize" or "keep your nose to the grindstone"? These clichés are worldly pieces of advice that are meant to be helpful in the pursuit of success. However, when our eyes remain on the end result—the prize—we can miss much along the way. Or if we keep our heads down, focused on our work, we cannot be guided.

Career paths, relationships, and financial decisions are only some of the areas that cause concern throughout all of life.

In all of these things, we shouldn't keep our eyes fixed on the end result, and we shouldn't keep our heads down and simply plow through. Instead, we must lift our eyes to the Lord. If we fix our focus on Jesus, we will see that He is prepared to lead and guide us through all of life's challenges.

Lord, I lift up my eyes to You. Please help me and guide me down the path of life. Let me never become so focused on my own goals or so busy about my work that I forget to look to You, for You are my help. Amen.

Spiritual Gifts

Now to each one the manifestation of
the Spirit is given for the common good.
1 CORINTHIANS 12:7 NIV

You are one of a kind, uniquely created by God. He has bestowed upon you at least one spiritual gift. Accept this gift, and don't try to be something you're not. If you don't know what your spiritual gift is, ask the Lord to reveal it to you. What are you passionate about? When do you feel the most alive and fulfilled? Look for opportunities to serve in that area.

As believers, we have received various spiritual gifts from the Holy Spirit. They are used to build up the body of Christ. All of the gifts are equally important, although some are more visible than others. Don't covet someone else's gift. Concentrate on developing your own. Pursue opportunities of service that emphasize your giftedness. Be willing to give up other endeavors in order to pursue God's call. You cannot serve everywhere.

Focus on exercising your spiritual gifts. As you learn and grow in these talents, you'll make a greater impact for the kingdom and fulfill God's purpose.

Dear Lord, reveal my spiritual gift. Help me
use it effectively to benefit the church body. Amen.

....
....
....
....
....
....
....
....
....

Treasured Daughter

"The Lord your God is with you, he is mighty to save. He will take great delight in you, he will quiet you with his love, he will rejoice over you with singing."

ZEPHANIAH 3:17 NIV

What an amazing verse to remind us of who God is and who we are in Him! He delights in and rejoices over us. He is our Father, and we are His treasured daughters.

Do you feel like a treasured daughter of the King? If not, what is keeping you from close communion with your heavenly Father?

We are all made perfect in Christ, and we can approach God's throne with confidence (Hebrews 4:16) because of what Jesus Christ did for us on the cross. Your heavenly Father loves you and wants to have a close father-daughter relationship with you. There is nothing you can do to earn His love. It is already there for you. There is nothing you can do to make Him love you more than He already does. His love is everlasting.

Take the time to write out this verse on an index card. Carry it with you today and meditate on it all day long. Ask God to reveal Himself to you through this scripture so that you can know Him more.

You are treasured!

Heavenly Father, thank You for being with me. Help me to know and feel that I am deeply loved by You. Amen.

....

....

....

....

....

....

....

....

The Light of Life

Your word is a lamp to my feet and a light to my path.
PSALM 119:105 NKJV

Imagine yourself camping in the woods with friends. There are no street or porch lights. The fire has been put out, and everyone has gone to bed. The darkness of night in the country has settled in, but you need to go from one tent to the other.

What would you do? Carry a flashlight, of course. Without it you can't see the tree roots, twigs, rocks, or uneven ground beneath your feet. There could be snakes, raccoons, coyotes, or bears lurking in the dark. Only a complete fool would step out into the dark without a flashlight to illumine her way.

The road of life sometimes has uneven ground, sharp turns, and dangers awaiting us. Foolishly, we try to walk it in the dark. Jesus said in John 8:12 (NKJV), "I am the light of the world. He who follows Me shall not walk in darkness, but have the light of life." Our light is the Living Word, Jesus Christ. He has revealed Himself in scripture, and His Spirit illuminates the scripture for us as we read it. With His Word He guides our every step.

Father, thank You for the gift of Your Son, who is the light of life. Give me the desire to study the scriptures and know You as revealed to me in them. By Your Spirit, bring the Word to my mind in times of need and temptation.

Leave Your Bags Behind

Give all your worries and cares to God, for he cares about you.
1 Peter 5:7 nlt

Imagine that your best friend has announced she's treating you to an all-expenses-paid cruise. All of your meals are included, and she's even throwing in a brand-new wardrobe.

"Leave your bags behind," she tells you. "All you have to do is show up."

Can you imagine arriving at the cruise ship with suitcases full of clothes, shoes, and food? "Why are you carrying all this junk?" your friend would say. "I told you I had it covered—don't you trust me?"

All too often, this is how we approach God. He invites us to give Him our burdens, but we show up, time and time again, weighed down with bags so full we can't even carry them. So we drag them behind us wherever we go. They slow us down so that we're not productive, just burdened. Worry, anger, resentment, anxious thoughts. . .sometimes the list is long.

God has told us to give all of our cares to Him. He promises that He has them covered, and yet we still hang on. What baggage are you carrying today that you can give to the Lord?

Father, thank You for the invitation to cast all my cares upon You. Help me to let go of the things that are weighing me down and to trust You to take them for me.

Pointing Fingers

They were very sad and began to say to him
one after the other, "Surely not I, Lord?"
MATTHEW 26:22 NIV

Picture yourself among the twelve apostles, sitting at the dinner table with Jesus and celebrating the Passover meal. Passover is always a serious event, but this evening seems even more somber, more so than other holidays you have celebrated together.

Then, as you are reclining at the table, Christ says, "One of you will betray me."

You're shocked. You look at the others on either side of you and across the table, then back at Jesus. Your voice joins the commotion. "Not I! Surely not I!"

It is easy for us to focus on Judas in this scene and lay all blame upon him alone. But later that same evening every one of the apostles flees the garden and deserts Jesus when the crowd comes to arrest Him.

Each of us must recognize our own capacity for betrayal and discover what tempts us the most. Perhaps the first temptation we must avoid is wanting to look around the table and search for parties more guilty than ourselves.

Lord, instill in me an honest humility. Strengthen my dedication to You so I am not so easily led astray.

A Life of Joy

*Satisfy us in the morning with your unfailing love,
that we may sing for joy and be glad all our days.*
PSALM 90:14 NIV

Webster's dictionary defines joy as "emotion evoked by well-being, success, or good fortune." When was the last time you experienced joy? Was it last month? Last week? Today?

There are many joyful occasions: a birthday, an anniversary, a job promotion, a wedding, the birth of a baby. . .the list can go on. But do we need a big event to give us joy? Many ordinary moments can bring joy as well: getting a close parking spot at the mall, finding a ten-dollar bill in your pocket. . .again, the list continues.

First Thessalonians 5:16 (NLT) tells us to "always be joyful." That doesn't mean we need to take pleasure when things go wrong in life, smiling all the while. Rather, God wants us to maintain a spirit of joy, knowing that He has provided happy times and will carry us through the hard times.

Ever notice how a joyful spirit is contagious? When you're around someone who is full of joy, it's easy to find yourself sharing in that joy. Maybe you could be that person today, bringing smiles to others. When you find delight in the ordinary moments, they will catch the joy.

*Heavenly Father, I thank You for being the source
of my joy. Please help me to share Your joy with
those whom I come in contact with today. Amen.*

Fruitful Living

*But the Holy Spirit produces this kind of fruit in our lives: love, joy, peace,
patience, kindness, goodness, faithfulness, gentleness, and self-control.*
GALATIANS 5:22–23 NLT

We've all had those days when nothing is going according to our plan. We might as well be beating our heads against the wall. What's the problem?

Because we are human, we tend to want to rely on ourselves to fix our problems. It's a constant battle. The apostle Paul describes this wrestling match in Romans 7:19 (NIV), "For what I do is not the good I want to do; no, the evil I do not want to do—this I keep on doing." Paul asks in verse 24, "Who will rescue me from this body of death?" His answer? Jesus Christ!

We need to recognize the problem. Frustration, resentment, and anger are red flags. They are by-products of our sinful nature, proving that we've bypassed the help and peace God offers. We want life to go according to our plan and agenda, but God's way is so much better. Jesus came to rescue us from ourselves. He came to enable us to walk in the Spirit by yielding control to Him. Once we do that, our lives will produce the spiritual fruit God wants us to grow. It's a better way to live!

*Dear Lord, help me realize when I am walking in the flesh.
May I yield to You so that I reap spiritual fruit. Amen.*

....

....

....

....

....

....

....

....

Conquer that Mountain

"I am the Lord your God, who teaches you to profit,
who leads you by the way you should go."
ISAIAH 48:17 NKJV

Life is full of ups and downs—mountain and valley experiences. There are times when you can get stuck or grow frustrated trying to conquer one specific mountain. Maybe you find yourself facing the same obstacle for the second and third time. Sometimes those mountains can present very difficult lessons to learn, so you climb them again and again, trying to understand something about yourself vital to reaching your next level of life.

If you feel like you're repeating the same lesson, go deep into your heart and ask yourself the hard questions. Why am I climbing this mountain again? What did I miss? What do I need to know or learn before I can go to the next level? Then ask the Lord to give you answers and show you things you might have missed.

God gave you a life to fulfill with a specific purpose to complete. He wants to see you moving forward. With your heart and mind open, ready to receive clear direction, you can conquer the mountain this time! You have an amazing destiny to achieve.

God, I ask for Your wisdom and guidance in my life.
Help me to see whatever it is I've missed and help
me to follow Your direction in all things. Amen.

A Faithful Example

"Surely your God is a God of gods and a Lord of kings and a revealer of mysteries, since you have been able to reveal this mystery."
DANIEL 2:47 NASB

King Nebuchadnezzar had a dream that neither he nor his magicians and sorcerers could explain. But God revealed both the dream and its meaning to Daniel. He, in turn, explained the dream to the king, who was so pleased with Daniel that he promoted him to a high position in his court.

What a day that must have been for Daniel! After years of remaining faithful to God—even in a foreign, unbelieving land—he was able to prove God's might to the king.

Maybe you have a friend or family member who has not yet put his or her faith in God. Perhaps you have been praying about it for many years. Don't give up hope! Daniel's faith allowed God to demonstrate His power to the king, and while the king did not immediately bow down to God, he saw that God was real and powerful.

Our faithful example is important. When we trust in God, those around us will see His power in us. Through our actions, others will come to know God.

Dear Lord, be with my friends who don't know You.
Help me to plant seeds of faith in their hearts.
Let me trust that You will make them grow. Amen.

Creative Fitness

Young people, it's wonderful to be young. . . . But remember
that you must give an account to God for everything you do.
So refuse to worry, and keep your body healthy.
ECCLESIASTES 11:9–10 NLT

"I know I should work out, but the gym is just so boring!" Rebekah said as she held up her sweatpants and tank top. She wanted to be healthy and take care of the body God gave her. Yet she also despised hitting the treadmill.

Going to the gym is great for some people, but for others it can be overwhelming, boring, or even too expensive. Luckily, there are plenty of other options for staying fit. Find a local hiking or biking trail and spend some time enjoying the beautiful world God created. Or take a class in martial arts, dance, or aerobics. Some local churches may even offer fitness courses for their members. Team sports like soccer, softball, or basketball are also a great option and are often organized through churches, businesses, or local recreation centers.

Still not satisfied? Simply put on your favorite Christian radio station or CD and dance or clean the house to some inspirational music. It makes working out less of a chore and gives you some quality time with God.

Dear Lord, I want to take care of the body You gave me.
Help me to find creative and enjoyable ways to stay fit,
while honoring You in the process. Amen.

More Than We Can Imagine

*Now to him who is able to do immeasurably more than all we
ask or imagine, according to his power that is at work within us.*
EPHESIANS 3:20 NIV

Sammie married her high school sweetheart right after college. A few years into the marriage, she sensed that her husband, Brad, was slipping away from her and from God.

At first, she panicked. But after talking to her pastor and spending time in God's Word, Sammie began to pray fervently—almost hourly—for her husband.

It didn't happen overnight, but within a few months, Brad began to open up to her. He revealed things he had been struggling with, and he agreed to see a counselor. Cautious yet hopeful, Sammie spent lots of time listening to and patiently encouraging her husband.

Slowly, Brad's chilly demeanor started to thaw, and he began to attend church with her again. A Bible study helped him further, as did a men's accountability group. Every day, Sammie praised the Lord that He chose to heal her husband and their relationship. She knew that her happy ending wasn't that common.

A few months into their renewed marriage, Sammie heard her preacher say, "God doesn't always answers our prayers like we expect." Sammie smiled through her tears and thought, *No—sometimes He does more than we can imagine.*

*Lord, thank You for Your amazing power—
power to do more than I can ask, think, or imagine.*

Pleasing God

*His pleasure is not in the strength of the horse, nor his delight
in the legs of a man; the Lord delights in those who
fear him, who put their hope in his unfailing love.*

PSALM 147:10–11 NIV

Americans value achievement. We measure our country by its various accomplishments. Scientific discovery, space exploration, technological advancement, and world economic and political power all attest to the hard work and achievement of people building a nation.

As individuals, we measure our days by how much we get done. We take pride in checking items off our to-do lists. We e-mail on handheld devices while sitting in airports and talk on phones while driving down the highway in an effort to get more accomplished in a day.

God does not place value on our achievements. He does not measure our days by how much we get done. He is not delighted by our efficiency or our excellence. This is pretty hard to believe because our culture places such value on self-reliance, but what pleases Him is our worship of Him. He wants our reverent fear, our wonder and awe at His great power and steadfast love. He desires our dependence. He enjoys our hope when we are looking to Him to meet all our needs.

*Great God, help me to remember that I do not have to perform
for You. You have redeemed me and made me Your own.
You desire my worship and my hope. Amen.*

....

....

....

....

....

....

A Life of Love

*Be imitators of God, therefore, as dearly loved children and live
a life of love, just as Christ loved us and gave himself up
for us as a fragrant offering and sacrifice to God.*
EPHESIANS 5:1–2 NIV

Are you living a life of love? Ephesians 5:1–2 tell us Christ loved us and gave Himself up for us. John 15:13 tells us there is no greater love than when you are willing to lay down your life for someone else.

How can you apply this to your daily life? By putting others first! Think of others' needs before you worry about yourself. Be others-minded instead of selfish. Wholeheartedly loving another person is one of the most selfless things you will ever do.

Do you love people enough to lay down your life for them? Putting others first can be difficult to do, but when we are being "imitators of God" He fills us with His Spirit and His power, and through Him we can do all things.

Dear God, show me how to love people selflessly and wholeheartedly. Help me to be willing to lay my life down for someone else if necessary. Amen.

Heavenly Treasure

*"But store up for yourselves treasures in heaven, where moth and
rust do not destroy, and where thieves do not break in and steal."*
MATTHEW 6:20 NIV

You've got ten minutes to leave your home before it is destroyed by fire. What will you take with you? Once you knew your loved ones were safe, you would likely grab the things that remind you of them—photos, heirloom jewelry, a precious family Bible.

Questions like these have a way of whittling our priorities down to the bare essentials. Most of what we own is easily destroyed and just as easily replaced. There are, however, a few things really worth having, and Jesus reminds us that these are things on which we can't put a price tag. Relationships. Eternal life. The assurance that our loved ones will live eternally with Him.

What will you take with you? This isn't a rhetorical question. The practicality of Jesus' words reminds us that the way we live our lives each and every day should be guided by this principle. Invest yourself in the things that matter. Take a look at your calendar and your checkbook. Do they reflect your desire to store up eternal treasures?

*Lord, You know it is easy to get distracted by earthly things—
things that will ultimately be worth nothing. Help me to shift
my focus to matters that have eternal significance and help me to
invest my life in those things that will bring eternal dividends.*

Look at the Heart

*For the Lord seeth not as man seeth; for man looketh on the
outward appearance, but the Lord looketh on the heart.*
1 SAMUEL 16:7 KJV

Stephanie entered the mall with one thing on her mind: She needed an outfit that would turn Alex's head. It wouldn't hurt to impress his friends, either. She'd been trying to get his attention for months. Now that he'd finally asked her out, she wasn't about to waste the opportunity.

After searching for some time, she found what she thought was perfect. She ignored the voice inside telling her that it was immodest and that her motives weren't pure. All she cared about was winning Alex.

The evening of the big date arrived. Stephanie applied her makeup and donned the new dress. The amount of skin she saw in her mirror shocked her, but she ignored the misgivings. Soon Alex arrived, and Stephanie's perfect evening began. It quickly became apparent that Alex viewed her attire as an advertisement. Stephanie realized that she had done both of them a disservice. Worse, she had revealed what was really in her heart. It was a backward step in her reputation, and it would take many forward steps to undo the damage, but Stephanie determined to make those strides.

*Lord, when I am tempted to draw attention to myself,
help me to remember that what is in my heart shows
who I really am. Let it be pleasing to You.*

Who's in Control?

The glorious God is the only Ruler,
the King of kings and Lord of lords.
1 TIMOTHY 6:15 CEV

Hannah was having second thoughts about her visit to Italy as a short-term missionary. Between the language challenges and cultural taboos, her jet-lagged brain was in overdrive. Things continued to worsen with each passing day.

On her second trip to the bureau to finalize some legal papers for her stay, she stood in the pouring rain to keep her place in line—in two inches of water. Once inside, the situation wasn't much better. The person she had to speak to wasn't there. He couldn't make it in; his car was under three feet of water. Hannah would have to make a third trip back. Disgruntled, she and her host left.

The street had become a lake. Everyone was trying to walk, wade, or swim their way to their cars and go home. Hannah saw one man who wasn't about to let the flooding best him. He walked down the street clothed in his T-shirt and underwear, holding his pants above the garbage-strewn street river.

Sometimes when we go on what we're sure is a God-ordained mission, bad things happen. In spite of inconveniences over which we've no control, we can rest in knowing God retains control. Some days we just have to trudge our way through—and look for a laugh along the way.

In my frustrations, Father, remind
me that You're in control. Amen.

....

....

....

....

....

....

....

A Lesson from the Bush

I am glad to boast about my weaknesses, so that the power of Christ
can work through me. . . . For when I am weak, then I am strong.
2 CORINTHIANS 12: 9–10 NLT

A cool breeze refreshed Anna's spirits, but when she took one look at her favorite hydrangea bush, her mood changed. How had the bush become so choked with vines? Dead flower heads hung limply among large glorious blooms. Disappointed with herself for letting busyness and procrastination take over life, she began pruning. With the dead parts falling away, the bush began to take on a different shape. The remaining blooms, having stretched high for sunshine through the strangling vines, stood sturdy and tall.

After cutting a dozen blooms, she couldn't help but smile. This gangly plant had produced incredible flowers—long, strong stems for glorious arrangements of the richest shades! What she had deemed dreadful turned out to be a delight. Her shortcomings actually provided an opportunity for God's goodness and grace to be revealed.

Anna thought about other areas of her life. Her attempts to be financially sound seemed to meet repeatedly with failure. But God always provided—even a car when hers died. Her weaknesses allowed His power to shine all the more. The less she had, the more she depended on Him.

Gracious Lord, help me to remember that when I am weak, then
I am strong. May Your power be revealed through me. Amen.

Using Time Wisely

See then that ye walk circumspectly, not as fools,
but as wise, redeeming the time, because the days are evil.
EPHESIANS 5:15–16 KJV

Is your testimony something you review on a regular basis? It should be. This world is full of darkness, and God needs dedicated Christians who truly love Him to shed His light on lost souls.

Our primary desire should be to bring people to Jesus. This doesn't mean that all we ever do is talk about God, but when He gives us opportunities, we should take them. No matter what we are doing or saying, it should always honor God.

Our time on earth is limited, and we must use every minute wisely. We will give an account of all our time, whether we waste it or use it for God's glory. That is why it is so important to look often at how we measure up to God's expectations for our lives.

Jesus is our ideal. It really doesn't matter if we are better or worse than someone else. If we don't measure up to Christ, there is work to be done. We must let God work in and through us that we might wisely use the time He gives us to make a difference for Him.

O God, give me a desire to make every moment I have count for You.
Help me be wise in how I conduct my life.

Put on the Armor

Finally, be strong in the Lord and in his mighty power. Put on the full armor of God so that you can take your stand against the devil's schemes.
EPHESIANS 6:10–11 NIV

As your relationship with the Lord grows closer, Satan will attempt to knock you off course. Has your soul ever felt oppressed for no particular reason? Satan is powerful and persistent, devising schemes that undermine the Lord's work in our lives. His attacks are more forcefully felt when we are on the front battle lines, fighting for the cause of Christ. He will go to great lengths to prevent the advancement of God's kingdom on earth.

Don't get discouraged. God has already won the battle! Christ claimed the victory by overcoming death, defeating Satan once and for all. He gives that victory to us.

Put on the spiritual armor Christ provides. We can't fend off Satan's attacks without it. We will triumph over him as we put on the belt of truth, breastplate of righteousness, helmet of salvation, shield of faith, and sword of the Spirit. Don't face your adversary ill prepared. Put on the full armor of God and stand!

*Dear Lord, remind me to wear the full armor
You have given me to ensure spiritual victory. Amen.*

Difficult People

He ransoms me unharmed from the battle
waged against me, even though many oppose me.
PSALM 55:18 NIV

There always seems to be that one person who opposes you. Maybe it's a manager you just can't seem to please, or a coworker who has to put her fingers in every project you are involved in, or a family member you just don't get along with.

Differences can really bring division between people. The enemy of your soul, Satan, has long tried to point out our differences—color of skin, political differences, gender, or religion. He'll use anything he can to divide people, specifically believers.

It's difficult to embrace those who oppose you, but with the Lord's help you can make a friend in the most adverse situations. Find something about that person you can be positive about. Show yourself friendly. The greatest gift you have to give is love. Let the love of God shine through you—and God will use you to change her or help you to find a way to be at peace with your differences.

Lord, I can't handle this difficult situation on my own.
Please help me find a way to create peace
and harmony and turn it for good. Amen.

Keep Short Accounts

Anyone who can be trusted in little matters can also be trusted in important matters. But anyone who is dishonest in little matters will be dishonest in important matters. If you cannot be trusted with this wicked wealth, who will trust you with true wealth?

LUKE 16:10–11 CEV

Credit cards seem like such a simple and easy way to buy all we want. Sometimes, though, plastic helps us acquire not only a bunch of stuff, but a mountain of debt as well. Good intentions can result in never-ending bills, interest charges, and minimum payments that barely chip away at the actual money owed. Buying on credit allows us to immediately fulfill our desires for things we want, but this isn't God's way. Instead, He desires us to be wise in our wealth.

When we prove to be faithful with our own finances, God will trust us with the bigger things in life. If we patiently wait for the blessings of life to come, we will reap the rewards of satisfaction, financial security, and the trust of others. Exercise godly principles by making sound financial decisions and faithfully honoring the gifts God gives.

Jesus, thank You for the rich blessings in my life. Please help me to be patient and wise with my finances. I want to be faithful with the little things so that I will be worthy of trust in the big ones. Amen.

Honor God with Healthy Habits

Honor God with your body.
1 Corinthians 6:20 NLT

The statistics are grim. More than half of Americans are overweight or obese. Only about a third of us get the minimum recommended amount of exercise each day. Health problems that were once reserved for elderly people—like diabetes and high blood pressure—are now affecting us at younger and younger ages.

The Bible says to honor God with our bodies. We often think of this verse in relation to sexual purity, and it certainly applies. However, we also have an opportunity to honor God with our bodies by taking good care of them—by getting enough rest and enough exercise.

Take a look in the mirror. You need at least eight hours of sleep each night so your body can function optimally. Do you make it a priority to get enough rest, or do you stretch yourself to the limit all week and then try to make up for it on the weekends? Adults should get 30–60 minutes of physical activity most days of the week. Is there time in your day for exercise? It sounds like a cliché, but you only get one body—make it a priority to honor God with it.

Father, thank You for blessing me with a body that does so much for me. Please help me to make it a priority to care for it in a way that honors You. Amen.

Fear and Dread

What I feared has come upon me;
what I dreaded has happened to me.
JOB 3:25 NIV

Job 3:25 tells us that for all the great stuff that was Job's before Satan ripped his life to shreds, deep down Job was always afraid of what might happen. When terrible times came to him—the loss of his children, his wealth, and his health—he says he expected it all along.

None of us looks forward to hardship. Some of us, quite frankly, don't expect it. If things are going well, why clutter our heads with the "what ifs"?

But then the "what ifs" intrude into our world. There's a bad diagnosis. We lose a job. Or there's a natural disaster. And too often our response is like Job's.

"I knew it was too good to last."

Do we have a secret fear or dread? God knew Job's secret fears, but still called him "blameless and upright" (Job 1:8 NIV). God doesn't withhold His love if we harbor unspoken dread. He doesn't love us any less because of secret anxieties. The Lord "is like a father to his children. . .he remembers we are only dust" (Psalm 103:13–14 NLT). God never condemned Job (and He'll never condemn us) for private fears. He encourages us to trust Him. He alone retains control over all creation and all circumstances (Job 38–41).

Father, please stay beside me when what
I dread most comes to me. Amen.

Daughters of the King

*"And I will be your Father, and you will be my
sons and daughters, says the Lord Almighty."*
2 CORINTHIANS 6:18 NLT

It is an amazing thing to know that we have a Father in heaven who loves us and calls us His daughters. And as a daughter of the King, you have some royal benefits!

John 3:16 tells us God loves us so much that He sent His only Son to die for us and take away all of our sins. Romans 8:39 asserts that we can never be separated from the love of God that is in Christ Jesus. Romans 8:28 says God works out everything for our good. Ephesians 1:4–5 remind us we were chosen by God and adopted as His children. 1 John 5:18–19 tell us we are children of God and the evil one cannot harm us. Psalm 57 tells us God sends us His love and faithfulness and fulfills His purpose for us.

Even if you have an earthly father who hasn't quite met your expectations, you can rest assured that your Father in heaven loves you and will never, ever let you down.

*Dear Father, thank You for loving me and choosing
me as Your daughter. Help me to live my life
in the comfort of Your loving arms. Amen.*

Life from Within

"Whoever believes in me, as the Scripture has said,
streams of living water will flow from within him."
JOHN 7:38 NIV

Andrea's days were long and demanding, stealing her vibrant life. Yes, it was where she wanted to be, doing what she always dreamed of, but she had not expected such a drain on her energy and time. Too many needs to meet, too many miles in the car, too little time for relaxation. How could days fly by yet seem so eternal at the same time? How would she manage to continue on for months before a break came? Where would the stamina come from when she'd already given all she could?

The Word speaks of a flow of spiritual refreshment, a steady rush of life from the streams of living water in Jesus Christ. An endless bubbling spring that reaches the mind, spirit, soul, emotions, and body, quenching deep needs, restoring life and energy to His children. God isn't a god of stuffy rules, stale dos and don'ts; He is a God of far-reaching resources. He provides a contentment that overflows to those who are parched, dry, and in need of refreshment.

Great Source of all life, fill me with Your steady flow
of living water. Make Your presence very real,
that I might overflow to those around me. Amen.

Go with God

"Therefore go and make disciples of all nations, baptizing them in the name of the Father and of the Son and of the Holy Spirit, and teaching them to obey everything I have commanded you. And surely I am with you always, to the very end of the age."
MATTHEW 28:19–20 NIV

Have you ever had to make a presentation? Maybe you had the opportunity to teach a class at your workplace or church. Wasn't it a boost to have a coworker or friend there for moral support? Even if that person just nodded occasionally in the audience, assisted with passing out papers, or adjusted the laptop or projector for you, it was a blessing to not go it alone.

Having the moral support of a friend is great, but the promise of the Great Commission scriptures is even greater. The God of the universe gives believers a command in these verses, but He does not tell us to go and teach the gospel on our own. He makes His intention very clear: He promises to be with us always.

Ask God to reveal to you the people in your life who need to hear the good news of Jesus. As He shows you lost friends and family members, share the gospel through word and deed and claim God's promise to be with you.

Father, thank You for the joy of sharing Christ with others. Remind me that You accompany me as I follow Your command to go and make disciples. Amen.

Working as a Couple

But Jesus said, "Not everyone is mature enough to live a married life.
It requires a certain aptitude and grace. Marriage isn't for everyone. . . .
But if you're capable of growing into the largeness of marriage, do it."
MATTHEW 19:10–12 MSG

Gina has been married for four years to Jon. At first, it was all roses and romance.. But after a couple of years the spark started to fade. They still love each other, but now it takes a little more work.

Marriage is a wonderful partnership between two people, but it isn't always easy. It takes work to keep any relationship going in the right direction—especially marriage.

Remember first that there should be three members of any marriage: you, your husband, and God. As long as you grow together in Him, you can continue to grow stronger with one another.

It's also important to set aside some time for each other. Have a regular date night with your spouse. It can be as simple as dinner and a movie at home or can involve going out for the evening, but it's important to have some alone time. The more you work on your marriage, the healthier it will become for the long run.

Dear God, help me to remember that marriage is a blessing,
but that it also requires work. Remind me to set aside
time for both You and my husband each day.

The Open Door

For everyone who asks receives; he who seeks finds;
and to him who knocks, the door will be opened.
LUKE 11:10 NIV

The whole process of looking for a job can be overwhelming—not just the first time, but every time. From preparing and sending out your résumé to the interviews, the fear of the unknown can weigh heavily on you. If only someone would just give you a chance to show what you can do.

You don't have to be a bundle of nerves. You can rest assured that God has prepared a place for you. He has the right environment for you to flourish and grow in, as well as people in that environment who need what you have to offer to help the company succeed.

Be confident in who He created you to be. Trust Him to place you in the right place. You do your best, and He'll do His part. Ask Him for direction and guidance to lead you to the right people, places, and choices. Don't become discouraged if what you want and what He wants for you are a little different. He perfects everything that concerns you. Place yourself in His capable hands.

Heavenly Father, please open the door to that fulfilling job that You've created just for me, one that will meet all my needs. Direct me to the right place and give me wisdom and favor. I'm trusting You! Amen.

God's Confidence

"Who gave man his mouth? Who makes him deaf or mute? Who gives him sight or makes him blind? Is it not I, the Lord? Now go; I will help you speak and will teach you what to say."

EXODUS 4:11–12 NIV

Moses was raised in Pharaoh's palace, but he remained loyal to his own people, the Israelites. As a result of killing an Egyptian, he was forced to flee Egypt. Much later, Moses saw a burning bush that was not consumed and suddenly, God began to speak. God called Moses to deliver the Israelites from Egypt, but Moses did not want to go.

Moses feared the rejection and scorn of both Pharaoh and the Israelites. Even when God allowed His reluctant servant to perform miraculous signs, Moses was still scared to go back to Egypt. After all, he was about to demand that the most powerful ruler in the world release more than a million slaves from bondage!

Like Moses, we might sometimes question God when He calls us to do something for Him. When we feel doubt setting in, we can find comfort in the words God spoke to Moses. We know He has given us all the abilities that we possess. God's confidence in us is not misplaced. He will help us speak, and He will teach us what to say.

Dear Lord, thank You for promising to help me do Your will. Teach me to trust Your confidence in me. Amen.

Display His Glory

But we have this treasure in jars of clay to show that
this all-surpassing power is from God and not from us.
2 CORINTHIANS 4:7 NIV

Many Christians struggle with the fact that they struggle. We forget our frailty. We don't remember that our spiritual growth is as much a work of Christ as our salvation. We find ourselves frustrated and disappointed because we fail to live up to our own high expectations of ourselves.

At the root of this thought pattern is our pride. We are trying to live out our faith in our own strength—but we can't. We forget that the Bible says we are clay pots. Our Father deliberately places the treasure of knowing Christ into a jar of clay.

Think of bright red geraniums filling clay pots in summer. Picture fuchsia blooms, waxy green leaves, and soft petals that stand in contrast to the rough pot that contains the plant. Drop the clay pot on the patio, and it will break. Leave it out in extreme cold, and it will crack. Place it in a wet, shady spot, and moss will grow on its sides. The pot alone is not valuable, strong, or beautiful, but when filled with blossoms it becomes a joy to behold.

Father, help me not to think too highly of myself. Help me to remember that I am made of dust, but that You have placed the treasure of Your Son in me to display His glory.

Wired for Fun

*All the days of the afflicted are evil: but he
that is of a merry heart hath a continual feast.*
PROVERBS 15:15 KJV

What do you do for fun? It seems that in our busy society, fun has been pushed out in favor of work accomplishments, acquiring stuff, and making sure our families are safe and cared for.

But God created us with a need for laughter and fun. Laughter relieves stress, bonds us with other people, and even promotes healing.

Some women love to play games with their friends for fun; others like to watch romantic comedies; and others love to shop, make scrapbooks, or quilt. There's no right or wrong way to have fun—whatever gives you relief from stress and makes you laugh is fun to you.

If you're stumped for fun ideas, watch children for a while. They instinctively know how to create lots of fun out of a little bit of material and time. Follow their lead, and play with modeling clay, blow bubbles, or toss a ball around in your backyard with friends. You'll be glad you did.

*Lord, thank You for making me with a need for fun.
Give me the heart of a child when I start to get too serious.*

Inside Out

Do not conform any longer to the pattern of this world,
but be transformed by the renewing of your mind.
ROMANS 12:2 NIV

Makeovers are fun. The effects of a new hairstyle, makeup, and wardrobe can be instantaneous and dramatic. Some makeovers are so good that it's almost impossible to recognize the person in the before photo. But no matter how trendy the haircut or how cute the clothes, it's always the same person underneath, and nothing can change the heart. This is the worldly formula for transformation: Change what's on the outside and maybe the inside will feel better.

The Bible presents a much more effective alternative. Paul tells us that true transformation radiates from the inside out. The word transformation means metamorphosis. This process does not happen overnight. The process of transformation begins with the attitudes of our minds. Our attitudes determine our thoughts. Our thoughts influence our actions, and our actions reveal our character.

Allow God to influence and shape your thoughts, and your character will gradually look more and more like His. Soon you won't even recognize the person you were before. Now that's genuine transformation.

Father, thank You that in You I am a new creature. Continue
to transform and change my character from the inside out.

The Same in a Changing World

*"True, the grass withers and the wildflowers fade,
but our God's Word stands firm and forever."*
ISAIAH 40:8 MSG

The world has changed so much in the past one hundred years. Electricity, indoor plumbing, airplanes, automobiles, computers, MP3 players, GPS, and countless other technologies have created an entirely new world. Perhaps you have flipped through a yellowed photo album with pictures of your great-great-grandparents and then looked at perfectly preserved digital photos on a computer. Or maybe you remember a day when you paid much less for a gallon of gas or cup of coffee. The world is changing, but our God is not.

God is the constant in our lives. His Word was, is, and will always be the same. It's amazing to think that while we cannot imagine life without electricity, someone hundreds of years ago read the same Bible we read and was learning to trust in God, just as we are learning to trust in Him. God's Word is for all people, regardless of the world they live in and no matter where they are in life. Hundreds of years before the birth of Christ, Isaiah proclaimed that the Word of our God stands forever. Praise be to the Lord that we are still able to proclaim that same message today!

*Dear Lord, thank You for Your unchanging Word.
Thank You for the comfort of knowing that You are
the same yesterday, today, and forever. Amen.*

Thunderous

God's voice thunders in marvelous ways.
JOB 37:5 NIV

One crew of the city's fire department was instructed to position the fire truck and themselves across the river from the launching barge. As the grand finale concluded the Independence Day fireworks celebration, the fireworks began raining down on the firefighters. Bowling ball-sized fireworks exploded at ground level instead of at skyscraper height. The firefighters covered their ringing ears and ran for their lives. As one of them was to say later, "We ran like cockroaches from a burning building!"

From a safe distance, Tammy and some of her young family watched the fireworks with rapt attention. But the thunderous booms didn't faze her son, Josiah. He fell asleep on their blanket, oblivious to the explosions of sound and color.

When God speaks, the word "thunder" shows up a lot. (See Job 37 and Psalm 29.) Fear is our first and understandable response. Even Job's friend, Elihu, admits his "heart pounds and leaps from its place" (Job 37:1 NIV). Yet in the thunder-heavy Psalm 29, we're told "the Lord blesses his people with peace" (Psalm 29:11 NIV).

Whether we find ourselves in the middle of a thunderstorm, booming fireworks, or thunderous personality clashes, God can be our peace. The Thunderstorm Maker who thunders when He speaks remains our source of peace. Unlike the scattering firefighters, but like Josiah, we can be at peace in thunderous times.

*Lord, thank You for bringing peace to my
heart when peace is hard to find. Amen.*

Keep Praying

Then Jesus told his disciples a parable to show them
that they should always pray and not give up.

LUKE 18:1 NIV

A story is told of a foreign missionary with a wife and six children. While on furlough in the United States, he asked local church leaders to pray that the Lord would provide a car upon his return to the mission field. Although he gladly walked to the store or church, his heart ached with the desire to reach more people with the gospel. When asked how long he had been praying for a car, he responded matter-of-factly, "Fifteen years." Imagine faithfully praying for something for fifteen years!

God answers our prayers in one of three ways: yes, no, or wait. "Yes" is the answer we most desire. However, sometimes out of divine wisdom God's response is "no." Although it's not the coveted answer, at least the matter can be put to rest. But what happens when God requires that we wait?

Jesus encourages us to be faithful in prayer. We are to be persistent. We are to not give up. We are to continue bringing our request before Him. Our faith grows as we pray and wait upon His perfect timing.

Do not become discouraged. God hears every prayer you utter. He sees every tear that falls. Continue to ask. Continue to seek. Continue to knock. The Lord will answer. Trust and persevere.

Dear Lord, thank You for Your love and faithfulness to me.
May I persevere in prayer as I trust You. Amen.

....
....
....
....
....
....
....

The Godly Marriage

Wives, understand and support your husbands
in ways that show your support for Christ.
EPHESIANS 5:22 MSG

We're told we can have it all: power, wealth, authority (in the workplace and in the home), and equality. While that may be true in some parts of life, God sees it a bit differently when it comes to marriage. Whether before entering a marriage or after a marriage has begun, we must seek God's will for godly wives, even in the midst of a world that demands women fight for power.

Wives are to support and submit to the authority of their husbands. And husbands are to love their wives as Christ loves the church, even to the point of laying down their lives. We like the part about love, but submission—that's a tough one. This selfless respect may require a wife to abandon her personal ambition in order to support the decisions of her husband—all for God's glory.

Following God's plans in the marriage relationship won't be understood by the world. But the truth is that the promise of a union that is blessed by Him far outweighs any personal cost that such humility and love requires.

Lord, I want to honor You in my role as a woman.
Help me to see the parts of me that I need to get under
control. Help me to reorganize my priorities so I can
be the wife that You have called me to be. Amen.

Christ Is Involved

Being confident of this very thing, that he which hath begun
a good work in you will perform it until the day of Jesus Christ.
PHILIPPIANS 1:6 KJV

When you accepted Jesus as Savior, that was just the beginning of His work in your life. Yes, salvation was complete through His grace. Your sins were forgiven, and your home in heaven was secured.

But Christ wants so much more for you. He wants you to grow in your faith. He wants to help you flee the temptations that you will inevitably face. He wants to give you strength to be joyful even as you go through trials. His ultimate desire is to help you become more like Him.

Do you allow Jesus to be as involved in your life as He wants to be? Unfortunately, a lot of people accept Him in order to get into heaven, but then they want little more to do with Him. Why not choose now to let Him be a part of everything you do and every decision you make? Go to Him in prayer. Seek answers from His Word and from the Holy Spirit. He will do a great work in your life. He will be faithful to complete what He started in you—and you will become like Him.

Dear Jesus, thank You for wanting to help me be
like You. Thank You for being involved in my
life and not leaving me to my own designs.

....

....

....

....

....

....

....

....

His Help for Our Holiness

*Do not bring shame on my holy name, for I will display my holiness
among the people of Israel. I am the Lord who makes you holy.*
LEVITICUS 22:32 NLT

Jamie sighed as she read the word in her Bible: holiness. She'd been a Christian for more
than a decade, but she felt as far from holiness as she ever had. "Lord," she prayed, "I want
to please you. But I'm always messing up! I feel like such a failure."

She cried as she mentally reviewed the sins she'd committed in just the past day. But
as she prayed, journaled, and confessed her sins, God reminded Jamie of a sermon she'd
heard the week before. "God doesn't just ask us to be holy and then leave us to figure it out
on our own," the preacher said. "He's the one who will make us holy if we daily surrender
everything to Him."

As she closed her Bible, Jamie smiled. God always brought the perfect words and
scriptures to mind at just the right time. It's not hopeless, she thought. God is working on
me and with me. I'm not the same as I was last year, and I will keep growing if I stay close
to Him.

"Make me like you, Lord," she prayed. "And thank you for never leaving me to figure
it out on my own."

*Holy God, I praise You for never leaving me on my own.
You are changing me to be like You. I want to
participate with—and not hinder—You.*

Swift Word

He sends his command to the earth; his word runs swiftly.
PSALM 147:15 NIV

A small dog sat by the glass door curiously watching a squirrel outside. She did not move a muscle of her twenty-pound body. She was concentrated and focused. Her muscles were taut and ready to spring into action. Her master opened the door. Like a shot from a rifle, the dog ran out of the house, across the yard, and to the base of the tree where the squirrel had escaped to the safety of a high branch.

God's Word is like that dog: ready, focused, concentrating, waiting for the right time. God speaks, and there is no stopping His purpose. Unlike the little dog that never catches the squirrel, God's Word accomplishes what He sends it to do. Design, order, and purpose are behind all He does. Creation came from nothingness at the sound of His voice. Daylight and darkness, winds and tides all move at His command. Isaiah 55:11 (NKJV) says, "So shall My word be that goes forth from My mouth; it shall not return to Me void, but it shall accomplish what I please, and it shall prosper in the thing for which I sent it."

Lord, when I am impatient or afraid, help me to remember Your Word is powerful to change me, and Your love is intently focused on me. Bring to my mind the scriptures that call forth new life in me.

Count the Cost

*Those who live only to satisfy their own sinful nature will harvest
decay and death from that sinful nature. But those who live to
please the Spirit will harvest everlasting life from the Spirit.*

GALATIANS 6:8 NLT

In decision making there is a cost factor associated with everything you do—and everything you don't do. Action or lack of action both cost you.

Take exercise for example. Regular physical exercise offers amazing benefits. It strengthens your body, boosts your immune system, and improves mental health. The cost to exercise includes the time you need to actually do it and the pain of putting your body through the motions to get in shape. But there is also a cost associated with not exercising, such as deteriorating physical and mental health.

When you make a decision, remember to take a look at the whole picture. What will it cost you if you act? What will it cost you if you fail to act? Everything you do—or don't do—carries consequences.

God made wisdom available to you to help you make good choices for your life. The next time you are faced with a decision, take a step back and count the cost!

*Heavenly Father, thank You for making wisdom available to me.
I ask You to show me how to count the cost in all my choices. Amen.*

Puffed Up

So, if you think you are standing firm, be careful that you don't fall!
1 Corinthians 10:12 niv

It's easy to fall into the trap of thinking that we have conquered a sin and it will never bother us again. Be careful! 1 Corinthians 10:12 is a warning not to puff ourselves up with pride. Allowing ourselves to think that we have completely overcome sin is prideful. We can only overcome sin through the power of Christ, relying on His power daily.

This passage continues, "No temptation has seized you except what is common to man. And God is faithful; he will not let you be tempted beyond what you can bear. But when you are tempted, he will also provide a way out so that you can stand up under it" (1 Corinthians 10:13 niv). This is a reminder that we are all human and are tempted. However, God promises to always provide a way out for us. It is only through Him that we can overcome!

Dear Lord, please help me not to be prideful. Help me to rely on Your power each and every day to overcome my shortcomings. Amen.

Rescued

*God rescued us from dead-end alleys and dark dungeons. He's set us up
in the kingdom of the Son he loves so much, the Son who got us out of
the pit we were in, got rid of the sins we were doomed to keep repeating.*

COLOSSIANS 1:13–14 MSG

It was as if she had fallen into a deep, dark pit. Sleep, withdrawal, and numbness were her coping mechanisms when she was stuck in the ugliness of her sin. She was simply going through the motions, trapped in despair; helpless, it seemed, to make change within herself. She had dealt with these same battles years before—conquered them, even. But her sins were again creeping through the chambers of her heart and mind like a dragon wreaking havoc on her spirit.

The message of the gospel doesn't leave us trapped in our sin and misery without hope. God sent the rescuer, Christ, who plucked us out of the dungeons of despair and into His kingdom of light and strength to overcome the dragons of sin. It's by the Father's grace that we are not stuck in our habitual ruts and dead-end alleys, living without purpose and fulfillment. We walk in His kingdom—a kingdom that goes counter to the world's ideas. We are out of the pit, striding confidently in Him, enjoying life to its fullest.

*Glory to You, Jesus! You have rescued me from the pit
and lifted me to Your kingdom of real life and victory.
Help me to walk in that fact today. Amen.*

....

....

....

....

....

....

....

....

Joyful, Patient, and Faithful

Be joyful in hope, patient in affliction, faithful in prayer.
ROMANS 12:12 NIV

Romans 12:12 tells believers to be joyful in hope, patient, and faithful. This is a tall order. The good news is that believers can be strong, even in weakness, because of Christ living in us. We can do all things through Him—including being hopeful, patient, and faithful in prayer.

Hope is sometimes described as "the present enjoyment of a future blessing." Even if your situation is difficult now and doesn't improve while you are on earth, you are promised eternity with Him.

Throughout our lives, we face trials both small and great. Whether your affliction is sitting in traffic or a cancer diagnosis, seek to be patient. Rest in Him and lay your anxiety at the feet of your Savior.

Faithfulness in prayer requires discipline. God is faithful regardless of our attitude toward Him. He never changes, wavers, or forsakes His own. We may be faithful to do daily tasks around the house. But faithfulness in the quiet discipline of prayer is harder. There are seemingly no consequences for neglecting our time with the Lord. Oh, what a myth! Set aside a daily time for prayer, and see how the Lord blesses you, transforming your spirit to increase your joyful hope, your patience, and your faithfulness.

Faithful God, find me faithful. Stir up the hope and joy within me.
Give me the grace I need to wait on You. Amen.

....

....

....

....

....

....

....

May I Have a Towel, Please?

*[Jesus] got up from the meal. . .and wrapped a towel around his waist.
After that, he poured water into a basin and began to wash his disciples' feet,
drying them with the towel that was wrapped around him.*
JOHN 13:4–5 NIV

Can you picture this scene? As Jesus and His disciples finished eating, He got up and wrapped a towel around His waist, poured water into a basin, and began washing their feet. Several jaws probably dropped to the floor as the disciples tried to comprehend what He was doing. Their feet, most likely dusty from walking on dirt roads, were being washed by the Master!

Jesus was giving us an example: Just as He served the disciples in washing their feet, we should serve others. He humbled Himself and commanded that His disciples do the same. In verse 16, Jesus tells them, "No servant is greater than his master, nor is a messenger greater than the one who sent him." This was a profound lesson in servant leadership.

Who can you serve today? Is there someone who needs a meal? Do you know of a shut-in who needs a ride to a doctor's appointment? Offer to help out, serving them in the name of Jesus.

Father, help me to be willing to serve others with a joyful spirit, just as You did. Lead me to someone whom I could serve, for Your glory. Amen.

Girls' Day Out

*Be friendly with everyone. Don't be proud and feel that you
are smarter than others. Make friends with ordinary people.*
ROMANS 12:16 CEV

Sometimes you just need a good girls' day out. It's nice to hang out with a husband or boyfriend, but sometimes it is also important just to spend time with the girls.

A good girlfriend can come from many places. Maybe she's a coworker who likes to have lunch but whom you don't see outside the office. Perhaps she's a church friend with whom you can attend church functions or a buddy you meet once a week at the gym. Maybe she's your sister or someone you've known since you sat next to one another on the kindergarten mat. It does not really matter where and when, but spending time with other women can be refreshing. They can provide support and understanding in a way that a member of the opposite sex may not always be able to relate.

When you find a good girlfriend, cherish her. Make time for calls and visits and let her know that you love being her sister in Christ.

*God, thank You for giving me good girlfriends. Help me to
be a sister in Christ with each and every one of my friends
and to spend time cultivating our relationship in You.*

How to Please God

I know, my God, that you test the heart and are pleased with integrity.
1 CHRONICLES 29:17 NIV

Of all the character traits we look for in a friend, a potential mate, a leader, and especially an auto mechanic, integrity sits at the top of the list. King David was a man of integrity (1 Kings 9:4). Even Jesus' sharpest critics called Him "a man of integrity" (Mark 12:14). Paul encourages teachers to "show integrity. . .so that those who oppose you may be ashamed because they have nothing bad to say about us" (Titus 2:7–8 NIV).

Not everyone, however, appreciates the honesty that characterizes the person of integrity. Proverbs tells us that "bloodthirsty men hate a man of integrity" (29:10 NIV).

Even though we don't know a lot about Hanani in the book of Nehemiah, one thing we're told is that "he was a man of integrity and feared God more than most men do" (Nehemiah 7:2 NIV). What a high compliment! To have that said of us prepares us for whatever challenges come our way. Whether we're given a pat on the back—or a push out the door—for our personal integrity, we can be confident that our integrity pleases God.

Lord, make me a woman of integrity so that I never bring shame to Your name or pain to Your heart. Amen.

Owning Your Faith

But the Helper, the Holy Spirit, whom the Father will send in My name, He will teach you all things, and bring to your remembrance all things that I said to you.

JOHN 14:26 NKJV

Is your faith deeper and stronger than when you first accepted Jesus?

We each must make the choice to continue to build our faith. Instead of expecting others to lead us, we need a personal desire for our own relationship with God. Rather than just taking things at face value, we now wrestle with issues so that we can own the truths and share them with others. It's no longer a simple, "because the Bible says so." It now becomes a matter of, "Where does the Bible say it and why?"

Jesus promises that the Holy Spirit will teach us and guide us if we allow Him to. He will help us to remember the spiritual truths we've learned over the years. Fellowship with other Christians also helps us to mature as we share our passions and are encouraged.

God wants you to own your faith. Make it real with words and actions.

Jesus, I want to know You intimately. Help me to mature in my walk with You daily. Guide my steps as I seek You through Your Word. Amen.

Greed

"Beware! Guard against every kind of greed.
Life is not measured by how much you own."
LUKE 12:15 NLT

Contrary to popular belief, material riches do not guarantee happiness. Beaming smiles often radiate from faces in third-world countries while depression soars in the lands of plenty. Many times prosperity breeds discontentment and dissatisfaction. Lottery winners have declared bankruptcy. Professional athletes have succumbed to drug abuse. Movie stars have become inmates. Greed is an insatiable appetite that destroys lives.

The Lord never meant for us to be satisfied with temporary treasures. Earthly possessions leave us empty because our hearts are fickle. Once we gain possession of one thing, our hearts yearn for something else.

Lasting treasure can only be found in Jesus Christ. He brings contentment so that the treasure chests of our souls overflow in abundance. Hope is placed in the Lord rather than our net-worth statement. Joy is received by walking with the Lord, not by chasing some fleeting fancy. Love is showered upon us as we grab hold of real life; life that cannot be bought, but that can only be given through Jesus Christ.

Jesus is enough. Jesus is everything. Find joy and contentment in Christ alone.

Dear Lord, may I be content with what You have given me. May I not wish for more material treasures, but seek eternal wealth from You. Amen.

Obedience

*"I did not know Him; but that He should be revealed
to Israel, therefore I came baptizing with water."*
JOHN 1:31 NKJV

God had told John the Baptist that the Messiah was coming, but John had limited understanding of God's plan. Yet long before God revealed to John who the Messiah was, John obediently preached repentance and baptized with water. When John did meet Jesus, he testified that He was the Son of God.

Too often we delay our obedience because we don't see the big picture. Unsure of what lies ahead, we question our calling and postpone doing what God wants because it doesn't make sense to us. At the root of our procrastination is pride. We don't want to do things until they make sense to us or until we can see how we benefit from them. Mostly, we want God to serve us and meet our needs. Even our will to serve Him is tainted by sinful desires to be important in His kingdom or to be useful to Him. Our only hope is the very message that John preached: repentance.

*Lord, forgive us for our selfish hearts and our prideful
thoughts, always deceiving us into believing we know
what is best. Give us grace to turn to You and trust You.
Help us to obey Your voice the way John did.*

Finding Trust

I trust in your unfailing love;
my heart rejoices in your salvation.
PSALM 13:5 NIV

Alicia found relationships hard. Well, maybe not the relationship, she thought, as much as the trust that is necessary for relationships. Past experiences provided very few reasons to give anyone a chance. She perceived people to be users, ready to take what they needed from her and leave her out in the cold.

Finally she found a way to escape the hard world she grew up in and ventured out on her own. Most of the people she encountered offered a nod, a smile, or a lighthearted hello, but when they tried to get close, she threw up a wall. That is, until she met Tracey, whom she somehow found easy to trust. There was something different about Tracey that she'd never noticed in anyone else. As she took time to know Tracey, she found Jesus— and allowed both of them into her heart and life.

Maybe you hold others at bay, never allowing them truly into your world. Begin to let your guard down. Trust your heart to the Lord and allow Him to lead and guide you in your relationships.

Lord, help me learn to trust people as I am learning to trust You.
Show me the right relationships for my life. Amen.

....
....
....
....
....
....
....
....
....
....

Return Blessings

"Everything we have has come from you,
and we give you only what you first gave us!"
1 CHRONICLES 29:14 NLT

We sometimes find it difficult to realize that the things we work so hard for are not really ours. The money we make is not ours. The car we drive and the house we live in are not ours. The food we prepare isn't ours. Not even our time is ours. In 1 Chronicles 29:14, the Israelites realize that nothing is ours! God has given us everything we have, and He has blessed us in inconceivable ways.

Sometimes we take for granted the blessings we have received. More often, we take credit for these blessings. Because we spend so much of our time working hard to provide for ourselves and our families, time and money can be two blessings we firmly believe we have a right to, and we jealously guard against giving any part of these blessings away. Instead, we must learn to freely give back to God that which He has already given to us. While the Israelites certainly did not get everything right, they did, at least for a moment, fully understand the blessings of God.

Everything we have comes from You; what we give back is already Yours!

Dear Lord, thank You for Your countless blessings.
I know that You have given everything to me.
Help me to unhesitatingly return it all to You. Amen.

Pour Out Prayers

Trust in Him at all times, you people; pour out
your heart before Him; God is a refuge for us.
PSALM 62:8 NKJV

Girl talk. Girls' night out. Girls' weekend getaway. Women's retreats. Women are relational creatures. We need each other. When we are in crisis, we seek consolation from one another. Friends let us vent when we are angry, listen to us think out loud, and offer advice. Our friendships are a gift from the Lord. This marvelous gift, though, should never become a substitute for the only relationship that can truly give us the help we need.

The psalmist tells us to trust the Lord at all times and to pour out our hearts to Him. There is nothing we think or feel that He does not already know. He longs for us to come to Him, spilling out our thoughts, needs, and desires. God invites us to an open-ended conversation. He made us for relationship with Him. He never tires of listening to His children.

The Lord is our helper. He is our refuge. No matter how good a listener a friend may be or how good the advice she gives, ultimately the Lord is our source of wisdom and counsel. He knows the solutions to our problems and the wisdom we need for living each day.

Lord, remind me of Your invitation to pour out my
problems to You. You are my refuge and my helper.
Help me to trust You with every detail of my life.

Creating or Destroying

Every wise woman buildeth her house:
but the foolish plucketh it down with her hands.
PROVERBS 14:1 KJV

Maddy had only been married a short time, but already she sensed that the honeymoon was over. She looked for all kinds of reasons to blame her husband, Kurt, and once her sob story was compiled, she called her mother to complain.

"Kurt never helps with the housework or suggests we go out to dinner," she whined, and continued with her list of Kurt's faults.

Her mother, a wise and practiced wife, offered some sound advice. "Maddy, the first thing you need to do is take your concerns to God. That is the most important part of building a godly home. If you try to handle this on your own, you will gradually tear your home to the ground," her mother said.

"Next, you should wait until you are calm. Then talk these things over with Kurt in a non-confrontational way. Chances are he doesn't even know what's bothering you. Find out what concerns he might have, and work through them together.

"Finally, regardless of what Kurt does, you should always strive to be a good and godly wife who builds her house rather than destroying it. Your situation might not be ideal, but it will be blessed by God."

O Lord, give me the strength and wisdom
to build a home that pleases You.

Jesus Never Fails

It is better to take refuge in the Lord than to trust in people.
Psalm 118:8 nlt

Trusting any human being more than the Lord will always prove futile. Even the most trusted people will eventually let you down.

Does this mean you shouldn't ever trust anyone or cultivate trust in any of your relationships? Of course not. It's just that when we trust another person with our thoughts and feelings more than we trust God with them, we get ourselves into trouble.

Do you have a relationship that you honor more than your relationship with God? Is there a person in your life you always run to before you run to the Lord? Confess that to the Lord and ask Him to be real to you. Ask Him for the desire to come to Him first with all of your thoughts, your dreams, and your problems. People will fail you time and time again, but Jesus never fails!

Father, I confess that I sometimes run to others before turning to You. Please give me the desire and the willingness to seek You first. Thank You for never failing me. Amen.

Redemption

*Put your hope in the Lord, for with the Lord is
unfailing love and with him is full redemption.*
PSALM 130:7 NIV

Jill and Mike's teen years were strewn with drugs and bad choices. Those choices culminated in Jill's pregnancy at sixteen. The couple decided their best course of action would be to surrender their son for adoption.

Years later, Jill and Mike married and became followers of Jesus. They entered full-time ministry. They had three children. Could they ever get back the son they had given up? They wanted to find out how life had turned out for Steve, their firstborn child. Their three grown children were just as eager to meet their oldest brother. The family began their search.

Meanwhile, Steve had begun his own search.

An extra blessing followed the reuniting of Mike and Jill's entire family. Steve's wife, unable to carry children, found a voluntary surrogate in one of Steve's biological sisters. Soon Steve and his wife will have a child of their own, lovingly carried by the biological aunt.

When God permits a redemption of lost years and relationships, we get a black-and-white snapshot of the colorful mural of God's redemption of us in Christ. When we one day stand in His presence, we'll understand more clearly the marvelous scope of God's redeeming love.

*I praise You, Father, for Your awesome redemption.
Thank You that I've yet to see the scope of it all. Amen.*

The Lord, Our Confidence

Have no fear of sudden disaster or of the ruin that overtakes the wicked,
for the Lord will be your confidence and will keep your foot from being snared.
PROVERBS 3:25–26 NIV

Melinda's husband, Tom, works as a firefighter. Even though she knows he has been well-trained and takes every precaution, she still worries about his safety. Each time Tom goes out on a fire, she's terrified that he will die or become permanently disabled—and leave her to care for their three children alone.

Tom has faced those same fears, but he doesn't worry about them any longer. "I gave my life to the Lord," he says, "and He has given me a sense of peace. I know this job is something I'm called to do—and He is with me, whatever happens."

Whether our loved ones are in harm's way daily or not, all of us live in a dangerous world. And while we should take physical precautions, our best preparation is spiritual.

When we spend time with God and learn about His love, we begin to realize that He will give us His grace when we need it. He promises to never leave us, and the more we come to know His love, the more we will rest in that promise.

God, thank You that You promise Your peace to those who seek You.
Help me to rest in Your love for my family and me.

Your Glorious Future

"No eye has seen, no ear has heard, no mind has conceived what God has prepared for those who love him."

1 CORINTHIANS 2:9 NIV

What if Cinderella had said no? The handsome prince breezes in, the slipper fits, but Cinderella says, "No thanks. I'd rather stay here and be doomed to a life of drudgery. It's sweet of you to want to take me away from all this, but I've grown accustomed to my little prison and I don't want to leave."

Not much of a fairy tale, is it? But when God offered the Israelites a trip to the Promised Land, they responded in much the same way. Since they couldn't see the future, they thought they'd rather continue working as slaves.

God's promise for our future is so magnificent we can't even comprehend it. He has great plans for each of us, but we often become paralyzed by fear. Why? Because the past seems more comfortable. Because the future is uncertain.

While God doesn't give us a map of what our future is like, He does promise that it will be more than we could ever ask or imagine. What steps of faith do you need to take today to accept God's glorious future for your life?

God, Your ways are not my ways and Your plans are too wonderful for me to even comprehend. Help me to never be satisfied with less than Your glorious plans for my life.

Smile, Smile, Smile

*"I will forget my complaint,
I will change my expression, and smile."*
JOB 9:27 NIV

Jenni had been having a bad day. Everything seemed to go wrong from the moment she awoke. Then something happened. A man on the sidewalk smiled at her and opened the door to her office. It wasn't much, but that small gesture helped lighten her mood. His attitude was contagious.

Days may not go just as planned. We are all human, and we can't always control our circumstances. What we can control, however, is our attitude. Remember each day that you are a representative of Jesus Christ. As a Christian and a woman, it is important to model a godly attitude at all times. Even a small look or smile can help show others the love of God. Just because we don't feel like having a good attitude doesn't mean we shouldn't try. God tells us to praise Him always—in good times and in bad. Let that praise show on your face today.

*Lord, I know I can choose my attitude. Help me to show
Your love to others by having a positive attitude each day.
Let Your glory show on my face. Amen.*

A Legacy of Praise

*We will not hide them from their children; we will tell the
next generation the praiseworthy deeds of the Lord,
his power, and the wonders he has done.*

PSALM 78:4 NIV

In Psalm 78, King Asaph recounts the early history of Israel. He speaks of times when the Israelites doubted and disobeyed God. He tells of their rebellion in the desert and the way they quickly forgot God had rescued them from slavery in Egypt. He describes their ungratefulness during the period of the judges.

Is all this negativity necessary? King Asaph thought so. He reviewed this history of disobedience and rebellion because he was determined that the next generation would not behave the way their ancestors had. Asaph wanted the story to change. He wanted the rebellion to end.

What is your heritage? How has your story begun? What legacy will you leave behind? Does your life story need some revision or even a drastic turn?

Maybe you are a mother. If so, choose to instill in your children a respect for God and a thankfulness for the good deeds He has done. Whether or not you are a mother, you influence those around you for the Lord. Make your story one of praise to your God rather than one lacking faith and obedience.

Father, reveal to me the places where my story needs revision and editing. Keep at the forefront of my mind the amazing works that You have done both in ancient days and in my own lifetime. Amen.

Feeling Alive

Good news makes you feel fit as a fiddle.
A cheerful heart brings a smile to your face.
PROVERBS 15:30, 13 MSG

Little ones gathered at Abby's feet. Shy ones sat along the edges on parents' laps. The classroom was packed. The community had come for this outreach event as the church had prayed they would. With enthusiasm, Abby told the story of Jesus. She kept these three-year-olds' attention throughout with well-placed pictures, noises, and actions. They were into this Jesus!

Parents also were enthralled, hearing the simple truths of salvation. Abby knew she had them. There was an intangible energy inside of her and inside this room! The sharing of truths to eager hearts pumped Abby's blood like nothing else. There was no other place she'd rather be, and her face showed it.

It wasn't the "Abby Show," though. No, it was the result of God using the gifts He gave her for His purposes. There was no thought of the late-night hours spent preparing to make this event a success. It was worth every bit of effort to be in the place where she knew she was supposed to be, doing what God created her to do.

Lord, use me in the spreading of good news. Show me creative ways I can use the gifts You've given me. May my face reflect a joyful heart because I'm accomplishing what You've designed me to do. Amen.

Pursuing Peace

Turn from evil and do good;
seek peace and pursue it.
PSALM 34:14 NIV

Too often we find ourselves burdened with heartaches—both of our own making and from our surroundings. These problems may keep us from experiencing peace, and if we're not careful, they may lead us to evil, to sin.

But God tells us it is not enough to simply "turn from evil"; we must also "seek peace and pursue it." Pursue peace. Reach for it, stretch for it. Peace isn't something that will come easily—it must be earnestly sought after and faithfully pursued.

A troubled heart has a difficult time finding peace. What are the burdens that haunt your life? What holds you back from the peace that God so desires you to find? Perhaps it is something that appears harmless. Is it your busy schedule? Your impatience? Your jealousy? Your negative attitude?

As Christians, our pursuit of peace is a persistent, lifelong saga. Some days peace seems within our grasp. Other days peace seems very far away. But don't let that stop you from seeking God's peace. The heavenly Father's truth can only be found by a tranquil and still heart.

Dear God, teach me to humble myself and my needs before others and to seek peace instead. Instill in me a quietness of heart so that I may in turn share it with others. Spread Your joy, Your love, Your peace through me. Amen.

Perspective

Each one of these people of faith died not yet having in hand what was promised, but still believing. How did they do it? They saw it way off in the distance. . .accepted the fact that they were transients in this world. People who live this way make it plain that they are looking for their true home. . .a far better country than that—heaven country.
HEBREWS 11:13–15 MSG

The nurse in the cancer unit sees daily how fragile life can be. The former homeless family has a newfound appreciation for their well-worn "new" home. The EMT sees firsthand why gaining a few minutes isn't worth charging through the just-turned-red light. Perspectives are different depending on your experiences.

Christians who realize this life is just the preface of a truly joyful eternal life live their lives differently in the here and now. People matter; possessions don't. Sacrifice and a job well done produce fruit; convenience and entertainment usually don't. Time isn't money, but it is an opportunity to make God known to others. Behind-the-scenes service is seen by God. Joy comes from giving—not keeping.

Faith looks forward to our true home. This perspective drives us forward, living triumphantly, looking ahead to a far better place.

Jesus, I can't wait to live in that far better country! You've gone ahead to prepare my place. Help me to see life now in light of that perspective, making an eternal difference to those around me. Amen.

Knowing Love

He knew what was in man.
JOHN 2:25 NKJV

We see how others act. We hear what they say. We then make reasonable judgments about their character and motives. Yet sometimes we are terribly surprised and disappointed by what they do.

Jesus knows all hearts and minds. He discerns what we can't or won't see in ourselves. He knows our thoughts and motives as well as those of our friends and family. In spite of all our sin, He died for us. His unconditional love led Him all the way through the Crucifixion and the Resurrection. He longs to rescue us, cleanse us, comfort us, and empower us.

He invites us to Him. We can come with our sins and our offenses. He knows our pain, as well as the minds and hearts of those who have wronged us. He sees all sides, inside and out, and He can repair relationships. His Spirit can search our hearts, show us our uncleanness, and put a new spirit within us.

Lord, help me remember You know all about me.
You see what I cannot. You are the discerner of hearts.
Help me to trust Your all-knowing love.

....

....

....

....

....

....

....

....

Circle of Friends

*You have heard me teach things that have been confirmed
by many reliable witnesses. Now teach these truths to other
trustworthy people who will be able to pass them on to others.*
2 TIMOTHY 2:2 NLT

Who you spend your time with says a lot about you. Take a look at your inner circle—those whom you allow to know you best and speak the most into your life.

Jesus chose twelve men to trust to grow with Him and learn from Him. They asked Him questions and made choices in their own lives that had an impact on His life and His ministry. And in the same way, His answers and decisions greatly influenced them. They knew Him well, and He knew them better than they knew themselves.

It matters who you spend time with because you usually become like those you are with the most. It's so important to choose friendships and relationships wisely and be aware of the influence that you have on others as well as their influence on you.

There are people God desires to use to help you live life with Christ at the center. Be certain those who speak into your life and help you make decisions are supporting and guiding you toward God and His design for your life.

*God, I want relationship that will bring me closer to You,
that keep me accountable in my daily walk with You. Amen.*

....
....
....
....
....
....
....
....

Overlooked and Unappreciated

My dear brothers, take note of this: Everyone should be quick to listen, slow to speak and slow to become angry, for man's anger does not bring about the righteous life that God desires.
JAMES 1:19–20 NIV

It's so easy to become irritated and angry when things aren't going our way—especially at work. Maybe you've been overlooked or inconvenienced in some way and it just makes you feel awful. Maybe your boss and coworkers aren't noticing or appreciating all the extra effort you put in.

It's our human nature to want to lash out somehow or at least get some kind of attention. But our selfish anger isn't God's will for us. We should be slow to speak and become angry, but quick to listen. Easier said than done sometimes, but we can reprogram our minds through Christ's help.

Start by memorizing James 1:19–20 and repeating it to yourself the next time you feel like lashing out. Other scriptures to remember are Ephesians 6:7 and 1 Corinthians 10:31, which remind us that everything we do should be done for the Lord. By keeping an eternal perspective, being overlooked and unappreciated by others doesn't seem like that big of a deal as long as God is pleased with us.

Dear Lord, please help me to keep my focus on You each day. Help me to be quick to listen, slow to speak, and slow to become angry, especially when things aren't going my way. Amen.

A Thing of Beauty

How beautiful upon the mountains are the feet of him that bringeth
good tidings, that publisheth peace; that bringeth good tidings of good,
that publisheth salvation; that saith unto Zion, Thy God reigneth!

ISAIAH 52:7 KJV

Did you realize that you don't need a pedicure to have beautiful feet? They don't even have to be clean, and you don't have to wear shoes. After the woman at the well received Christ's salvation, she ran back to her town saying, "Come, see a man. . .is not this the Christ?" (See John 4:29 KJV.) Her feet were either bare or sandal-clad. They were hot and dusty from running, and maybe they were even chapped—but they were beautiful.

They were beautiful because they were carrying the news of God's salvation to souls who might never have heard or believed it otherwise. After all, there must be something about this man if He could create such a change in this woman of ill repute.

You, too, will have opportunities to reach souls others might not reach. You have the most wonderful news ever proclaimed. Will you share it with others? It is your opportunity to have beautiful feet. You won't incur the cost of a salon, and the results will be much more rewarding.

Dear Jesus, make my feet beautiful as
I share the glorious gift of Your salvation.

Looking Good

*Don't be concerned about the outward beauty of
fancy hairstyles, expensive jewelry, or beautiful clothes.*
1 PETER 3:3 NLT

A 3:00 a.m. emergency in the ICU brought the attending physician and the medical resident running.

Later, the physician and resident sat down to write their notes. The nursing staff couldn't help but notice the difference in the doctors. The physician looked like she had just gotten out of bed. The resident had all the appearance of a fashion model just back from a photo shoot. Her secret, the nurses learned later, was permanent makeup.

Professionally applied cosmetics may have been the medical resident's secret to a flawless appearance, but beauty begins before any makeup—permanent or water soluble—goes on. Spite, bitterness, or jealousy quickly distorts the face of even the most attractive woman. The Bible tells us that interior beauty is unfading and "is so precious to God" (1 Peter 3:4 NLT). We can be made to look outwardly beautiful with enough cosmetics or plastic surgery. But the right blush or perfectly lined eyes can't hide or cover up petulance or pride for long.

Beauty that people remember, that pleases God, and that shines through—day or night—comes from within. That kind of deep beauty, the Word tells us, comes from trusting God (1 Peter 3:5). In Christ each of us can have that kind of beauty, no matter what kind of cosmetics we use.

*Father, I want to be beautiful in Your
eyes and in the way I treat others. Amen.*

You Are What You Eat

Since we have these promises, dear friends, let us purify ourselves from everything that contaminates body and spirit, perfecting holiness out of reverence for God.

2 CORINTHIANS 7:1 NIV

Stacy isn't much of a breakfast eater—she usually grabs a donut and washes it down with a cup of coffee on the way to work. Lunch is hit or miss. If it's a good day she buys a sandwich from the vending machine. Her frozen dinner tastes like cardboard, but at least it's filling.

What have you eaten today? Our diets are often driven more by what's convenient and available than what's best for us.

Scripture tells us that our bodies are temples. It's true that we'll get new bodies in heaven, but we only get one on earth, and we need to take care of it. When we eat right, our bodies function more efficiently, making it easier for us to do the things God created us to do.

Often, eating right means planning ahead—making a sandwich at home instead of driving through for fast food. It might mean packing fresh fruit instead of buying a candy bar from the vending machine. Making healthy food choices is not only good for our bodies, but it also demonstrates reverence for their Creator.

Creator of all good things, thank You for my amazing body. Help me to honor You with the foods I choose to eat.

Prayer

Jesus often withdrew to lonely places and prayed.
LUKE 5:16 NIV

The crowds relentlessly followed Him. The sick pressed upon Him, longing for a miracle cure. Needy men and women sought Jesus continually. Jesus responded by pouring Himself out like a drink offering. Yet He also knew the importance of refilling His spiritual cup. He knew that He could not give what He didn't have. So He often withdrew to lonely places, such as the Mount of Olives, to reenergize Himself through prayer.

Jesus, the Son of God, felt the great need to commune with His heavenly Father. During these times, His soul was refreshed. His spirit was restored. Jesus is our perfect role model. If He withdrew often to pray, shouldn't we? Do we think we can continually give to others without getting replenished ourselves?

Make prayer a priority. Recognize that the Lord must daily fill your cup so that you will have something to give. Set aside a specific time, a specific place. Start slow. Give Him five minutes every day. As you are faithful, your relationship with Him will grow. Over time you will crave the time spent together as He fills your cup to overflowing. Follow Jesus' example and pray!

Dear Lord, help me set aside time to pray each day. Please fill my cup so that I can share with others what You have given me. Amen.

Break the Cycle of Divorce

"So they are no longer two, but one. Therefore what
God has joined together, let man not separate."
MATTHEW 19:6 NIV

Virtually everyone is affected by divorce. Whether it's your own parents, an aunt and uncle, grandparents, or anyone else you look up to, divorce is painful, and it often leads to more divorce. When one couple in a family divorces, splitting up may seem to others like a reasonable way out of a tough situation.

If you have faced a divorce in your family, you need to realize that, no matter how brave a front your family members put on, it was horribly difficult for them. It is not an easy way out, and it's not God's way out. God's desire is that marriage be a lasting covenant between two people He joins together. Determine in your heart now to make your marriage or future marriage a permanent, godly priority. Pray for your husband and prepare yourself to be a wife who honors God in your marriage.

Jesus, please help me to be a godly wife. Show me where I need to change my thinking and submit to Your will so that I am able to fully commit to a marriage, never making divorce an option. Amen.

Loyalty to Family

Then Orpah kissed her mother-in-law good-by,
but Ruth clung to her.
RUTH 1:14 NIV

The story of Naomi and her two daughters-in-law, Orpah and Ruth, is a favorite of many women. After the death of their husbands, the three women had decisions to make. It was customary for a childless young widow to marry her husband's brother so that the deceased might have an heir. Naomi had no more sons. It didn't make sense for the widows to remain with her.

Orpah went back to her homeland, but Ruth remained with her mother-in-law. "Where you go I will go, and where you stay I will stay. Your people will be my people and your God my God," Ruth told Naomi in Ruth 1:16 (NIV).

Ruth refused to worry about the future or to look out only for her own good. She put a high priority on the welfare of her mother-in-law. She stood by her in her time of need.

Do you have a family member who needs your loyalty? Perhaps there is someone in your family who has been a blessing to you and whom you can bless in return. Or maybe you have a relative who has let everyone down, someone who truly does not even deserve your faithfulness—but who desperately needs it. Pray that God will show you the Naomi in your life. He will honor your faithfulness to family.

Father, help me to be faithful to my family. Amen.

....
....
....
....
....
....
....
....

School's Out?

"Take my instruction and not silver, and knowledge rather
than choicest gold. For wisdom is better than jewels;
And all desirable things cannot compare with her."
PROVERBS 8:10–11 NASB

At age thirty, it was hard for Monica to imagine going back to school. Still, she longed for more knowledge, more instruction, and more education.

The prospect of going back to school can be daunting—whether you've never been to college, are hoping to go back for a second degree, or are aiming for a graduate degree. It may be scary, but taking the leap of faith into the world of education can also be extremely worthwhile.

If you're considering going to school, remember to do so prayerfully. Explore education options for your potential career, as well as how education could benefit you in your current position—in work and life.

Remember, however, that the most important area of study is that of God's Word. Just as you carve out time for homework, also make time to read the words of our ultimate teacher—Jesus Christ.

Jesus may have been the Son of God, but He still made time for study and prayer. He spent time in the temple, read scriptures, and spoke with God daily. That type of study will enrich any education.

Lord, thank You for giving me the ability to learn.
Help me to follow Your will. If that plan includes
additional education, help me to take that leap of faith.

Overflowing with Thanksgiving

Just as you received Christ Jesus as Lord, continue to live in him. . .
strengthened in the faith as you were taught, and overflowing with thankfulness.
COLOSSIANS 2:6–7 NIV

When Annie was in college, she assumed she'd graduate with honors and land the job of her dreams. But in spite of her impressive transcript, the perfect job never materialized. An obscure major, a lack of experience, and a struggling economy meant Annie was lucky to get a job making a modest hourly wage, barely enough to pay the rent.

After a few months of working hard for little income, Annie was discouraged. A chance encounter with an old family friend changed everything. This elderly woman had outlived two husbands and was now alone. Social security provided little income, but the woman didn't seem to mind. When asked how she managed, the dear woman's response was simple. "Life's a lot better when you focus on what you do have instead of what you don't."

It's easy to get caught up in the things we don't have or things we wish we had. However, a simple change in perspective can open our eyes to the many ways God has blessed us. Take a moment to make a list of your blessings. Soon you'll be overflowing with thanks!

Dear Father, I confess that I sometimes focus too
much on the things I don't have. Help me not to
miss the wonderful gifts You give to me each day.

Freedom

Exercise your freedom by serving God, not by breaking the rules.
Treat everyone you meet with dignity. Love your spiritual family.
Revere God. Respect the government.
1 PETER 2:16–17 MSG

As Christians in the United States, we can be thankful that we live in a free nation. Galatians 5:13 tells us that we were called to be free. We have freedom in Christ, because of what He did for us on the cross. It's so important to remember that with this freedom comes great responsibility.

Paul tells us in 1 Corinthians 10:23 (NIV) that " 'Everything is permissible'—but not everything is beneficial. 'Everything is permissible'—but not everything is constructive." We must be careful and responsible with our freedom. Paul warns us not to cause anyone to stumble, and that everything we do should be done to the glory of God.

Are you a responsible Christian? Is there anything in your life that is causing someone in your life to stumble? Could it be the television shows you watch, the types of movies you frequent, or maybe even your spending habits? Take this to the Lord in prayer and ask Him to search your heart and show you anything that may be hindering another person in her walk with Christ.

Father, help me to be responsible with my freedom.
Please help me to change anything in my life that
might be causing someone else to stumble. Amen.

....
....
....
....
....
....
....
....

A Good Reputation

Now when Jesus came into the district of Caesarea Philippi,
He was asking His disciples, "Who do people say that the Son of Man is?"
MATTHEW 16:13 NASB

Jesus stirred things up in His generation. His actions caused people to talk. His ministry—His love, compassion, and miracles of healing—were heard of all over the land. Many of the leaders of the day saw His popularity and influence as a threat to their position and power and tried to silence Him. Those who sought and believed in Him found healing, salvation, and a better life.

Just as people watched Jesus in His lifetime, people are watching you. What are people saying about you? What do your actions tell them about you and your relationship with God? Jesus' words and teachings were powerful, but it was His actions that caused others to stop and take notice.

What matters most isn't really what you say—it's what you do that speaks the loudest in the lives of those around you. Who do others say you are? And does what you do each day point people to Christ? Your reputation precedes you. Take inventory of your influence today.

Lord, thank You for reminding me that I represent You in everything I do. Help me to make godly choices and good decisions to influence others to see You in my life. Amen.

....
....
....
....
....
....
....
....

Attention and Prayer

Pray in the Spirit at all times and on every occasion.
Stay alert and be persistent in your prayers for all believers everywhere.
EPHESIANS 6:18 NLT

The instructions in Ephesians 6:18 regarding prayer are perhaps more radical than we first think. Sometimes we find ourselves praying only when we need to—when we're hurt or sick, worried, or sitting down to dinner. Prayer becomes a crutch that we use when bad things happen or a habit we thoughtlessly employ.

Paul must have known how difficult prayer could be. He realized the kind of prayer he describes in Ephesians is demanding, but he also knew that it is the most fulfilling and valuable type of prayer.

Persistence and consistency are difficult, but possibly Paul's most challenging instruction is to pray for all Christians everywhere. In today's society, getting wrapped up in our own lives is all too easy to do. Even when we look outside ourselves, we often limit prayer to our family and friends, or at most, our local church family. We must look further, though. God wants us to love and pray for our Christian family whether they are around the corner or around the world.

Dear Lord, teach me to pray according to Your will.
Help me to be consistent in my prayers, and help me to remember
to pray for my Christian family throughout the world. Amen.

God's Word—Our Road Map

The Law of the Lord is perfect; it gives us new life. His teachings
last forever, and they give wisdom to ordinary people.
PSALM 19:7 CEV

Jen hung up the phone and shook her head. What seemed like a dream only a few months ago—a job offer from a groundbreaking company in her field—now seemed more like a huge question mark.

After finishing her internship and placing her résumé with several companies—some far away from her college friends and family members—Jen began dating a godly guy, Neil, from her church's singles ministry. Over the past few months their relationship had gotten serious, and now she was faced with a dilemma: Choose the guy or choose the job.

What is God's will? Jen wondered. *Would Neil be open to a long-distance relationship? Would God give me this great guy and then expect me to move halfway across the country?* She didn't think so. Yet she hadn't received even a call from any of her other potential employers.

Jen decided to do what she knew. She got on her knees, prayed for wisdom and discernment, and then opened her Bible. *Show me what You want, Lord,* she prayed. *I will trust and obey You.*

After her time with God, she still wasn't sure what to do, but she had peace.

Lord, thank You for the Bible, Your road map for my life.
Remind me to go to Your Word when I'm confused or stressed.

....

....

....

....

....

....

....

Love Banishes Fear

*There is no fear in love. But perfect love drives out fear, because fear has
to do with punishment. The one who fears is not made perfect in love.*
1 JOHN 4:18 NIV

Light dispels darkness. No matter how dark the room, turn the light on and darkness is chased away. The tightest corner cannot escape the flood of light.

Perfect love is like light. God's love for us is perfect. It is complete. The sacrifice of His Son to reconcile us to Himself is the ultimate act of this love. He came to us in our sinfulness, loving us first, so that we could love Him.

If we are so loved, why do we fear? We worry about the future: Is a job in jeopardy? A relationship rocky? Fear for our family grips us. We fear old age, poor health, or poverty. We fear rejection by others, so we say yes to more than we should. We fear failure, so we shy away from callings and responsibilities.

Perhaps it's difficult to trust God because we have not truly basked in how much He loves us. Romans 8:35–39 (NASB) says nothing can separate us from the love of God which is in Christ Jesus—not tribulation, distress, persecution, famine, nakedness, peril, or sword. Daily we need the light of His love shining into the dark corners of our mind, chasing away fear that seeks to dwell there.

*Lord, help me to know more of
Your deep and complete love for me.*

....

....

....

....

....

....

....

....

Best of the Best

And at the end of ten days their countenances appeared fairer and fatter in flesh than all the children which did eat the portion of the king's meat.
DANIEL 1:15 KJV

It was the third job Brigit had tried, and she hoped she had finally found a good fit. It was a new opportunity for her, and she was determined to let God have control. She knew it wouldn't be easy, so her first step was to seek godly friends who would encourage and support each other. She wanted to meet people who shared her standards and convictions because she knew it wouldn't be long before her faith would be tested.

Almost immediately a manager began to push his worldly agenda. He expected his staff to embrace his beliefs, but Brigit was ready for him. With God's help and the prayers of her good friends, she was able to address the manager wisely. He didn't change his beliefs, but he didn't try to force Brigit to change hers, either. He could see that she had put much thought into the subject and that she was indeed a wise person.

Brigit was so grateful that she had supportive, Christian friends. Otherwise she might have buckled under the pressure. Now she truly felt she was in the right place.

Dear Lord, help me choose friends who will encourage me to do right, and help me be that kind of friend.

....

....

....

....

....

....

....

....

Breeze of Peace

*Make every effort to keep the unity of
the Spirit through the bond of peace.*
EPHESIANS 4:3 NIV

The two adult sisters kept the squabbling out of their mother's hospital room, but as soon as they were out of range, each went for the other's jugular. Intense animosity circulated between them. Disagreement about their mother's health care was only one more brick on an already developed wall of dissension.

Jenna, the evening shift nurse, tried to ignore the problem, but there was no way to avoid the women. Especially with them individually confiding in her—griping, really— it was impossible to remain indifferent. Jenna knew God had led her to be a vessel of peace in this charged atmosphere. Her prayers each morning were for specific ways to help defuse the tension and restore His peace and presence to the family that so desperately needed Him.

You are placed where you are for specific purposes. As a Christian, being a channel of peace is part of that purpose. A heart restored to its Maker is at rest and reflects His presence. Your peace-giving efforts can be a balm to soothe splintered hearts. Be that open window for God's breeze of peace to blow gently through.

*Prince of Peace, first, keep my heart in union with Yours.
Second, enable me to share Your peace with those around me.
Let Your breath of life blow through me. Amen.*

Quiet Time

"Study this Book of Instruction continually. Meditate on it day and night so you will be sure to obey everything written in it. Only then will you prosper and succeed in all you do."

JOSHUA 1:8 NLT

Perhaps the word "study" makes you cringe, followed closely by the question, "When am I ever going to use this stuff, anyway?"

God, our teacher, has given us an assignment: study the Bible. Rather than viewing it as a chore, however, we should consider what He's asking. He wants us to get to know Him better. We know He would never ask us to do anything unless it drew us closer to Him.

Our task is to study God's Word, and we are to obey it, as well. When we abide by His commands, we will benefit by receiving God's blessing. As we study God's Word, we don't need to wonder, "When am I ever going to use this stuff, anyway?" Instead, we will enjoy getting closer to our God and living in harmony with those around us.

Lord Jesus, help me to take the time to read Your Word. I want to obey Your command, and in doing so, draw closer to You. Thank You, too, for Your promise of reward. Amen.

"Yes" Is Enough

"Simply let your 'Yes' be 'Yes,' and your 'No,' 'No';
anything beyond this comes from the evil one."
MATTHEW 5:37 NIV

It's a very difficult, awkward situation to be wrongly accused, especially when it seems that everyone believes the accuser. When your reputation is on the line and rumors begin to spread, it's maddening since you know the accusations are false. As a Christian, it's even more difficult because your desire is to maintain a pure example of Christ, and that can be sullied easily by false accusations.

It's important to live above reproach and not allow any room for doubt among unbelievers. But when you've done all you can and are still wrongly accused of something, consider Jesus' example. He was falsely accused of many things and even sentenced to death in front of the people He had lived to serve, yet He said nothing. He let His life speak for itself. His Father protected His witness, and He will do the same for you if you ever face a similar situation.

Father, please help me to live a life above reproach, one that honors You in all things. Please help me to choose my words carefully and to remain silent when it is Your will that I do so. Amen.

God Does It Again!

*"Now we are all here, waiting before God to
hear the message the Lord has given you."*
ACTS 10:33 NLT

Does God ever do anything in the twenty-first century like He did in the first century of the Christian church? Barb wondered. When she went on a mission trip to Malawi in southeastern Africa, she found her answer.

Barb and her evangelism team approached a remote village. The village chief was on his prayer mat. Like Cornelius in Acts, this nominal Muslim was "waiting before God to hear the message" of the one true God. Barb and her team shared the gospel message with the chief. Before Barb came back home to the United States, he and hundreds more had prayed to receive Christ.

In the Bible we read of people speaking in languages they never knew. We learn of people like Cornelius having visions (Acts 10:1–7). We read that about three thousand people were added to the Kingdom roster in one day (Acts 2:41).We wonder if things like that happen anymore. Barb doesn't question it any longer. She's lived it!

God is still in the business of bringing men and women to Himself. Sometimes one at a time, sometimes with all the drama of the book of Acts. Jesus promised, "Anyone who believes in me will do the same works I have done, and even greater" (John 14:12 NLT).

*Lord Jesus, I praise You because You're
still a miracle-working Savior. Amen.*

Sweating the Small Stuff

Blessed are all who fear the Lord, who walk in his ways.
You will eat the fruit of your labor; blessings and prosperity will be yours.
PSALM 128:1–2 NIV

It was just one of those days. Alice couldn't find one thing worth smiling about. She was stressed out and stretched to her limit. She thought her life couldn't get any worse.

The Lord showers us with many blessings each day—family, friends, education, job, good health, and a beautiful earth. But despite the gifts He gives, it's easy to get bogged down in the little things that go wrong. Maybe the car broke down or the bus was late. Perhaps your boss yelled at you for no reason or your boyfriend or husband forgot the date you had planned. The bills could be late or gas prices too high.

We're all human, and we sometimes focus on all the negatives rather than the positives in life. Next time you're feeling that "woe is me" attitude, remember that you are a child of God. Spend some time counting all the wonderful blessings that come from the Lord rather than the headaches from this earth.

Father, thank You that I am Your child. Remind me each
day to count the many blessings You shower upon me,
rather than focusing on the negatives of this world. Amen.

Fill Up My Cup

"But whoever drinks the water I give him will never thirst. Indeed, the water
I give him will become in him a spring of water welling up to eternal life."
JOHN 4:14 NIV

Imagine never being thirsty again! No more water bottles or Gatorade. Your thirst would always be quenched.

The woman at the well in John 4 was just a little confused when Jesus offered to quench her thirst forever. She thought Jesus was talking about making her life simpler by eliminating her need to return to the well for water all the time. It took her some time, but she eventually understood. Jesus was really offering her spiritual water for her soul. She ran back to her town wondering if He was the Christ.

Jesus offers us that same spiritual water today. We come to Him for eternal life, and then He continues to fill us with His Spirit forever. When you think of your life as a Christian, are you bubbling up with love for the Lord, or are you a little dried up? Return to the well and ask Him to fill up your cup.

Dear Jesus, let my life overflow with love for You. Fill me up and let others around me see the difference You make in my life. Amen.

....
....
....
....
....
....
....
....
....
....

Seasons of Change

The Spirit of God, who raised Jesus from the dead, lives in you.
And just as God raised Christ Jesus from the dead, he will give life
to your mortal bodies by this same Spirit living within you.
ROMANS 8:11 NLT

God created you to grow and mature, just as He created the earth to develop and produce. Much like the earth goes through seasons, you live a lifetime of seasons. Some look similar and some very different, but all require change on your part.

Change can be exciting or fearsome. Changing a habit or moving beyond your comfort zone can leave you feeling out of control. Maybe you want change but feel powerless to make it happen. But you don't have to do it in your own strength. With God's help you can achieve the things you want—you can do things better and live smarter.

The power of God that formed the world, brought the dry land above the waters of the sea, and raised Jesus from the dead is alive and active today. Imagine what it takes to overcome the natural laws of gravity to put the earth and seas in place. Imagine the power to bring the dead to life again. That same power is available to work out the details of your life.

Lord, help me to accept change and depend on Your
strength to make the changes I need in my life today. Amen.

Praying for Loved Ones

"Therefore I tell you, whatever you ask for in prayer,
believe that you have received it, and it will be yours."
MARK 11:24 NIV

One of the best things a woman can do for her loved ones is pray for them. And while we don't find one simple formula for effective prayer in the Bible, how we pray may be just as important as what we pray.

As we talk to our heavenly Father, do we ask Him to change our friends or family members—or to change us? Do we take responsibility for the hurts we have caused, as well as forgiving our friends for the hurts they have caused us? Or do we pray with anger in our hearts, asking God to make our family member different out of frustration and not love?

Do we beseech God with faith, believing that He can do anything? Or do we pray with hesitation, believing that nothing is going to change? God is honored and willing to work when we pray with faith.

The most beneficial times of prayer often come when we make time to listen to God, not just talk "at" Him. He can give us wisdom and insights we would never come up with on our own.

Though we can't always see it, He is at work, in our loved ones' hearts and in ours.

Lord, thank You for Your concern for my friends and family members. I know You love them even more than I do.

....

....

....

....

....

....

....

....

Rest for the Weary

*"Come to me, all of you who are weary and
carry heavy burdens, and I will give you rest."*
MATTHEW 11:28 NLT

Smash! Crack! The task before her seemed endless. With a chisel in one hand and a hammer in the other, the Nepalese woman squatted along the roadside crushing rocks to make gravel. This monotonous, painstaking labor continued from sunup to sundown, day after day with no end in sight.

Have you ever felt like that Nepalese woman, repeating the same monotonous tasks over and over until you felt like screaming? Life has worn you out. You feel like throwing in the towel. You are on your last nerve.

The Lord wants to lighten the load you bear and give your soul rest. How can you receive the rest He offers?

Humbly come to Him by admitting your need. Pride insists that you can handle everything without help. Instead, be honest with the Lord about your struggles. Allow Him to shoulder your burdens and strengthen you in your areas of weakness. Invite Him to be your helper, your advocate, your friend. The Lord desires to be yoked with you in life. Regardless of the size of your rock pile, He yearns to be a part of your labor. Come to Him and receive the rest you crave in the midst of life's journey.

*Dear Lord, I am weary. I humbly
come to You, asking for rest. Amen.*

....

....

....

....

....

....

....

....

Sense of Belonging

"All that the Father gives Me will come to Me,
and the one who comes to Me I will by no means cast out."
JOHN 6:37 NKJV

A child belongs to his parents. Mothers and fathers happily give their child love and attention. They meet his needs and look out for his safety. Parents plan for their child's future. A child doesn't have to worry about providing his next meal or getting enough rest. He knows that his parents will see to his well-being. His sense of belonging to them provides him with peace and security.

We belong to Christ. When the Father calls us to come to Jesus, we belong to Him. This is an irrevocable transaction. We are His, given to Him by the Father. He does not refuse to save us. He will not refuse to help us. No detail of our lives is unimportant to Him. No matter what happens, He will never let us go. Like the enduring love of a parent—but even more perfect—is the love of Christ for us. He has endured all the temptations and suffered all the pain that we will ever face. He has given His very life for us. We can live peacefully and securely knowing we belong to Him.

Lord Jesus, I confess I often forget that I belong to
You and how much You love me. Help me to rest
in Your everlasting love and care. Amen.

....

....

....

....

....

....

....

....

Our Rock and Savior

"The Lord lives! Praise be to my Rock!
Exalted be God, the Rock, my Savior!"
2 SAMUEL 22:47 NIV

When David assumed the throne of Israel, he might have had more temptations than most for forsaking God. The people of Israel loved him, his troops fought valiantly for him, and he had all the power and money he could need. But David did not forsake God. Instead, he chose to maintain a personal relationship with Him.

Throughout the Psalms, we read that David not only worshipped and praised God, he also complained to Him, was honest with God about what he was feeling, and even admitted to being angry at God. Perhaps the most amazing thing about David, though, was his constant devotion and reliance on his Creator.

Even though David is the powerful king of Israel, he praises God in 2 Samuel 22:47, calling Him his Rock and Savior. David knew that God was alive, and he also knew that he needed Him more than anything else in the world.

It's the same for us today. Find strength in the fact that you can rely on the same powerful God that David relied on.

Dear Lord, You are my Rock and my Savior. You are alive, and I praise You as God above all else. Thank You for Your love and power. Amen.

Moving On?

Let every detail in your lives—words, actions, whatever—be done in the name of the Master, Jesus, thanking God the Father every step of the way.
COLOSSIANS 3:17 MSG

LeighAnn held a few temporary jobs before she landed what she thought was her dream gig with a big company. Now less than a year later, she's having second thoughts. Is this really the place where God wants her?

Some human resource managers call it "the seven-year itch." But for some people it happens much sooner than that. It's a sense that something else exists out there that you may need to explore.

As a Christian, it's important to focus on what God wants in your career—not just what feels right. If you're thinking about leaving a job, make sure you consider it prayerfully. Seek guidance in His Word. Examine your own motives before making the move. Why don't you like your current job? What's making you think you should move on? If you're considering a new job, what makes it better?

No matter where you are in your career, make sure you're honoring God each day. Your work is His work. Even if you aren't where you think you should be, use your position to show His love to others.

Lord, help me to make my career what You would like it to be. Remind me to examine my motives and come to You in prayer before making any changes in job direction.

One Thing

"Therefore do not worry about tomorrow, for tomorrow will worry about itself. Each day has enough trouble of its own."
MATTHEW 6:34 NIV

Suzanne was exhausted. Pressures at work had become increasingly intense. She tossed and turned at night, wondering how she was going to get it all done—on top of keeping up with things at home.

Do you ever feel this way? Life can often be overwhelming. Deadlines, commitments, details—it's enough to make you want to crawl back into bed and pull the covers over your head. Jesus understood that life could be busy and overwhelming. His advice in this regard is simple—do not worry about tomorrow . . . each day has enough trouble of its own. Looking too far ahead into the future—even one day—can paralyze us with worry and exhaustion, so much so that we don't feel like doing anything at all.

Jesus taught that it's far more effective to tackle life one step at a time. Simply do the next thing that needs to be done. Not only does this keep our worry at a minimum, it enables us to trust God to help us accomplish what we cannot do on our own. Living in the moment takes practice, but it's a worthwhile investment of your time.

Father, help me not to worry about the future. Teach me to live for today and trust You for tomorrow. Amen.

Releasing Your Hold on Anxiety

Search me, O God, and know my heart;
test me and know my anxious thoughts.
PSALM 139:23 NIV

We live in an age of anxiety. Worry and stress pervade our lives, and most of us accept it as a given that we will not live in a personal state of peace.

This is not how God intended it to be. He asks us to place our trust and our hope in Him. If we worry, we are not trusting. If we let the cares of this world weigh on our hearts and distract us from participating in God's work, then that worry becomes sinful.

What is it that weighs you down? Financial issues? An unhealthy relationship? Your busy schedule? Surrender these misgivings to a God who wants to take them from you. Ask Him to search your heart for any and all anxieties, for any and all signs that you have not truly put your trust in Him. Find the trouble spots in your life to which you direct most of your thoughts and energy, and then hand these troubles over to One who can truly address them.

Realize that you are only human, and that God is infinitely more capable of balancing your cares than you are.

Lord, take from me my anxieties, big and small. May I remember to give these to You daily so that I will not find myself distracted by the things of this world.

Hold His Hand

"For I am the Lord, your God, who takes hold of your
right hand and says to you, Do not fear; I will help you."
ISAIAH 41:13 NIV

Holding hands communicates love and protection. Courage and strength are imparted from one person to another. Holding hands acknowledges that a strong bond exists between two people.

Imagine facing surgery, a new job, divorce, or a financial setback. Many circumstances may cause us to become fearful. We need to feel love and protection. We yearn for courage and strength to face another day. If only we had someone's hand to hold!

God desires to help us. When we walk through life hand in hand with God, we can face anything. His love covers us. His presence is our guard. We can do all things through Christ because we are given His strength.

Do you feel as though you're walking through life alone? Do not fear. Are you in need of love, protection, courage, and strength? Reach out your hand. Allow Jesus to take hold of it. Receive His love and protection. Bask in His courage and strength. Take hold of His hand!

Dear Lord, thank You that I do not have to fear.
You will help me by taking my hand. Amen.

....
....
....
....
....
....
....
....

God's Unstoppable Plan

*"I know that you can do anything,
and no one can stop you."*
JOB 42:2 NLT

Melinda's passion is music. Ever since she was a little girl, she has loved to sing and play the piano. As a teen, she won several competitions, and her college of choice offered her a scholarship to study music.

For years now, Melinda has prayed for a way to make money from her passion, but she hasn't been able to find a job in music.. She has a good job in sales, an area in which she is naturally gifted but it doesn't excite her much. However, she does sing in a community chorus and participates in music groups at her church. And she continues to pray for a way to get paid to do what she loves. During her times with God, He assures her that He has a plan and that He will open a door for her, in His time and way.

While Melinda waits, she holds onto His promises with faith, knowing that the same God who parted the Red Sea can bring her the perfect job.

*Lord, thank You for giving me unique talents. Help me
to trust You to open doors for me to use them for Your glory.*

....

....

....

....

....

....

....

....

....

....

Born to Laugh

A cheerful heart is good medicine,
but a crushed spirit dries up the bones.
PROVERBS 17:22 NIV

"The Queen of Comedy," Lucille Ball, won the hearts of television viewers with her hit sitcom, *I Love Lucy* which first aired October 15, 1951—a show that can still be seen on television reruns today. It seems Lucy was born to make people laugh.

When was the last time you laughed so hard that your belly shook and tears streamed down your face, the real, rolling on the floor, uncontrollable laughter? It feels good to laugh, and it is a wonderful stress and tension reliever. Sometimes the most awkward situations or stressful circumstances can be simply avoided when laughter erupts. It sets our hearts and minds at ease.

As children of the Creator Himself, we were made to laugh—to experience great joy. Our design didn't include for us to carry the stress, worry, and heaviness every day.

Maybe it's time you had a really good laugh. Take a break—push the concerns and worries out of your mind for the moment. Go ahead! Have a good time! Ask God to give you a really good laugh today.

Lord, help me to realize every day every opportunity You bring to see the joy in life and the humor in the world around me. Amen.

More Blessed to Give

*"Give, and it will be given to you. A good measure, pressed down,
shaken together and running over, will be poured into your lap.
For with the measure you use, it will be measured to you."*
LUKE 6:38 NIV

When Cassie learned that her church's homeless ministry needed help, she volunteered, anxious to give what she could. Lending a hand seemed like the right thing to do, and she expected to find lots of needy people with whom she could share her gifts. She found plenty of needy people, and she definitely lent a hand. However, what she hadn't expected was to be blessed so much. Not only did she make some new friends, but they taught her a great deal about thankfulness, contentment, and how to make the best of a hard situation.

In God's economy, giving means receiving. When we give to others, we receive more than the satisfaction of a job well done. Jesus promises blessing when we give to others. They can be simple blessings, such as a smile or a kind word of thanks. Blessings can also be life-changing, such as making a new friend or acquiring a new skill. Getting something shouldn't be our motivation for serving others, but it is an added bonus. What can you do today to be a blessing to others?

*Lord, thank You for the promise of giving and receiving.
Help me to bless others as You have blessed me.*

Prayers for Boldness

Pray that I may declare [the gospel] fearlessly, as I should.
EPHESIANS 6:20 NIV

The apostle Paul was an amazing follower of Christ. He endured countless hardships, all in order to preach the gospel to those who had never heard it. He was in prison when he wrote to the Ephesians.

One might think Paul was fearless about his faith, courageously overcoming obstacles, and boldly preaching the good news. In Ephesians 6:20, however, Paul asks the Ephesians to pray for him. He realized that without the prayers of the saints and the faithfulness of God, he would not be an effective ambassador for Christ.

In today's world, proclaiming our faith can be difficult. Our family, friends, and coworkers can make us feel shy about sharing the gospel. We might feel unworthy to talk about our faith, or we may be worried that we will not use the right words. Paul's request for prayer should encourage us. Paul, too, worried about his ability to effectively communicate the gospel to those around him. He relied on his brothers and sisters in Christ to lift him up to God. In the same way, we should rely on our brothers and sisters to pray for us, that we may declare the gospel fearlessly, as we should.

Dear Lord, thank You for Your Word. Surround me with people who will pray for me, and place people in my life for whom I can pray. Together let us boldly proclaim Your name. Amen.

Keeping Up with the Joneses

My little group of disciples, don't be afraid!
Your Father wants to give you the kingdom.
LUKE 12:32 CEV

Emily had a good job in a nice city. But she looked around at her tiny apartment and thought, *I want more.*

It's easy to look around at all the stuff that everyone else has—the nice house, new car, designer clothes—and wish for something more. But we must remind ourselves as Christians that God wants more for us than the treasures of this earth. He wants to give us His kingdom.

Not only is storing up treasures in this world a bad decision spiritually, it's also financially irresponsible. We may want the better house or easier lifestyle that we see wealthy people have, but that might not be God's plan for us. It's important to live within our means and plan for the future. That rainy-day fund may come in handy sooner than we ever plan.

Just because we don't have the latest trendy item or the nicest home or newest car doesn't mean we're not blessed. Trends come and go, but our blessings in heaven will last forever.

Dear Father, You give me so many blessings. Help me not to want more stuff or to store up my treasures on earth. A heavenly reward is so much greater than anything of this world.

What Is Required

He hath shewed thee, O man, what is good; and what doth the Lord require
of thee, but to do justly, and to love mercy, and to walk humbly with thy God?
MICAH 6:8 KJV

Micah has pretty much summed up what God expects of us. We are to do justly, and we are to be merciful and humble. It really isn't difficult to understand, but it is often hard to put it into practice.

So many times we ignore God's instructions and try to find other ways to please Him, but what He really wants is obedience. By society's standards, God's expectations don't make sense. Our idea of justice is that what works for me is fine, and what works for you is all right, too, as long as you don't bother me with it.

True mercy is virtually unheard of. Many people have the attitude that they are number one, and anyone who interferes with their desires is in danger. In a world where we are taught that we deserve everything, humility is not a priority. We are actually taught to be proud.

These are not God's ways. He expects us to be fair, merciful, and humble, and He will give us the strength to be so.

Father, You've made clear what You require of me.
Please help me live according to Your way.

Sniper on the Fifty-Yard Line

Nothing in all creation is hidden from God's sight.
HEBREWS 4:13 NIV

Tiffany's boyfriend, Brett, asked her to come out to the fifty-yard line with him after his victorious college football game. Brett assured Tiffany this was a brief meeting with a sports editor.

"It will just be a few minutes."

Once on the fifty-yard line, Brett went down on one knee and took Tiffany's hand. This wasn't a meeting with a sportswriter. Brett asked Tiffany to become his wife.

Tiffany didn't see their families—still in the stands—witnessing Brett's carefully planned surprise. And there was one other person hidden from the new fiancée, too. Brett gently turned Tiffany around. There, crawling across the field like a sniper, was Tiffany's future sister-in-law, snapping picture after picture.

We can hide all kinds of things from one another. We cannot, however, ever surprise God or hide anything from Him. He knows us inside and out—all the good and all the not-so-good. He needs no camera. He knows us intimately and individually. That knowledge can be our incentive for right living and our comfort when we're wronged. There's both warning and assurance that "everything is uncovered and laid bare before the eyes of him to whom we must give account" (Hebrews 4:13 NIV).

*Lord, teach me to live and rest in the knowledge
that I can't hide anything from You. Amen.*

Daily Confidence

For I can do everything through Christ,
who gives me strength.
PHILIPPIANS 4:13 NLT

Philippians 4:13 isn't talking about being able to do anything you set your mind to do. It's not about having super powers or amazing abilities to serve your own purposes. Philippians 4:13 is about being able to complete the tasks God has given you through His strength and power.

Do you feel a gentle nudging from the Spirit to do something about which you are unsure and insecure? Maybe the Spirit is urging you to talk to the new girl at work and invite her out for coffee. Or maybe the Lord is prompting you to reconcile a difficult family relationship, start a new ministry, or even stand up for your convictions in class or at work.

You won't be able to accomplish any of those things without the strength that comes only from Christ living and working in you. If the Lord asks you to do something, you can count on Him to give you the strength and the resources to accomplish His will.

Dear Lord, please give me the confidence that I need to do Your will each day. I pray that You would work in my heart so that I can know what it is that You want me to do, and that You would give me the strength to do it. Amen.

....

....

....

....

....

....

....

Peace Is a Guard

*Do not be anxious about anything, but in everything, by prayer
and petition, with thanksgiving, present your requests to God.
And the peace of God, which transcends all understanding,
will guard your hearts and your minds in Christ Jesus.*
PHILIPPIANS 4:6–7 NIV

A guard stands at the gate of the White House. His job is to protect and defend the nation's president.

Most of us do not need a bodyguard. What we do need is a guard over our hearts and minds. Anxious thoughts and worry will try to attack us on a regular basis. Fear can so easily creep into our thinking and rob us of joy, the very treasure we hold because we know Christ.

Thankfully, we have been given the key to protecting our minds and hearts—prayer. In coming to God with our petitions and in giving thanks to Him for all He has already done for us, we receive His peace. Beyond our ability to understand or explain, a heaven-sent peace will abide with us.

What a beautiful picture: the soldier of peace standing at the door of our hearts and minds, guarding the treasure of fellowship with Christ. It is ours for the asking when we go to our Father with all our requests.

*Father, cause me to remember that Your peace is available
to guard me night and day. Help me to bring everything
to You in prayer, trusting in Your faithful provision.*

....

....

....

....

....

....

You Are a Masterpiece

*For you created my inmost being; you knit me together
in my mother's womb. I praise you because I am fearfully and
wonderfully made; your works are wonderful, I know that full well.*
PSALM 139:13–14 NIV

We women often believe we should look like the models on magazine pages. Every day we're sent messages that outward appearance is what matters most. We feel we should be stick thin—yet curvy in all the right places. If our skin isn't perfect, we can purchase the newest skin care cosmetics for a flawless airbrushed look. We contemplate surgeries to alter our appearance. We avoid mirrors because they reveal our imperfections rather than perfect bodies.

God made your body. He designed you and knew you fully before anyone else ever laid eyes on you. And He thinks you are just right. He loves you no less and no more based upon your weight, your height, or the blemishes on your face. He sees you as His beautiful daughter, made righteous through Christ's blood that was shed for you on the cross. He sees your heart.

Praise God for the woman you are. He has great plans for you and desires to use your gifts for His purposes. Be confident in who you are!

*God, enable me to see myself as Your daughter,
designed by Your hand to be exactly who I am. Amen.*

Lose to Gain

"If you cling to your life, you will lose it;
but if you give up your life for me, you will find it."
MATTHEW 10:39 NLT

Life is precious. It has been said that life is but a dash, as represented by the hyphen between one's birth and death dates on a tombstone. Certainly, our physical lives are a mere dash compared to eternity. How will we choose to spend this gift of life that our Creator has given us?

Some selfishly cling to possessions and spend their entire lives trying to get more. They use people to gain possessions. They use time to pursue worldly passions. They use God to advance their cause. They are blind to truth. Someday, when their physical life closes in death, they will lose everything.

Others believe that physical life is just the beginning. Jesus came to give spiritual life, as well. These people use their possessions to reach people with the love of Jesus. They willingly sacrifice time and talent by allowing God to use them to advance His kingdom. When they draw their last breath on earth, they will be ushered into eternal life. Having given their life on earth for God's purposes, they will live forever.

Are we clinging tightly to what God has given us? Or are we willing to give it back to Him and gain so much more? Let's lose to gain.

Dear Lord, use my life on this earth for Your glory.
Help me unselfishly give myself to be used by You. Amen.

....
....
....
....
....
....
....

The Necessity of Loyalty

Ruth replied, "Don't urge me to leave you or to turn back from you.
Where you go I will go, and where you stay I will stay."
RUTH 1:16 NIV

Loyalty is fast becoming a dying virtue. In our fast-food, instant-message society, "stick-to-it-iveness" appears quaint and old-fashioned. But God doesn't look at loyalty that way. In fact, God praises and encourages it all through the scriptures. After all, He is loyal to us—even when we are not faithful to Him.

In the book named after her, Ruth's loyalty played out as she stuck with her relative, Naomi, after the deaths of both their husbands. Ruth could have gone her own way, as her sister-in-law did. Naomi even begged Ruth to leave, sure that her daughter-in-law's future would not be bright with a mother-in-law in tow.

What does loyalty look like in today's world? For a wife, it could mean not gossiping about her husband when she's at dinner with her girlfriends. For an employee, loyalty might equal sticking with a struggling company because of their godly mission statement. For a church member, loyalty might mean years of faithful service in a thankless volunteer position.

If we are to be all God wants us to be, we must cultivate loyalty. And when we do, the world will notice.

Lord, I praise You for Your unshakable loyalty to me.
Help me to be loyal not only to You, but also to
my family, friends, church, and my employer.

....

....

....

....

....

....

....

Truth

"You will know the truth, and the truth will set you free."
JOHN 8:32 NLT

Have you ever believed a lie about yourself? Perhaps someone told you that you weren't beautiful or that you'd never amount to anything.

When God called Moses to lead the children of Israel, Moses responded that he was "slow of speech." He doubted that people would listen to him (See Exodus 3–4). However, in Acts 7:22, Stephen says that Moses was "powerful in both speech and action." Moses didn't have the same confidence in himself that God did. If he had acted on the lies he believed, he never would have been able to lead the children of Israel out of slavery.

Many of us struggle to believe the truth about ourselves. The lies we believe ultimately come from Satan. Jesus says that Satan is the Father of Lies and that there is no truth in him.

What lies do you believe about yourself? How might those lies be preventing you from experiencing God's plan for your life?

The next time you're tempted to believe a lie, find a scripture passage that speaks truth over the situation. Commit the truth to memory. Over time, God's Word will transform your thinking and you'll begin to believe the truth. Then something amazing will happen—you'll be set free.

Father, thank You for the truth Your Word speaks about my life. Open my eyes to the truth and help me to believe it. Amen.

It's about Time

There's an opportune time to do things,
a right time for everything on the earth.
ECCLESIASTES 3:1 MSG

Our schedules keep us moving from early in the morning until late at night. Every task—and often free time—needs to be penciled into our calendar.

What makes the top of your list of priorities? Is it spending time with friends? Working a second job? Going to the gym? What about reading the Bible? Spending time in prayer? Attending church?

While there is nothing wrong with doing any of these things, we do, on occasion, need to step back and assess whether we have our priorities in order. We only have twenty-four hours in each day to eat, sleep, work, and do anything else that needs to be done.

Of course, God needs to be given first place. That doesn't necessarily mean that devotions should be done first thing in the morning, but it does mean that devotional time should be set apart. After determining the best time for that, list your activities and prioritize them. You may find that you need to eliminate some things from your schedule, in order to slow down the pace of life a bit. Pray about it—God will help you with the choices you need to make.

Dear Father, please be the Lord of my schedule. Give me
the wisdom I need in determining my priorities. Amen.

....
....
....
....
....
....
....
....
....

Never Lost for Long

For "whoever calls on the name of the Lord shall be saved."
ROMANS 10:13 NKJV

No one gets lost on purpose. It's easy to do, though—miss a turn off the freeway in an unfamiliar city, forget where you parked your car in a busy shopping mall, or lose your way off a hiking trail. The disconnect from the familiar is unsettling and, like a child separated from his mother in the grocery store, you probably call out for help.

Your spiritual journey is no different. It's a path that can seem familiar, and then a distraction—even for a moment—occurs and you find yourself in unfamiliar territory. The path seems lost, and the night grows dark. You feel alone and confused. You call out to God, but maybe for a little while you don't hear anything. You may have to listen intently for a while, but eventually you are reassured by His voice.

When He calls your name you know you are safe. You may have to take a few steps in the dark, but by moving toward Him you eventually see clearly. A light comes on in your heart, and you recognize where you are and what you need to do to get back on the path God has set before you.

Heavenly Father, help me to stay focused on You. Show me how to remove distractions from my life so I can stay close to You. Amen.

Seeking Rest

*It is vain for you to rise up early, to sit up late, to eat
the bread of sorrows; for so He gives His beloved sleep.*
PSALM 127:2 NKJV

Bills. Dirty dishes. Unexpected phone calls. Family responsibilities. Projects and assignments. Thing after thing, chore after chore demands your attention, day after day after very long day.

So you set your alarm clock for an hour earlier. You work through your lunch break and hurry through dinner. You stay up an hour later than you had intended. Saturday and Sunday serve as catch-up days, and then the week begins again.

Are you tiring yourself out? Do you find yourself exhausted at each day's end? To work without rest is not only physically unhealthy; it is also spiritually unhealthy. God intends for us to find a balance between work and rest. He commanded that we keep the Sabbath for just this purpose. This day should be set aside for praise and worship, certainly, but we are also to rest—to take quiet personal time for ourselves and to reflect upon our busy lives.

Take time for solitude, for reflection, for being still. The time spent away from your work will serve to rejuvenate you—physically, mentally, and spiritually—so that you may approach life directly and positively, as you should.

*Lord, give me rest. Take my anxieties over the
trivialities of life and give to me instead Your
peace so that I may act graciously toward others.*

Abandon All

*Jesus looked him hard in the eye—and loved him! He said,
"There's one thing left: Go sell whatever you own and give it to the poor.
All your wealth will then be heavenly wealth. And come follow me."
The man's face clouded over. This was the last thing he expected to hear,
and he walked off with a heavy heart. He was holding on tight to
a lot of things, and not about to let go.*
MARK 10:21–22 MSG

This wasn't the response the rich young ruler wanted to hear. But hearing these words so straightforward—so piercing—blended with the love in Jesus' eyes troubled his soul. It just was too much. He understood what was being asked of him—everything! His broken heart was obvious in his distraught face and slumped posture as he walked away. Facing the truth, he was not ready to relinquish it all for Christ.

What has Christ asked you to give up? What are you holding on to tightly? Are you giving up anything to serve Him? On the inside, are your motives pure? Is your thought life following God's will? Do your daydreams reflect a discontented heart? Let us face the truth to see what we cling to as a hindrance—whatever keeps us from fully serving Him.

*Jesus, show me what I need to relinquish to You. Help me
to abandon all to freely and joyfully serve You. Amen.*

Carry Each Other's Burdens

*Carry each other's burdens, and in this
way you will fulfill the law of Christ.*
GALATIANS 6:2 NIV

Christian women wear masks. We pretend everything is great. Admitting that we have less-than-perfect lives would be humiliating. We assume that we are the only ones experiencing problems, so we remain tight-lipped and reserved. Superficial talk dominates our conversations, allowing us to hide from each other what is really going on.

The truth is that Christians are not immune to worldly pressures. Believers suffer through divorce, addictions, eating disorders, and prodigal children, not to mention loneliness and depression. Everything is not all right. When will we be honest with one another?

God's Word instructs us to carry each other's burdens. Before that can happen, walls that hinder intimacy must be torn down. Learn to be vulnerable. Embrace honesty and affirm one another with unconditional love. There is no room for judgment. We all need the Lord so that masks can come off and burdens can be unloaded. Heartfelt prayer can be a blessing as we carry each other's burdens. We become examples of Christ. Let's take off our masks and allow someone to carry our burdens.

*Dear Lord, help me to be real with others. May I
allow others to carry my burdens so that I will
have the privilege of carrying theirs. Amen.*

Power-Packed and Personal

Thou hast magnified thy word above all thy name.
PSALM 138:2 KJV

Of all the wonderful graces and gifts God has given humankind, there's nothing that touches the power and truth of that all-time bestseller, the Bible. Unlike many of God's gifts, the Bible is one thing we can touch, see, and hear.

God says the Bible we hold in our hand is something that will endure forever. "Your word, O Lord, is eternal" (Psalm 119:89 NIV). "In your light we see light," wrote the psalmist (Psalm 36:9 NIV).

Through God's Word we experience salvation (James 1:18). The Bible provides healing, hope, and direction (Psalm 107:20; 119:74; 133). If we want wisdom and the desire to do things the right way, God's Word equips us (2 Timothy 3:16–17).

From the scriptures we can make sense of a confusing world. We can get a hold on real truth. God has given us His eternal Word to know Him and to know ourselves better. To know and obey the Word of God is to honor what God honors above all. "For the word of God is alive and powerful" (Hebrews 4:12 NLT).

Teach me not only to read, but also to obey Your living, powerful Word every day, Lord God. Amen.

....
....
....
....
....
....
....
....
....
....

A Valuable Deposit

He anointed us, set his seal of ownership on us, and put his
Spirit in our hearts as a deposit, guaranteeing what is to come.
2 CORINTHIANS 1:21–22 NIV

Payday may just be the best day of the week. Nothing beats knowing that a big hefty check was deposited into your account.

When we accept Jesus Christ as our personal savior, the Holy Spirit comes into our hearts and lives in us, showing us how to live a godly life. The Bible tells us God puts a deposit into our very own hearts. This incredibly valuable deposit guarantees we have a place in heaven some day.

When we commit our lives to Christ, He doesn't let us flail around in this mixed-up world without any help. We have the deposit of the Holy Spirit with us all the time, and He also gives us His Word and the help of other Christians to keep us strong in the Lord. So whenever you feel alone or overwhelmed with life, remember that God has anointed you, set His seal upon you, and deposited the Holy Spirit right inside your heart. That is the most valuable deposit of all!

Dear Lord, thank You for depositing Your Holy Spirit
in my heart to lead and guide me. Help me to listen. Amen.

Press On

I do not consider myself yet to have taken hold of it. But one thing I do: Forgetting what is behind and straining toward what is ahead, I press on toward the goal to win the prize for which God has called me heavenward in Christ Jesus.
PHILIPPIANS 3:13–14 NIV

A runner never looks back. She presses on toward the finish line in order to win the race. This is God's Word for us through the apostle Paul in the book of Philippians.

Paul had previously been known as Saul, a relentless killer of Christians. One day while walking a dusty road, he was blinded by a great light. His life was forever changed after he met the living Lord. His name became Paul and his mission the preaching of Christ.

What a turnaround! Paul preached the gospel as diligently as he had denounced it in his former life.

If Paul didn't think he had arrived spiritually, then certainly we haven't, either. The goal is to press on. Don't look back. There may be all sorts of sin in your past. Maybe you can relate to Paul. But no matter what your past, remember, as Paul said, to "press on toward the goal to win the prize."

Father, help me to never look back at the mess my life was before I met You. I want to look forward, just like Paul. Your promise of eternity is the prize I strive for. Amen.

The Hardest Person to Forgive

*This then is how we know that we belong to the truth,
and how we set our hearts at rest in his presence whenever our hearts
condemn us. For God is greater than our hearts, and he knows everything.*
1 JOHN 3:19–20 NIV

Felicia had been a Christian since she was a little girl, but she struggled with the concept of forgiveness—and not in the way you might expect. Felicia loved her friends and family members intensely, forgave them easily, and didn't hold grudges against anyone else.

But Felicia had trouble forgiving herself. Even after she had confessed her sins to the Lord, she didn't feel forgiven. Whatever the reason, she existed with a shadow of guilt constantly hanging over her. It was a miserable way to live.

But one weekend at a women's retreat, Felicia heard the speaker say, "If God promises something in scripture, and you don't take Him at His word, you're sinning."

The realization hit her like a lightning bolt, and Felicia almost laughed out loud. *In not receiving forgiveness, I've been sinning even more,* she thought. *Oh Lord, I'm such a mess!*

And then she heard the Lord speak to her heart. "*That's okay,*" He said. "*I love you anyway.*"

Right then and there, Felicia chose to believe Him. And that was the beginning of a renewed walk of faith.

*Father God, thank You for Your sweet forgiveness.
Help me to forgive others—and myself.*

....

....

....

....

....

....

....

....

Light in the Dark

The light shines in the darkness,
but the darkness has not understood it.
JOHN 1:5 NIV

A mother turns on the closet light in her toddler son's bedroom before switching off his bedside lamp. He is not afraid of the dark, he says, as long as there is a little light in the room. This boy knows that darkness cannot put out light. Even a candle or the smallest night-light will triumph over the darkness surrounding it.

The world around us can seem very dark at times; so can the circumstances of our lives. Is it really dark, or are we failing to look toward the true Light?

Jesus said in John 12:46 (NIV), "I have come into the world as a light, so that no one who believes in me should stay in darkness." He also promised that He is always with us. Because we have Him, we have light.

If we fail to perceive it, if we seem to be living in darkness, perhaps we have turned our backs to the light of His countenance. Maybe we are covering our eyes with the cares of this world. Clouds of sin may be darkening our lives, but He has not left us. He promises us that in following Him we will not walk in darkness but have the light of life.

Lord Jesus, where am I covering my own eyes or walking
away from You? Turn me back to You, the Light of life.

....
....
....
....
....
....
....
....

What's in a Name?

Whatever happens, conduct yourselves
in a manner worthy of the gospel of Christ.
PHILIPPIANS 1:27 NIV

Many families take pride in their family name. A name that has been around for a long time often commands respect; perhaps it is associated with money, power, or fine workmanship. When someone from the family enters the community, he often is expected to be careful to represent his family name well, behaving with dignity and honor, or he runs the risk of sullying the family name. In the same way, an employee must act in a manner that reflects well upon her boss or her company, or she risks damaging the reputation of the entire firm.

As Christians, we are called to conduct ourselves in a manner worthy of the gospel. We must uphold the name of Christ while accurately representing the gospel. Just like an employee who loses her temper and reflects badly on her company, when we succumb to sin we may tear down the gospel we work so hard to advocate. Our conduct, no matter the situation, should worthily reflect the gospel of Christ.

Dear Lord, thank You for Your Word.
Please help me to conduct myself in a worthy manner.
Let my life be a reflection of You. Amen.

Enter through the Narrow Gate

"Enter through the narrow gate. For wide is the gate and broad is the road that leads to destruction, and many enter through it. But small is the gate and narrow the road that leads to life, and only a few find it."
MATTHEW 7:13–14 NIV

Although peer pressure is often associated with teenagers, adults also have to deal with this phenomenon. Human beings instinctively embrace a mob mentality. Following the crowd comes easy. Acceptance by others is important. From wearing the latest fashions to watching the most popular TV shows, we hate being viewed as weird. We'd rather blend in with those around us by getting lost in the crowd.

Jesus warns us that the crowd is traveling the road that leads to destruction. Paul describes the masses in Philippians 3:19 (NIV) by saying, "Their destiny is destruction, their god is their stomach, and their glory is in their shame. Their mind is on earthly things." Believers are challenged to focus on the eternal—on things that have spiritual value. A choice is before us: embrace worldly values or adopt God's truth.

Dare to enter through the narrow gate. For it is through the narrow gate that true life is found. Embrace the life that God has for you by choosing the road less traveled.

Dear Lord, give me courage to enter through the narrow gate and experience life as You intended. Amen.

....

....

....

....

....

....

....

....

Web Savvy

*Pray for us. We are sure that we have a clear
conscience and desire to live honorably in every way.*
HEBREWS 13:18 NIV

Once you're out on your own, meeting new people can be difficult at best. Dating relationships are no exception.

Internet dating is a popular way to meet others for friendships or dating relationships. Dating sites, social-networking sites, and even local online classifieds offer a way to connect with other people. All of these can be great ways for Christians to meet other people—particularly on Christian-based sites.

But it's also important to exercise caution online. Though we may strive to have a clear conscience and "act honorably in all things," (Hebrews 13:18 ESV) not everyone on the Web has such pure purposes and godly motives. Make sure to never put personal, identifying information online. Set profiles on blogs and networking sites to private. Trust your instincts. If a situation feels wrong, log off immediately.

Before you put anything on the Web, check a site's credentials. Just as you would in the "real world," stick to familiar and safe places, and look for Christian values in the places you spend time.

*Dear Lord, I know that not everyone I meet has Your
purposes in mind. As I venture out, help me to seek
Christian friendships and stay safe in everything that I do.*

Jumping Hurdles

God's way is perfect. All the Lord's promises prove true.
PSALM 18:30 NLT

Sandy Allen prayed to be like the other girls, but she knew she never would. Throughout her childhood she was ridiculed for her size and appearance. At over seven feet seven inches tall, Sandy holds the world record as the tallest living woman. She learned to confront adversity and accept her place in life. And with much determination she learned to overcome the major obstacles she faced.

Obstacles appear in your path every day. The enemy of your soul wants to keep you from fulfilling your purpose and achieving your dream. You don't have to face challenges alone; you can depend on God to help you make it over the hurdles—tough decisions, physical pain, or financial insecurity.

Maybe there are times when you just don't think you can take one more disappointment or hurt. That's the perfect time to draw strength from God and His Word. Meditate on encouraging scriptures, or play a song that you know strengthens your heart and mind. Ask God to infuse you with His strength, and you'll find the power to take another step, and another—until you find yourself on the other side of that challenge you're facing today.

God, give me strength each day to face the obstacles I am to overcome. I am thankful that I don't have to face them alone. Amen.

Strong Words

"If you do not forgive men their sins,
your Father will not forgive your sins."
MATTHEW 6:15 NIV

Tina's hatred of her grandfather had simmered over the years. No one knew it was there. She'd never admitted the childhood abuse or her feelings that surfaced as she grew older. He wasn't worth a moment's thought anyway. It was in the past, and her spiritual life seemed to be okay. But lately the anger consumed her. Why couldn't she shake this? It was so many years ago. He was dead. She was over it.

Grudges and past hurts are difficult to overcome. The truth is, we have injured God just as others have injured us. Our sins separate us from God the very same way as everyone else's do—including those who hurt us. The sins may be different, but everyone is guilty and in desperate need of God's mercy—mercy that none of us deserves. Christ paid our sin penalty with His own blood on the cross. Every human stands on the same ground looking up at the cross for redemption. Christ Himself commands that we forgive others because of the forgiveness we experience from the Father. Who are we to withhold that forgiveness?

Christ, You suffered willingly for sinners like me.
I don't deserve Your forgiveness. Help me to remember
that when others sin against me. Only with Your help
can I forgive them as You forgave me. Amen.

God Will Not Change

For I am the Lord, I change not.
MALACHI 3:6 KJV

One of the most important truths is that God doesn't change. Often we are guilty of trying to bring God down to our level so we can be comfortable in our worldly standards.

"God understands that society changes," we say. "If we are going to reach today's people, we must incorporate some of their behaviors."

Yes, God knows that society changes, and what is sad is that His people change right along with it. God, however, does not change. His standard for purity, friendship, entertainment—and the list goes on—are the same that He established from the beginning. Yes, He wants us to reach those around us, but His power is great enough that He can help us do so through godly behavior. Unfortunately, it is more often our desire to fit in than a true desire to win others that causes us to adopt the world's standards.

It's time for us to acknowledge that God remains the same. We must ask ourselves whom we want to please. It's not always easy to choose modesty over style. It can be difficult to turn down a social opportunity that is contrary to God's design. But when we choose God, the satisfaction is more rewarding.

Dear God, I know You had my best interest at heart when You established Your standards. Help me to flee temptation.

Here You Are!

Two are better than one. . . .
If one falls down, his friend can help him up.
ECCLESIASTES 4:9–10 NIV

Jodie lived in a predominantly Muslim country where she became a student of Arabic. She was invited to teach English to women in a mosque basement kindergarten classroom. For five months she met regularly with these women—Jodie wrestling with Arabic and those dozen women doing their best to learn English. They had only met a few times when the women's questions took on an added dimension of challenge for Jodie: They wanted to know about Christians and Christianity.

Do foreigners pray? Are Christians like the ones we see in movies from America? Do you believe that Isa is the Son of God?

Jodie struggled to answer their questions in her own weak Arabic. But she did the best she could, trusting God to use her in exposing these women to the truth of Jesus Christ. An unexpected blessing came from one of the young women in her group.

"I have prayed all my life that God would give me a Christian friend so I could understand her better," she said. "And here you are!"

Sometimes we pick our friends; sometimes our friends pick us. We may be years into a friendship and not recall how it started. But how wonderful to have a good friend! Maybe today is the day to tell someone, "I'm so glad you're my friend." Those few words may make her day.

Thank You, Lord, for true friends. Amen.

....

....

....

....

....

....

....

....

My Future Is in Your Hands

The Lord says, "I will guide you along the best pathway for your life.
I will advise you and watch over you."
PSALM 32:8 NLT

Plans are running wild inside my head.
Lord, I know first I should come to you,
But I dream alone instead.
Still, I know inside my heart
You're always there for me,
And every time I fall,
I'll just wind up on my knees.
'Cause I know that if I trust you

You'll be true,
I can follow you.
You're always there for me;
You'll help me stand.
Lord, I need you;
My future's in your hands.
—lyrics by MariLee Parrish

Are plans running wild in your head? Remember that the Lord is watching over you, and He is there to guide you. He wants you to seek Him out. Don't try to make your dreams happen all by yourself. Get on your knees and ask Him to direct your plans each morning. Don't be afraid to put your future in His hands!

Father, thank You for always being faithful to me.
Continue to watch over me and direct my path. Amen.

Loving Friends

The heartfelt counsel of a friend
is as sweet as perfume and incense.
PROVERBS 27:9 NLT

Caitlyn's friends often came to her for advice. She always seemed to know just the right words to say, whether friends needed help with relationship or job troubles. Lately though, she was feeling overwhelmed because it seemed all of her friends needed her at once. What she really wanted was some time away—from her friends and their problems.

Caring for others, listening to them, and offering wise counsel is what God wants us to do. But it can become overwhelming to constantly care for the emotional needs of others. It drains us, and more importantly, it can keep them from seeking answers directly from God. We need to remember that our job is to point others to Christ, not become a substitute for Him. Allowing our friends unlimited access to our advice and counsel is one way this can happen. Sometimes the wisest words of advice we can offer are, "Let's take it to Jesus."

Father, help me to be a good friend, a good listener, and a person who offers wise counsel. I pray that I would ultimately turn my friends to You—the One who will never let them down.

Learn Contentment

I am not saying this because I am in need,
for I have learned to be content whatever the circumstances.
PHILIPPIANS 4:11 NIV

The time had come. The elderly woman, called Mamo by her grandchildren, could no longer live alone. She now required the medical supervision of a nursing home. On moving day, her family reluctantly pushed her wheelchair down the hall to her new room. As they entered, stark reality stared them in the face. Mamo's sparse furnishings included a bed, dresser, and chair. A semi-comatose roommate occupied the other half of her room. Peacefully looking out her window, Mamo said, "How could I want anything more?" The amazing thing was, she meant it!

How do we find contentment like this? The secret is found on the plaque quoting Philippians 4:11 that hung above Mamo's bed. Contentment is learned and cultivated. It is an attitude of the heart. It has nothing to do with material possessions or life's circumstances. It has everything to do with being in the center of God's will and knowing it. Contentment means finding rest and peace in God's presence—nothing more, nothing less. It is trusting that God will meet all of your needs.

At the end of her life, Mamo could rest in God's provision completely. May we learn to say confidently, The Lord is my shepherd, I shall not want. That is the secret of contentment.

Dear Lord, teach me how to be content in You,
knowing that You will provide all that I need. Amen.

Fellowship with Others

*They devoted themselves to the apostles' teaching
and to the fellowship, to the breaking of bread and to prayer.*
ACTS 2:42 NIV

Natalie felt at home in the outdoors. She loved to hike and bike and spend hours sitting by the lake. She wondered if, instead of going to church, she could just experience God where she was—outside.

It's true we can experience God everywhere and should seek Him daily wherever we are. But God still reminds us in His Word that we must devote ourselves to learning His instructions and seeking Him in prayer. That also means coming together with other believers in fellowship.

A church doesn't have to be big or formal or even meet in a traditional worship building, but as Christians, we still need to gather together as a church and worship. Other believers can keep us accountable and provide support. They can also give us different perspectives on the Word and lift us up in prayer.

Even if we don't always feel like going to church, it's an important part of our Christian walk. Find a group of believers that you can join and study with together. You'll grow in God and as the body of Christ.

God, I may be able to experience You everywhere, but I also need the fellowship of other believers. Jesus surrounded Himself with disciples; help me to seek a community of believers as well.

A Woman Who Fears the Lord

*Charm is deceptive, and beauty is fleeting; but a woman
who fears the Lord is to be praised. Give her the reward she
has earned, and let her works bring her praise at the city gate.*

PROVERBS 31:30–31 NIV

Proverbs ends as it begins—speaking of the fear of the Lord. When God repeats Himself in scripture, certainly we should take notice. The book's final chapter, Proverbs 31, presents the characteristics of a capable wife. Her description reminds us that the fear of the Lord is central in a godly woman's life.

Charm and beauty are not the attributes that God values in His daughters. Clearly, it is a healthy and holy respect for the Father that sets apart believers from the lost. Through Bible study and prayer, we get to know God better. In the Old Testament, He is a God of order, a jealous God. Seek Him in the New Testament and find Him consistent and faithful, offering up His great sacrifice in His Son, Jesus.

Ask the Lord to help you develop a true reverence for Him. He wants us to call Him Abba Father ("Daddy"), but He also demands respect, reverence, and a holy fear. He is the God of the universe—the same yesterday, today, and tomorrow.

*God, make me a woman who respects
You deeply, I pray. Amen.*

Confession

The Lord has heard my supplication;
the Lord will receive my prayer.
PSALM 6:9 NKJV

Where does faith like David's come from? How can he make such a bold and confident statement? Wrought with emotion, David cries out to God in Psalm 6. He feels punished by God. He describes himself as languishing, in need of healing, his bones trembling in terror. His soul is also afraid. He begs God for deliverance and says he is weary with moaning, flooding his bed with tears every night. He begs God for mercy and pleads for Him to save his life.

David's confession empties him. His weakness, sorrow, and fear gush forth. He reaches the end of himself. He sees that his only hope is God's steadfast love. Remembering that God's love never gives up or gives out, David is refreshed and renewed in spirit. His confidence in God is restored.

"Confession is good for the soul," says an old Scottish proverb. David shows us the truth of this. It is in our open, honest moments before God that we are restored. When we confess our weakness, we can receive His strength. When we admit our fear, He will calm us with His Spirit. When we give Him our sadness, He will turn the weeping to joy. Remembering Him, our faith and our confidence are restored.

Father, help me to come before You honestly confessing my weak and helpless state. Thank You for Your mercy and Your steadfast love.

Competition—the Good Kind

*"And whoever of you desires to be first shall be slave of all.
For even the Son of Man did not come to be served,
but to serve, and to give His life a ransom for many."*
MARK 10:44–45 NKJV

Possessions, clothes, appearance, cars, jobs, friends, family—these are all things that can drive a competitive spirit among women. In our insecurities, we want to be the best and have the best. Somehow the world has decided that those worldly things are a measure of the value of a person. But we each need to ask ourselves where we really want our successes to come from.

In answer to a competitive discussion among His disciples, Jesus explained that the greatest person was the one who places himself last. Jesus places value on others and their needs instead of His own. To be like Him, we need to serve others rather than only seeking the best for ourselves. Our competitive spirits should be driven by the goal to make Jesus happy—not to make the world happy. Serving others is the only way to be first in His eyes.

Father, forgive me for trying to compete over worldly things and help me to focus on honoring You by serving others in Your name. Amen.

....
....
....
....
....
....
....
....
....
....
....

Shut the Door

When you pray, go into your room, and when you have
shut your door, pray to your Father who is in the secret place.
MATTHEW 6:6 NKJV

We all have lists: things to buy, things to do, even a list for God. Lord, I want. . .God, I need. . .and if You could please. . .

He meets your needs because He loves you and wants to give you His best. Have you ever wondered what God wants? He wants you—your attention, affection, praise, and worship. He wants to be included in your life.

Prayer isn't just a time to give God our list, but a time to enjoy each other's company, just as you would if you were to take time with a close personal friend—and that's really who He is. In the busyness of life, we must be careful that our "quiet time" never becomes insignificant because it's limited to the needs we feel we must tell God about. We must remember our most precious desire—just spending time with Him.

Find a moment today, shut out the rest of the world, and discover truly how little anything else matters but God. No one knows the path He's chosen for you quite like He does. Let Him point you to the truth and bring about the results He destined for you before the beginning of time.

Father, forgive me for not taking time to spend with You.
Help me to listen and include You in my life at all times. Amen.

Rejoice

This is the day the Lord has made; let us rejoice and be glad in it.
PSALM 118:24 NIV

Her heart had been shattered. Tears streamed down her cheeks. She thought he was the man of her dreams. But earlier that evening he dropped a bombshell. Marriage would not be in their future. She felt as though she had just wasted two years of her life. Sitting in a chair late into the night, she stared out the bedroom window at the pitch-black sky. How could she have let her emotions get so out of hand? She focused on the one thing she knew for certain. The sun would rise in the east. And as it did, the reminder of God's faithfulness allowed her to rejoice.

Have you ever experienced a time when you felt overwhelmed with sorrow? Life can be confusing and painful, and rejoicing with gladness is not always possible. Take heart. The Lord cares. He empathizes with our pain. With the birth of each new day, He reminds us that His mercies are new every morning. He provides sufficient grace and turns our weakness to strength as we trust Him.

Experiencing trials enables us to grow deeper in our relationship with the Lord. We realize that He is enough. Others may leave us, but He never will. He alone becomes the cause of our rejoicing and gladness. Let's worship our Creator, even in our darkest days.

*Dear Lord, help me rejoice in You
regardless of my circumstances. Amen.*

He Is Faithful

If we are unfaithful, he remains faithful, for he cannot deny who he is.
2 TIMOTHY 2:13 NLT

Have you ever said you'll do something, knowing full well you probably wouldn't get it done? We humans have a knack for letting each other down; deals fall through, plans crumble, agreements are breached.

Sometimes we treat our relationship with God the same as we do with other people. We promise Him we'll start spending more time with Him in prayer and Bible study. *This time, it will be different—I'll stick with it,* we think. Soon the daily distractions of life get in the way, and we're back in our same routine, minus prayer and Bible study.

Even when we fail to live up to our expectations, our heavenly Father doesn't pick up His judge's gavel and condemn us for unfaithfulness. Instead, He remains a faithful supporter, encouraging us to keep trying to hold up our end of the bargain. Take comfort in His faithfulness, and let that encourage you toward a deeper relationship with Him.

Father, thank You for Your unending faithfulness. Every day I fall short of Your standards, but You're always there, encouraging me and lifting me up. Please help me to be more faithful to You— in the big things and in the little things. Amen.

Seek First

> *"But seek first his kingdom and his righteousness,*
> *and all these things will be given to you as well."*
> MATTHEW 6:33 NIV

What do you seek? Wealth, harmonious relationships, an impressive home, a devoted husband, a fulfilling career? The list can go on and on. We spend much time, energy, and resources chasing after what we think our hearts desire. Yet when we get what we want, are we truly content? Or do we simply pause until another tempting carrot is dangled before us?

Our Creator knows where we will find true contentment. Seeking the things of this world will never be enough. Our hearts yearn for more. Our souls search for everlasting love and inner joy. God meets our need in the person of Jesus Christ. If we attempt to fill the emptiness of our soul with anything or anyone else, it's like chasing after the wind. We will come up empty-handed and disillusioned.

Seeking His kingdom begins by entering into a relationship with our heavenly Father through the person of Jesus Christ. Accept Jesus as your Savior. Then honor Him as Lord in your daily life. Focus on God's priorities. Value people above possessions, eternal riches over earthly ones. When we seek first His kingdom and righteousness, we have obtained the most treasured possession. He will take care of the rest.

Dear Lord, may I have the desire to
seek You above everything else. Amen.

Who's in Your Path?

*Make a careful exploration of who you are and the work you
have been given, and then sink yourself into that. . . . Each of you must
take responsibility for doing the creative best you can with your own life.*
GALATIANS 6:4–5 MSG

Emily was overwhelmed. She had recently taken an interest in social issues. Hunger, poverty, war. The more she became aware of them, the more depressed she became. She desperately wanted to help everyone in need, but nothing she did seemed to make a dent in the enormous problems.

Many people today look at the seemingly dismal conditions of the world and become paralyzed by the enormity of it all. However, it's not our responsibility to solve the whole world's problems. Instead of becoming overwhelmed to the point of paralysis, we are far more productive when we focus on the people God brings across our paths each day.

Look around you. What are the needs of the people in your life? Perhaps it's a neighborhood food pantry or homeless shelter. Maybe a person on the subway or bus you ride could use a listening ear. You can't solve the world's problems on your own, but you can make an enormous difference in the life of just one person. Why not start today?

*Father, help me to reach out and make a
difference in at least one person's life today. Amen.*

....

....

....

....

....

....

....

....

Changed from Inside Out

*We also thank God continually because, when you received the word
of God, which you heard from us, you accepted it not as the word of men,
but as it actually is, the word of God, which is at work in you who believe.*

1 THESSALONIANS 2:13 NIV

Caroline prayed for patience and wisdom as she nursed her mom back to health after surgery. The balance of caring for her mom, working a demanding job, homework with the kids, and sporadic sleep was taking its toll. Irritability, anxiety, and rash responses were becoming the norm.

A friend handed Caroline a CD to listen to on the way from work one day. Smooth jazz tunes eased her troubled mood, but it was spoken scripture accompanying the music that gave her a quiet assurance deep within. Morning and evening commutes became a refreshing time. Impatience and worry lessened; more peace and gentleness resulted.

God's Word is active and living within every believer. God is at work in us through scripture. Whether it's through reading, hearing, or singing the Word, we must let it sink into our souls.

*God, Your Spirit is alive within me as a believer.
Continue to work Your righteousness in me as
I immerse myself in Your Word. Amen.*

We Need Friends

Let the peace of Christ keep you in tune with each other, in step
with each other. None of this going off and doing your own thing.
COLOSSIANS 3:15 MSG

Jo had friends galore in high school and college. But when she took a job in a new town, her free time was limited, and she found it hard to meet other Christians. At times, her loneliness threatened to overwhelm her.

God created us to live in community, not just with a spouse or family members, but with people who aren't related to us by birth or marriage. Jesus, the only perfect person who ever lived, chose twelve disciples and brought three of those disciples close to His heart. He also spent lots of time with the family of Mary, Martha, and Lazarus. And if the Son of God needed friends, how much more do we!

And though friendships can be difficult to maintain with our fast-paced lifestyles, we need to make time for relationships. The right kind of friend comforts, encourages, challenges, listens to us, and laughs with us. They are true gifts from God. When we're blessed with friends, we should give thanks—and strive to be a good friend. When we're lonely for companionship, we should pray expectantly, knowing that God created friendship and will meet our need for it.

Father God, I praise You for being a friend to me.
Make me a good friend, and provide me with godly relationships.

Where Is Your Heart?

For where your treasure is, there will your heart be also.
MATTHEW 6:21 KJV

When others look at you, what kind of woman do you want them to see? There may be many things you would wish to include in the list of adjectives that describe you. Maybe you aren't yet who you want to be, but you know you are a work in progress. Whatever the case, who you are is a very good indication of where your heart is.

For example, your attitude about your career is something people notice. Are you driven to succeed in order to obtain high position or salary? There's nothing wrong with desiring to succeed as long as you give God the glory and maintain a godly testimony. In fact, God could use a lot more God-fearing people running businesses and managing His finances.

If, however, you are willing to compromise God's standards in order to obtain position or wealth, your heart is not where it belongs. It is on corruptible things that will not last, but that might destroy you if your attitude goes too far in the wrong direction.

Think about where your heart is in every decision you make. Ensure it is with those incorruptible things that matter. And as you direct your heart toward God, you will become the kind of woman He wants you to be.

*O Lord, give me wisdom to direct my heart
to lasting treasure that will honor You.*

Humble Servant

*Jesus, knowing that the Father had given all things into His hands,
and that He had come from God and was going to God, rose from supper
and laid aside His garments, took a towel and girded Himself. After that,
He poured water into a basin and began to wash the disciples' feet,
and to wipe them with the towel with which He was girded.*

JOHN 13:3–5 NKJV

Imagine the twelve disciples in the upper room. Among them is the Son of God, with all authority given to Him by the Father. He has come to earth as a man and soon will return to heaven to sit at the Father's right hand. He puts a towel around His waist, pours water in a bowl, and kneels down before His disciples. He begins to wash feet—one of the lowliest jobs of that day. The Lord of the universe, the Living Word who speaks things into being and commands all things, makes a deliberate choice to get down on His knees and serve others. He handles their dusty feet, getting dirty Himself in order to make them clean. In word and deed, He teaches the disciples to follow His example. His humility is rooted in the quiet confidence of His relationship with His Father.

Are we willing to make a deliberate step to humble ourselves to serve others? Would we do the lowliest job? Will we enter into the messiness of each other's lives?

*Lord, help me to follow Your example.
Make me a humble servant.*

Heavenly Appreciation

God is not unjust; he will not forget your work and the love you have shown him as you have helped his people and continue to help them.

HEBREWS 6:10 NIV

Sometimes it seems our hard work is ignored. We sell a record number of lattes at the coffee shop only to be told that we need to sell more pastries, or we spend days working on a presentation that the boss barely acknowledges. Our hard work seems unimportant, and we feel unappreciated.

Unfortunately, our work in the church can often feel the same way. We dutifully assume the role of greeter every Sunday, or we consistently fill communion cups each week. We spend each Sunday afternoon visiting the sick, or we serve weekly Wednesday night meals. Yet our work seems to go overlooked, and we wonder what the point is.

When our work for Christ seems to go unnoticed by our church family, we can be assured that God sees and appreciates it. We may not receive the "church member of the month" award, but our love for our brothers and sisters in Christ and our work on their behalf is not overlooked by God. The author of Hebrews assures us that God is not unjust—our reward is in heaven.

Dear Lord, You are a God of love and justice. Even when I do not receive the notice of those around me, help me to serve You out of my love for You. Amen.

Private Prayer

*After sending them home, he went up into the hills by
himself to pray. Night fell while he was there alone.*
MATTHEW 14:23 NLT

Jesus gave us a perfect example of prayer to follow. Not only can we learn how to pray from the Lord's Prayer, but we can also discover where to pray.

Although there is no magical place where we need to be to talk with Him, we should find a quiet, secluded location. He wants us to focus our thoughts on Him only—not the television program coming on in fifteen minutes, the ringing telephone, or the household chores that need to be done—just God, and God alone.

Look again at the verse above. Jesus went up into the hills. You certainly don't need to go that far—although it can be an option—but your place of prayer should be free of distractions. Night fell while Jesus was there, indicating that it wasn't a hurried time of prayer. He took the time to commune with His Father, giving Him priority.

We can pray at any time, in any place, but it will benefit you and honor God when you follow Jesus' example and find a special place to talk with Him.

*Lord, thank You that You listen to me at any time
I come to You. Help me to find someplace that can be for
just You and me, where I can pour my heart out to You. Amen.*

Soul Cravings

As the deer pants for streams of water, so my soul pants for you,
O God. My soul thirsts for God, for the living God.
PSALM 42:1–2 NIV

Jen didn't understand how Stacy could be so blind. One relationship would end, and Stacy was on to the next. Couldn't she see that guys wouldn't fill her deeper needs?

Jen wondered if she was doing the same thing. Wasn't she angry because she felt unappreciated by her husband? Hadn't his recent overtime kept him from devoting time and attention that she wanted? Her heart ached. Was this just longing for time with her hubby, or was it a heart's cry for something else?

Our hearts have some indefinable yearnings. We look for fulfillment from people, titles, achievement, chocolate. We may attempt to squelch the longings with distractions of busyness, fashion, an extra drink, motherhood, or even church work. But the longing is a thirst for intimate connection with our God. Our souls pant for Him! He alone quenches our needs.

The Spirit knows our subtle moods, our hearts' aches, and our soul-cravings. We must turn to Him in transparent prayer, mulling the Word over in our minds, allowing it to penetrate the hidden recesses of our souls.

God, You are the headwaters of life for me. Reveal the substitutes I look to for fulfillment. Help me to drink deeply from Your Word and Your abiding Spirit that I might be complete in You. Amen.

Too Good to Be True

*The woman was convinced. She saw that the tree was beautiful and
its fruit looked delicious, and she wanted the wisdom it would give her.*
GENESIS 3:6 NLT

It sounded like King David's son Absalom was finally going to bury the hatchet.

Absalom carried a grudge against his half-brother, Amnon, for two years. When Absalom threw a party, he made a point to invite Amnon to the festivities. King David was a little suspicious about the whole situation, but he allowed Amnon to attend.

The whole thing turned out to be a ruse. Absalom did what he had intended for years. He got his revenge and killed his brother (2 Samuel 13).

As David suspected and most of us know, if something sounds too good to be true, it probably is. Eve faced this dilemma in the Garden of Eden. When Satan whispered that she could be more like God by partaking of the forbidden fruit, the thought may have crossed her mind that it was too good to be true. But instead of walking away, she decided to take Satan up on the offer.

When our conscience or our common sense tells us something doesn't sound right, we should heed the warning. It may keep us from throwing away hard-earned money. It may keep us from a relationship that's long on excitement but short on commitment. It may keep us from long-lasting, painful consequences of poor choices.

*Lord, give me wisdom in the simple
and complex decisions I make. Amen.*

....

....

....

....

....

....

....

....

Spirit and Truth

"But the time is coming—indeed it's here now—when true worshipers will worship the Father in spirit and in truth."
JOHN 4:23 NLT

Are you a true worshipper?

God's Word tells us that if we are true worshippers, we will worship in spirit and in truth. John 4:24 continues and tells us that "God is Spirit, so those who worship him must worship in spirit and in truth."

God is everywhere all the time, and He doesn't just want to be worshipped at church. Yes, church is a place to worship, but it is not the only place we can worship. We should be living a life of worship.

You can worship God on your way to work, during class, as you clean your house, and pay your bills. Worship is about living your life in a way that is pleasing to the Lord and seeking Him first in all things. Paying your bills? Ask God how He wants you to spend your money. That is pleasing to Him, and that is worship. In the middle of class? Be respectful of your professors, and use the brain God gave you to complete your studies.

If you are living your everyday life to please God, that is worship!

Father, help me to live my life in ways that please You.
Let my focus be on worshipping You in everything I do. Amen.

A Living Hope

*[Jesus] died for us, a death that triggered life. Whether we're awake
with the living or asleep with the dead, we're alive with him!
So speak encouraging words to one another. Build up hope so
you'll all be together in this, no one left out, no one left behind.*

1 THESSALONIANS 5:10–11 MSG

What do we have to lose? Christians are either on earth or dancing on streets of gold in heaven with God. Do you see the power of that? Hearts that yearn for heavenly eternity radiate contagious hope and encouragement for others.

As a believer in Christ, you are in a position to give that hope and be that boost people need. Your well-placed words can build up when you share your life with needy hearts. Their world may be darkened by hopelessness, discouragement, or disillusionment. Your words of grace convey the reality of a life beyond what we see here on earth.

Your life has purpose, meaning, and a glorious future! Smile, look the lost squarely in the eye, and speak the truth of His love to them. As you go about daily life, look for opportunities to build up hope in others. Bring them along on this joyful journey.

*Father, will You give me specific words of encouragement
for those I am with today? May the hope within me
be contagious, infecting them with Your life. Amen.*

Prayer Reveals Our Dependence

Then Jesus went with his disciples to a place called Gethsemane,
and he said to them, "Sit here while I go over there and pray."
MATTHEW 26:36 NIV

Independent. Self-reliant. In control. These attributes are considered important in today's culture. Revealing weakness and depending on others is unacceptable. Sadly, this worldly mind-set often seep into spiritual matters. Christians don't want to be perceived as needy or weak. Yet, what did Jesus model? Did He desire spiritual independence?

Jesus was humble. He conceded that He needed help. He admitted His human weakness. He acknowledged His struggle in the Garden of Gethsemane. Confiding in His disciples, He revealed His anguish and pain. Then He turned to His heavenly Father. Jesus knew He needed God's help to endure the cross. Prayer revealed Jesus' utter dependence on God.

How much do you really need God? Your prayer life reveals your answer. If an independent attitude has crept into it, prayer may seem a ritualistic exercise. But if you realize your weakness and acknowledge your need, then prayer will become vital to your existence. It will become your sustenance and nourishment—your lifeline. Prayer reveals your dependence upon God. How much do you need Him?

Dear Lord, I truly need You. May my prayer
life demonstrate my dependence upon You. Amen.

Wisdom or Beauty

As a jewel of gold in a swine's snout,
so is a fair woman which is without discretion.
PROVERBS 11:22 KJV

Karis was used to having her way. She was beautiful and well-dressed and turned heads wherever she went. She knew her boss found her attractive, so she naturally assumed that the newly opened supervisor position would be hers.

As the time approached for the new supervisor to be named, she flirted, dressed provocatively, and did all she could to draw attention to herself. She began to wonder why she was never called to the office to be informed of her promotion.

Finally she learned that another woman, Teri, had been named to the coveted position. Karis pouted for a while and refused to speak to Teri. Her coworkers could easily read her emotions, and finally, one tactfully approached her.

"Look, Karis," Rob said. "We all know you wanted that spot that Teri got, but you were relying on your looks, since they've always gotten you your way. You are gorgeous, but it takes common sense, punctuality, and a proper work ethic to make a good supervisor. You have to admit those haven't been your strong points."

Karis was angry at first. Still, she thought about what Rob said. It was too late this time, but maybe another opportunity would come.

Lord, I know many women desire beauty,
but help me to make wisdom more of a priority.

....
....
....
....
....
....
....
....

Saying Good Things

Oh, magnify the Lord with me, and let us exalt His name together.
PSALM 34:3 NKJV

It's so wonderful when people say nice things about you. It puts a smile on your face when someone notices you or the things you do. We all enjoy a word of encouragement and a little praise now and then. It takes a little thought to say something good about someone else, but it's worth it and much appreciated when it's heartfelt.

Now imagine how it must make God feel when you say good things about Him. He has given so much to us. He created a world for us and then gave His only Son to repair the breach between us and Him so we could have a relationship with Him.

There are so many ways to praise Him. Tell Him how much He means to you and how thankful you are for all He's done for you. Brag on Him to others in your life—sharing His goodness and love with them and expressing how faithful He's been to you. God's goodness makes it easy to find good things to say about Him. Make time to praise Him today!

Dear heavenly Father, I could never say enough good things about You, but I want to try. I am thankful for Your mercy and unfailing love. Your goodness is endless, and the way You express Your love to me is without measure. Thank You, Lord. You're awesome. Amen.

Eternal Treasure

"Wherever your treasure is, there the desires of your heart will also be."
MATTHEW 6:21 NLT

For Melissa's parents, love meant providing for their children's physical needs. They had a comfortable home, drove late-model cars, and never had to worry about whether their children could have a college education.

Unfortunately, this also meant both parents had to work long hours. Throughout their childhoods, Melissa and her sister wanted nothing more than to take a walk in the evening or go on a picnic on the weekends as a family, having their parents' undivided attention. Sadly, Melissa's father died suddenly when he was in his early 50s, and Melissa never did receive the attention from him that she craved.

Fast cars, luxurious homes, travel, high-paying jobs, working hard to get ahead. . .these are the values that drive many people today. Most of us know logically that these things aren't the key to happiness, but it's easy to get caught in worldly trappings of success.

It's not that owning comfortable homes or driving nice cars is wrong, but as Christians we are called to live our lives differently. Jesus challenges us to place our value in things that have eternal significance and to make choices that have an impact on our spiritual lives—not just our physical lives. What investments are you making today that will have eternal significance?

Father, thank You for the promise that there is more to life than material success. Help me to invest my life in things that have eternal significance. Amen.

Standing Still

"The Lord will fight for you; you need only to be still."
EXODUS 14:14 NIV

The Israelites were panicking. They had just marched out of Egypt, leaving the tyrant king and slavery behind. Now they were stuck between the entire Egyptian army on one side and the massive Red Sea on the other side. Their leaders, Moses and Aaron, had seemingly led them to this dead end where death or captivity were the only options. They were scared, angry, and completely hopeless.

Moses knew exactly how the Israelites were feeling. But he remained faithful to God, even in the midst of his fear, and he commanded the Israelites to stop panicking and stand still. Then God held back the waters of the Red Sea, and the Israelites were able to walk across on dry ground! When the Egyptians tried to follow them, the waters rushed in and drowned them all.

Sometimes when we stress and panic, we rack our brains trying to figure out solutions to our problems. We find ourselves confronted with horrible options, and instead of standing still and praying to God, we become even more panicked. Moses' words still apply to us today. When we face our fears we should be still, trusting in God and relying on Him to bring us through the struggle.

Dear Lord, please teach me to be still and to trust in You.
Thank You for Your constant faithfulness. Amen.

....
....
....
....
....
....
....
....

By Obedience Blessed

Behold, for thus shall the man be blessed who fears the Lord.
PSALM 128:4 NASB

Do you ever wonder if serving God is worth it? After all, acclaim tends to follow those who adopt the world's beliefs. Movie stars who bare their bodies in front of cameras make millions of dollars per film. Politicians who trade favors for votes inherit power and prestige. And people and companies who cheat on their taxes rack up even more wealth. Sometimes it seems nonbelievers prosper and those who serve the Lord suffer.

But God doesn't sit idly by while people flaunt their sinfulness and mock His righteousness. He sees everything—even those acts that the wicked prefer to keep secret.

And as the Psalms state over and over again, God delights in His faithful children. He sees their suffering, notices their obedience, and revels in their steadfastness. He will never leave the righteous.

Eventually, because He is a God of justice, love, and compassion, He will honor and reward His children. Either on earth or in heaven, the scales will be balanced. He will turn every bit of evil they've experienced into good. And because He made us for Himself, His presence will be His sons and daughters' greatest gift.

God, I praise You for being a God of justice and mercy.
Help me to keep my eyes on You and not on the world.

What a Rush!

*Likewise, I say unto you, there is joy in the presence
of the angels of God over one sinner that repenteth.*
LUKE 15:10 KJV

There's no feeling quite like an adrenaline rush. Experiences like riding a roller coaster, bungee jumping, graduation, or getting a new job can result in the heart-pounding excitement adrenaline brings. It's intoxicating! And it always, always makes you want more.

Luke 15 tells us the angels experience that sort of rush when even one sinner repents and turns to God. Do we all feel that way? Are we driven to feel that same rush by witnessing to unbelievers and seeing sinners repent as they turn to God as their Savior? Challenge yourself to reach out and experience what the angels do when your lifestyle, words, and efforts cause an unbeliever to turn to God. There is no adrenaline rush that even comes close to that one!

Father, please give me boldness to reach out to others and lead them to You. Give me the words to say and make the hearer receptive to whatever You lead me to say or do. Amen.

....
....
....
....
....
....
....
....
....

Say No to Blabbermouths

Gossips can't keep secrets, so never confide in blabbermouths.
PROVERBS 20:19 MSG

If you're like most people, every day you're surrounded with the temptation to gossip. Whether it's at work, at church, in a circle of close friends, or simply out in the community, the rumor mill is always turning.

The wisdom in Proverbs spells plainly its warning: A gossip can't be trusted to keep her mouth shut, so don't share secrets with her!

As Christians, we need to take this attitude a step further and stand up against gossip. Don't be afraid to voice your displeasure—in love, of course—when your friends talk about others. Introduce encouragement and uplifting words into your conversations, and resist the temptation to fall into old habits.

Words are powerful. If you've ever been the victim of having your secrets blabbed behind your back, you know the pain they cause. Commit yourself to cutting gossip from your life, and your relationships will be strengthened.

Father, please forgive me for talking about others behind
their backs. I don't want to be known as a blabbermouth.
Help my words to always be encouraging to others. Amen.

Resolute

"Why all this weeping? You are breaking my heart! I am ready not only to be jailed at Jerusalem but even to die for the sake of the Lord Jesus."
ACTS 21:13 NLT

Heather and Leon are a young couple who both felt called to be missionaries. Now in their midtwenties, they're completing their ministry training as youth leaders in a church. They recently received word of their assigned mission field: the Middle East.

Their assigned country is quickly becoming a hotbed of conflict. But the few Christians who are there are calling for help to start a church. Heather and Leon eagerly anticipate going.

Others are not so excited, especially the people at Heather and Leon's church.

"How can our mission board even think of sending you there?"

"You have a mission field here. With us."

"Our kids need good, young role models and leaders like you."

Paul's experience with his closest friends was similar to Heather and Leon's. He had been warned of bad things ahead, but he was also "compelled by the Spirit" to go (Acts 20:22 NIV).

When God calls us to a task or ministry, we have to shut out the well-meaning entreaties of others. That's neither easy nor painless. But the time comes when, like Heather and Leon and the Lord Jesus Christ, we must "resolutely set out" in obedience to our Father (Luke 9:51 NIV).

Father, help me to be obedient to the task to which You've called me. Amen.

....

....

....

....

....

....

....

Changing Our Perspective

Turn my eyes away from worthless things; preserve my life according to your word.
Psalm 119:37 niv

Read a few greeting cards targeting women, and you will soon get the message: Most things can be fixed with chocolate or shopping. Pick up a magazine and learn what fashion purchases will transform your size and shape or how a spa weekend can change your outlook on life. The media and the mall are full of answers before we even ask ourselves the questions. Underneath the slick pages are messages that we deserve whatever we want and that the accumulation of possessions will fulfill us.

The book of Psalms offers hundreds of verses that can easily become sentence prayers. "Turn my eyes from worthless things" whispered before heading out to shop, turning on the television, or picking up a magazine can turn those experiences into opportunities to see God's hand at work in our lives. He can change our perspective. He will show us what has value for us. He can even change our appetites, causing us to desire the very things He wants for us. When we pray this prayer, we are asking God to show us what He wants for us. He knows us and loves us more than we know and love ourselves. We can trust His love and goodness to provide for our needs.

Father, imprint this scripture in my mind today.
In moments of need, help me remember to pray
this prayer and to relinquish my desires to You.

Little Things Become Big Things

"His master replied, 'Well done, good and faithful servant!
You have been faithful with a few things; I will put you in charge of many things.'"
MATTHEW 25:23 NIV

Megan answered a newspaper ad looking for freelance writers, confident that it was perfect for her. Unfortunately, the editor chose to not hire her because of her lack of experience.

Megan faced a dilemma common to many people her age. "We'd love to hire you, but we need someone with experience." But how is a person supposed to get experience if no one ever hires her?

Jesus addresses this issue from a spiritual perspective with the parable of the talents in Matthew 25. Essentially He says that as we demonstrate trustworthiness with little things, God will gradually increase our responsibilities, entrusting us with bigger and more important tasks.

If you lack life experience, there are many things you can do to show your trustworthiness. Take on small jobs in your field of interest—even if they are low-paying or provide little recognition. Look for places to volunteer—even after you're earning a regular paycheck. Pray for opportunities to showcase your talents. It may not feel like it at the time, but those little efforts will be rewarded and will add up to a lifetime of worthwhile experience.

Father, help me to be willing to use my gifts and
abilities in small ways. Thank You for rewarding
even the smallest of my efforts. Amen.

Did You Hear. . . ?

*Though some tongues just love the taste of gossip,
those who follow Jesus have better uses for language than that.*
EPHESIANS 5:3 MSG

Our tongues can sing the highest praises of someone or destroy them—all in the matter of a few seconds. And once those negative words slip past our lips, there is no way to erase them, no matter how much we wish we could.

Have you ever been a victim of gossip? It hurts when we hear what someone has said about us! The words can tear us up inside. A close friendship can easily be ruined as a result of breaking a trust.

One more question to consider: Have you ever spread gossip? You may have thought it harmless, perhaps even sharing it only as a "prayer request." However, the words you spoke may have injured someone deeply. Before speaking, take a moment to consider whether what you are about to say would be considered gossip or not. Those few seconds could spare a lifetime of grief!

If we have given our life to Jesus, our whole body is His—including the tongue. Commit it to Him, and ask Him to help you to control the words that come from your mouth. Remember, "Those who follow Jesus have better uses for language than [gossip]."

*Dear heavenly Father, please guard my tongue so I won't
be guilty of spreading gossip. Help me to seek forgiveness if
I have, and to be forgiving when gossip is spread about me. Amen.*

Genuine Article

"He who speaks on his own does so to gain honor for himself,
but he who works for the honor of the one who sent him
is a man of truth; there is nothing false about him."
JOHN 7:18 NIV

Amy is solid and true. She isn't swayed by the opinion of others or what's in style. She doesn't have to always be the center of attention. Knowing the job is done for God's glory is enough. Is she stiff or boring? On the contrary—she's refreshing! There is nothing fake about her. She has the freedom to be who God created her to be. She is liked and respected for her strength of character, which is actually Christ shining through her.

Recognition, achievement, money, fame—that's what matters to many people. While there is nothing wrong with these, how they're achieved does matter. Self-promoters push their way through. Christ-promoters are secure in not having to receive accolades. This brings freedom and an authenticity that, in the long run, outshines the self-absorbed heart. By focusing on Christ and the glory He deserves, we allow God to touch others as well as produce in us an enriched life as a person of truth.

God, sometimes I find I am promoting myself rather
than You. Help me to be all I am created to be
because You are foremost in my heart. Amen.

A Roaring Fire

For the word of God is living and active. Sharper than any
double-edged sword, it penetrates even to dividing soul and spirit,
joints and marrow; it judges the thoughts and attitudes of the heart.
HEBREWS 4:12 NIV

The world is filled with books on every topic and in many languages. You can find pages at your fingertips on a computer keyboard and can explore volumes of information that provide you with entertainment and knowledge, but only the Bible—the Word of God— can truly speak to you.

No matter what you are facing, there is always something in the Bible to help you find your way. There is simply no other book like it. Other books can encourage, inspire, and motivate—but the Bible gives life. The Word of God can infuse you with strength, sustain you in battle, and uphold you during the darkest days you'll ever face.

Maybe for you the fire of God's Word starts out as a small glowing ember. You could read for days, and then suddenly you stumble upon that scripture—those amazing words—written so many years ago that seem written specifically to you. You know it the moment the Word comes alive as it ignites your heart. It comforts you, provides an answer to the questions you've been asking, and consumes you with a hunger for the truth.

Lord, I want to read Your Word and hear Your voice as it speaks
to me. Ignite me with a passion for the Bible. Amen.

....
....
....
....
....
....
....
....

The Blues

Why are you downcast, O my soul? Why so disturbed within me?
Put your hope in God, for I will yet praise him, my Savior and my God.
PSALM 42:11 NIV

Tabitha had been in a funk for days. From the moment she woke up in the morning until she closed her eyes at night, she felt the burdens of life. Newspaper headlines screamed doom and gloom; gas and food prices continued to rise; and the stress of job, family, and church ministries were wearing her thin. Every burden in her life seemed unending, with no relief in sight.

Has your soul ever felt weighed down like this? Everyone experiences times when frustrations seem to outweigh joy, but as Christians, we have an unending source of encouragement in God.

That's great, you may think, *but how am I supposed to tap into that joy?* First, pray. Ask God to unburden your spirit. Share your stress, frustrations, and worries with Him. Don't hold back; He can take it. Make a list of the blessings in your life and thank the Provider of those blessings. Choose to not focus on yourself; instead, praise Him for being Him.

Soon you'll feel true, holy refreshment—the freedom God wants you to live out every day.

Rejuvenate my spirit, Lord! You alone can take away the burden
I feel. You are my hope and my redeemer forever. Amen.

Releasing Your Worries

"Look at the birds of the air; they do not sow or reap or store away in barns, and yet your heavenly Father feeds them. Are you not much more valuable than they? Who of you by worrying can add a single hour to his life?"
MATTHEW 6:26–27 NIV

God loves you so much. You are His precious daughter, created in His image. He longs for you to find rest in Him. Over and over in His Word He reminds you that you need not worry. He calls you to cast your cares upon Him because He cares for you. He offers a special peace that the world cannot give. He vows that He has plans to prosper and not to harm you. He says you are His sheep and He is the Good Shepherd. He does not want you to worry.

Worry is a human thing. It is not of God. As Matthew 6:27 points out, worry cannot add a single hour to one's life. It is, in other words, pointless and a waste of time.

Rest right now. Still your mind and heart before God. Consciously release to Him all the worries that you cling to so tightly. Ask your Father to take care of you as He does the birds of the air and the flowers of the fields. He made you. He knows just what you need.

When your mind begins to race, remember that God has you in the palm of His hand. Worry not. God is good.

Father, take the worries that I am burdened by today. Give me rest.

The Truth about the Holy Spirit

And I will ask the Father, and he will give you another
Counselor to be with you forever—the Spirit of truth....
You know him, for he lives with you and will be in you.
JOHN 14:16–17 NIV

To some Christians, the Holy Spirit is a mystery. To others, He is a frightening part of the Trinity. And for even mature believers, the Holy Spirit is often misunderstood.

Jesus called the Holy Spirit a comforter, counselor, and friend. In Acts, the Spirit fell on the early church with power. He made the new Christians bold, authoritative, and fearless. And the Spirit longs to do the same for us.

Are you lonely? Let Him be a friend to you. Are you grieving? The Holy Spirit will comfort you. He can guide you to the perfect scriptures for your grief, and He will pray to the Father for you when you don't have the words. Do you want to make a difference for Christ? Pray for the Spirit to give you opportunities to share your faith with seekers.

Jesus longs for you to understand the One who came to be with the church after He ascended to heaven. And instead of frightening you, the Holy Spirit wants to be as second nature to you as your next breath.

Will you let Him?

Father, thank You for providing the Holy Spirit.
Make me aware of Him and help me to understand Him.

Worthwhile Suffering

For I reckon that the sufferings of this present time are not
worthy to be compared with the glory which shall be revealed in us.
ROMANS 8:18 KJV

At times the things you endure for the cause of Christ will bring a great deal of suffering. Family, friends, and coworkers will not understand the decisions you make or the convictions you hold dear. This is especially true if the situation directly involves them. They might mock or reject you. They might try to inflict feelings of guilt. There are many ways they'll react, and few are pleasant.

Determine today to stand strong in your convictions. God's ways are the right ways even when you don't understand them. You might suffer for a while, but think of the rewards that await.

It might be challenging to determine God's will in some circumstances. It's true that universal things that God expects from all believers are revealed in His Word. However, issues specific to your own life are sometimes harder to determine. You might think you know what He wants, but someone you love—at times even other believers—have other ideas. These differing convictions can be confusing and discouraging. That is why it is so important to stay close to God. He will guide and bless you in His time.

Lord, sometimes I suffer as I try to do Your will. It hurts,
but I know You make all things beautiful in Your time.

Hold Tight to Him

Reverently respect God, your God, serve him,
hold tight to him. . . .He's your praise! He's your God!
DEUTERONOMY 10:20 MSG

Deuteronomy 10:20 holds three commands and an eternal truth we can apply to our everyday lives. The first tells us to live with respect for our God. Several times God's Word states that reverent fear or respect for the Lord is the beginning of wisdom and knowledge. The second command tells us to serve Him. That is our purpose here on earth: to serve and worship the Lord. The third tells us to hold tight to Him. This command makes the verse so much more personal. God is our loving Father who wants to comfort us and hold us throughout life—the good and the bad.

The verse ends with a reminder that God is our praise. He is a good and loving God worthy of our affection. James 4:8 tells us that if we draw near to God, He will draw near to us. So hold tight to the Lord and experience His presence in your life.

Dear Father, help me to live with respect for You in all areas of my life. I want to serve You with all my heart. Thank You for wanting to draw near to me as I hold tight to You. Amen.

Break the Mold

Ephraim's daughter was Sheerah. She built the towns of
Lower Beth-Horon, Upper Beth-Horon, and Uzzen-Sheerah.
1 CHRONICLES 7:24 CEV

She began her life as the only child of parents who immigrated to the United States from Jamaica. Like her mother, she became a pianist, with a dream to become a concert pianist.

In college, however, she discovered a new interest: political science. She went on to become one of the world's most powerful women of color. She earned her nickname, the "Warrior Princess," while serving in the administration of President George W. Bush. In 2005 Dr. Condoleezza Rice began her tenure as the first black woman to hold the position of U.S. Secretary of State.

In the Bible we're told little about Sheerah except that misfortune marked her family. Yet she took a position of political leadership and built three cities. She established settlements for her decimated family, clearly showing herself to be a woman of purpose and action. A woman, like Condoleezza Rice, who broke the mold.

You may be a woman like Sheerah or Condoleezza. Your aspirations exceed those of your peers. You suspect God has gifted you uniquely, and you want to honor Him in your life accordingly. If you're this kind of woman, go for it! Try something new and bold. If the Lord is in it, be confident in His leading.

Lord, whatever You've called me to, embolden
me to do it with tenacity and wisdom. Amen.

God as He Really Is

The Lord is compassionate and gracious, slow to anger, abounding in love. . . .
He does not treat us as our sins deserve or repay us according to our iniquities.
PSALM 103:8, 10 NIV

In Matthew 25, Jesus tells the story of three servants who are given different sums of money by their master. The servants' attitudes toward the master influence how they use the money. The first two knew their master trusted them, so they invested the money wisely. The last one feared the master and failed to understand his true character. As a result, he made a bad decision and lost the money he was given.

Our attitude toward God can influence the way we handle what He has given us. Some people perceive God as a harsh and angry judge, impatiently tapping His foot, saying, "When will you ever get it right?"

People who see God this way can become paralyzed by an unhealthy fear of Him. However, the Bible paints a very different picture of God. Psalm 103 says He is gracious and compassionate, that He does not treat us as our sins deserve. What difference can it make in your life to know that you serve a loving God who is longing to be gracious to you?

Lord, thank You for Your compassion,
Your grace, and Your mercy.

Where's Our Focus?

*Since, then, you have been raised with Christ, set your hearts
on things above, where Christ is seated at the right hand of God.
Set your minds on things above, not on earthly things.*

COLOSSIANS 3:1–2 NIV

Worldly concerns can distract us from godly pursuits. Although we live in the world, God calls us to be separate from it. What a challenge we face! The world demands our attention: Jobs are necessary to survive financially; daily living activities require our time. Since we have to clothe ourselves, shouldn't it be in a fashionable way? At what point do these things become distractions that prevent us from experiencing God's best?

The answer depends on our hearts and minds. If earthly possessions and accomplishments are the goal, our focus becomes temporal. But even when we focus on the spiritual, temptation lurks around every corner. We must be purposeful, intentionally focusing on the Lord.

Begin the day by tuning in to God with prayer and quiet time. Then throughout the day allow the Holy Spirit to reveal spiritual truth. The Lord will impart spiritual insight into everyday activities. When our hearts and minds seek Him, our focus will be on things above because that is where He is. So, keep your eyes on Jesus!

*Dear Lord, help me walk in the world with a heavenly perspective.
May my focus be on You. Amen.*

Great Gain

But godliness with contentment is great gain.
1 TIMOTHY 6:6 KJV

As a society, we demand our rights. We want what's coming to us. In reality, what our sinful natures deserve is eternal separation from God. But our Father in His great mercy provided a glorious escape from that end, and that alone should give us great contentment. His salvation is the most precious thing we could ever hope to possess.

Television, newspaper, and billboard ads say different. They tell us spa getaways and lavish vacations bring more pleasure. Owning a certain kind of car guarantees success, and high fashion can bring a desired result. These clever ad campaigns insist we deserve these things, and we hear the claim of entitlement often enough that we sometimes begin to believe it.

Usually there isn't anything wrong with the products themselves. It is normal for us to want to look and feel our best, but the commercials engage in false advertising by urging us to make the items our focus and to believe we deserve them.

Material things bring only temporary joy. The effects of the massage wear off. The memories of vacations fade. The car transmission goes out. Clothes lose their appeal. Only striving for godliness and truly Christlike living can bring any lasting gain, and you can and should have these even if you don't have all the world offers.

Sometimes, Lord, I feel jealous when I don't have all the trinkets my neighbors have. Then I remember: I have You, and that's far more precious.

One Hundred Percent

They were utterly astonished, saying, "He has done all things well;
He makes even the deaf to hear and the mute to speak."
MARK 7:37 NASB

You've probably heard someone say, "Well, that's good enough," which usually means they did a "good enough" job. It wasn't their best—maybe it wasn't well-planned or thought out, but it got done.

What if you knew the mechanic who worked on your car did a "good enough" brake job. Would you feel safe? Would you believe his work was worthy of what you paid him? What if a surgeon told another doctor, "That's good enough, let's sew her up!"

Life is busy, and with so much to accomplish, you might be tempted to do something "good enough." It might get you through, but what does "good enough" really do for you? What does it say about you and how you value the person you halfheartedly serve? "Good enough" is an attitude that can eventually cost you.

Maybe what you do each day doesn't seem that important, but God created you to do your best. Become determined to do all you do with a passionate pursuit of pleasing God. It will bring you satisfaction in knowing that in all you do, you do it well.

God, You created me for greatness. Forgive me when I don't give 100 percent, and help me to always have the integrity and passion to do all things to the very best of my ability. Amen.

Look Up

*In the morning will I direct my
prayer unto thee, and will look up.*
PSALM 5:3 KJV

"If you look at the ground, you'll be on the ground," the riding trainer says. Over and over the young girl hears this as she canters her horse and learns to jump fences of graduated heights.

"Steer with your eyes" is another expression she hears regularly from her teacher. As the horse and rider leap over one hurdle, her eyes are on the next fence ahead, giving the horse motivation to keep moving and go over it. It is this fixed gaze that keeps the twosome moving together and springing over the fences.

The psalmist knows something about the importance of fixing one's gaze. "I will look up," he says. In the morning he directs his prayer to God and then watches and waits.

By going to God in prayer early in the day, we set our perspective for the entire day. Once we have given Him our problems and cares and listened for His voice to speak in our hearts, we have set our eyes for the day on Him as the place we are going for whatever we need.

*Father, cause me to seek You early each day, to remember
to fix my gaze on You, and to watch You work in my life.*

....

....

....

....

....

....

....

....

....

Rock Solid

"Therefore everyone who hears these words of mine and puts them into practice
is like a wise man who built his house on the rock. The rain came down,
the streams rose, and the winds blew and beat against that house;
yet it did not fall, because it had its foundation on the rock."
MATTHEW 7:24–25 NIV

It could have been different. Sadly, her life began spinning out of control. She had endured one storm after another: a failed marriage, a sudden job loss, and her mother's unexpected death. In desperation she turned to pills, alcohol, and even exercise—anything to numb the pain and help her cope. As the sand shifted beneath her, she felt herself slipping away She had never laid a solid foundation, and her life shattered into a million pieces.

Prepare for tomorrow's storms by laying a solid foundation today. Rain and wind are guaranteed to come. It is only a matter of time. We need to be ready. When our foundation is the Rock, Jesus Christ, we will find ourselves still standing when the storm has passed.

Rain will come. Winds will blow and beat hard against us. Yet, when our hope is in the Lord, we will not be destroyed. We will remain steadfast. Stand upon the Rock today so that your tomorrows will be secure.

Dear Lord, help me build my foundation today upon
You so I can remain steadfast in the storms of life. Amen.

....

....

....

....

....

....

....

....

....

A Pure Heart

"For out of the overflow of the heart the mouth speaks."
MATTHEW 12:34 NIV

Did your parents or teachers ever use the line, "Garbage in, garbage out," especially in reference to less-than-stellar TV shows? This little proverb did not originate with the invention of the television. Christ, too, warns us to beware of what we allow to take root in our hearts, because the heart will inevitably tell what it holds.

Our thoughts reflect what is stored within our hearts, and our words and actions reflect our thoughts. Before we can stand up for the oppressed, we must look outside ourselves and recognize their needs. Before we can speak words of encouragement, we must think well of others.

However, it is difficult to think well of others if we do not first think well of ourselves. What picture of yourself do you hold within your heart? If you think ill of yourself, your words and actions will reflect that negativity. If you're overly proud of yourself, others will know it. Practice instead a humble confidence, a confident humility.

Commit yourself to furnishing your heart with the affirming truths of Christ rather than the lies of our popular culture. Good things come only from goodness of heart. Strive for goodness.

*Lord, restore my heart to a true state of purity,
so that my heart may better reflect Yours.*

A Song of Praise

*You have turned my mourning into joyful dancing. You have taken
away my clothes of mourning and clothed me with joy, that I might sing
praises to you and not be silent. O Lord my God, I will give you thanks forever!*
PSALM 30:11–12 NLT

The psalmist can hardly contain himself in Psalm 30:11–12. God has taken away his sadness and made him not just joyful but ecstatic! He cannot merely offer thanks, he must dance. He cannot simply be glad, he must sing songs of praises. He certainly cannot remain silent—he must praise with passion!

We serve a mighty God—a God who transforms and makes us new. When we are brought low, God raises us up. When we are downcast, God fills us with joy. We serve a God of restoration. We were made to worship Him and be glad. When we mourn, we need God to bring us back into wholeness and worship. Most of all, our God is faithful. The faithfulness of God is so perfect that it compels us to sing with joy and praise before Him.

Worship God and give Him thanks. Raise your voice and praise Him! Indeed, we must sing praises, for God has made us whole; He has taken away our mourning and replaced it with His joy!

*Dear Lord, thank You for Your transforming joy. May
I always sing Your praises with joy and thanksgiving. Amen.*

Freedom Reigns

*For the Lord is the Spirit, and wherever
the Spirit of the Lord is, there is freedom.*
2 CORINTHIANS 3:17 NLT

We are free in so many ways because of what Christ did for us on the cross: free from death, free from sin, free from guilt, free from shame—and the list goes on. If you have ever felt trapped by someone or something in your life and then were set free, you know that amazing feeling of relief!

That is how living our lives through Christ should feel each day. Freedom reigns in Christ. We can breathe again.

Your past doesn't have to haunt you anymore. The Lord can use it to help change the life of someone else, so don't be ashamed any more. You are truly free. John 8:36 (NIV) says, "If the Son sets you free, you will be free indeed."

If you are still struggling with thoughts of guilt and shame, ask the Lord to free you from your past, and begin to live a life where freedom reigns!

*Dear Jesus, thank You for taking away my sin and making me free.
Help me to live like I believe that. Amen.*

A Woman of Integrity

Love and truth form a good leader;
sound leadership is founded on loving integrity.
PROVERBS 20:28 MSG

If you're a reality TV watcher, you've seen many examples of a lack of integrity in the contestants. Honesty falls by the wayside, as it's often every man for himself. The backstabbing, gossip, putting others down for the benefit of self, and many other actions exhibit a lack of morals.

God wants us to live a life of integrity. Many benefits come as a result of establishing and living by godly morals. One is mentioned in the book of Proverbs: sound leadership. A good leader has most likely achieved that position because she has integrity. It's a quality that is attractive to those around her, and she will be respected because of her example. She will be known for holding to a strong moral code, treating others in an honorable manner.

Ask God today to help you to live a life of integrity. Spend time in His Word and in prayer, so that you can develop the godly principles that others will see in you. In doing so, you will be a shining example for Him.

Dear Father, make me a person of integrity, so that I can bring honor to Your name, as well as bring unity to my workplace. Amen.

God's Work

The Lord will perfect that which concerns me; Your mercy,
O Lord, endures forever; do not forsake the works of Your hands.
PSALM 138:8 NKJV

From childhood we are taught to finish what we start. This is an important part of our maturity. Yet as adults we all have our list of unfinished projects. There are New Year's resolutions, diets, and home improvement projects that we never quite complete. We have dreams we haven't accomplished and goals we've yet to meet. More importantly, we have attitudes and habits we need to change and sins we continue to commit. It's easy to look at what we have not done and become discouraged.

The psalmist offers hope when he tells us the Lord will complete things that concern us. We are the work of His hands and He has enduring mercy toward our failures. He is as active in our sanctification as He is in our salvation. Philippians 1:6 (NKJV) says, "Being confident of this very thing, that He who has begun a good work in you will complete it until the day of Jesus Christ." The power to change or to see difficult things through to the end comes from the Lord who promises to complete the work He begins.

Lord, remind me of this word when I am discouraged by my lack of progress. Help me remember Your eternal love and mercy to me. Give me confidence that You will complete me.

Living a Complete Life

It is a good thing to receive wealth from
God and the good health to enjoy it.
ECCLESIASTES 5:19 NLT

You've probably heard the term "workaholic," but you may be surprised to find that people really can work themselves to death. The Japanese word *karoshi* is translated literally as "death from overwork," or occupational sudden death. The major medical causes of karoshi deaths are heart attack and stroke due to stress.

It's vital to find a balance in your life between hard work and rest. While you need to earn a living to provide finances to meet your needs, you also want to listen to your physical, mental, emotional, and spiritual needs as well.

God has promised to supply all your needs, but it takes action on your part. Seeking wisdom for your situation and asking God to direct you in the right decisions will help you find a well-balanced life that will produce success, coupled with the health to enjoy it. It may be as simple as realizing a vacation is exactly what you need, instead of working throughout the year and taking your vacation in cash to pay for new bedroom furniture.

Know when to press forward and when to stop and enjoy the life God has given you for His good pleasure—and yours!

Lord, I ask for Your wisdom to help me balance my
life so I can be complete in every area of my life. Amen.

A Thankful Heart

*Let them give thanks to the Lord for his
unfailing love and his wonderful deeds for men.*
PSALM 107:8 NIV

Every day is a day to be thankful for all God has given us: family, friends, home, jobs, and country. Are you having trouble counting your blessings in this season of your life? Remember we serve a God who promises to work all things together for our good (Romans 8:28).

If you are going through a hard time right now, you can be thankful that God uses everything in our life—the good and the bad—to make us more like Him. How can you cultivate a thankful heart? Start each day by thanking God for His blessings. As you drive to work, thank Him for a car that runs. Thank Him for a healthy body as you work out, thank Him for food to eat as you prepare a meal. Be mindful that the Lord is always with you and listening, and thank Him often throughout each day.

Do you have a thankful heart? If not, focus on who God is and all that He has done for you. Praise Him and He will fill your heart with thankfulness.

*Heavenly Father, thank You for all that You are
and all of the blessings You have given me. Please fill
my heart with thanksgiving today and every day. Amen.*

Faith and Action

And I keep praying that this faith we hold in common keeps showing up in the good things we do, and that people recognize Christ in all of it.

PHILEMON 1:6 MSG

Philemon owned a runaway slave named Onesimus. After his escape, Onesimus met Paul and received the gospel of Christ. Upon his conversion, Paul sent Onesimus back to Philemon with a letter that urged Philemon to exercise forgiveness and love toward his slave. Paul realized that only through the generosity of his faith could Philemon accept Onesimus back as a brother, not just as a slave.

Paul was aware that Philemon would experience conflicting emotions when Onesimus returned. He would be angry that Onesimus ran away, and his initial reaction might be to punish him. But as a generous and loving Christian, Philemon would wish to welcome Onesimus back as a brother in Christ. Paul recognized that Philemon's reaction was crucial; if Philemon chose anger over love, he might jeopardize Onesimus' understanding of his new faith.

Our actions and reactions are a powerful gauge of how serious we are about our faith. When others wrong us, do we refuse to forgive, and risk misrepresenting Christ, or do we freely offer forgiveness as an expression of our faith? God calls us to faith and forgiveness in Christ Jesus.

Dear Lord, please let me remember that people look to me for a glimpse of You. Let my actions always reflect my faith in You. Amen.

....

....

....

....

....

....

....

More Than Conquerors

*Nay, in all these things we are more
than conquerors through him that loved us.*
ROMANS 8:37 KJV

Daria glanced around her apartment and cringed. It had been a stressful day at work, and she longed to brew a cup of tea and sink into a bubble bath. Reality struck as she saw the dishes in the sink and the clutter on her table. She knew also that her accounting book and notes awaited her attention if she wished to do well on tomorrow's exam.

I am never going to survive this, Daria thought as tears of frustration came to her eyes. She was so exhausted she couldn't help the feelings.

Instead of diving immediately into her tasks, Daria collapsed onto the couch. She picked up her Bible and flipped to the ribbon marker.

"We are more than conquerors through him that loved us," she read. *Yes, I know God loves me,* Daria thought. *Through His strength I will conquer this year.*

Daria knew she couldn't snap her fingers to get the dishes done. She couldn't sleep with her accounting book and hope that osmosis would help her prepare for the test. But she could trust God, who would give her the energy and clarity of mind to accomplish all that must be done.

Dear Jesus, sometimes the sheer volume of my workload overwhelms me. Help me not to give up. Instead, help me remember that through You I can conquer this.

....

....

....

....

....

....

....

....

Who's on the Throne?

When Jesus heard this, he said to him, "You still lack one thing.
Sell everything you have and give to the poor, and you will
have treasure in heaven. Then come, follow me."
LUKE 18:22 NIV

When the rich young ruler approached Jesus, he was sure he'd covered all the bases. The young man knew the law and had followed it to the letter since he was a boy. However, Jesus threw him a curveball.

"All this stuff you love," Jesus said, "get rid of it. Then follow me." Jesus' candid answer made the young man very sad because he had great wealth. This man had it all. He'd arrived. He was, perhaps, at the pinnacle of his career. Who was Jesus to ask him to give it all away?

The rich young ruler was devastated because his stuff was more important than following Jesus. Scripture tells us that anything in our lives that we put in place of Christ is idolatry. We are far too easily pleased by wealth, material success, fame—the things that many people value and envy in others.

Is there anything in your life that is taking the place of Jesus? What is He asking you to give up? The cost of following Him is high—perhaps too high for some—but the rewards are eternal and far too wonderful for words.

Father, help me to put You first, before
everything I have and everything I do. Amen.

....
....
....
....
....
....
....
....

Holding the Line

When I said, "My foot is slipping," your love, O Lord, supported me.
When anxiety was great within me, your consolation brought joy to my soul.
PSALM 94:18–19 NIV

Lightning began streaking across the sky as the mountain climber hung from the rope, desperately trying to rappel down a sheer bluff she had climbed. The wet, slick rock made for tricky footing. Her heart pounded as her white-knuckled hands gripped the lifeline that attached her to safety. Her only comfort was knowing her experienced guide secured the end of that long rope. Even if she did slip, she'd only fall a few inches before the guide would snap the rope tight, keeping her safely suspended to continue the journey down.

Often we may feel that our feet are slipping in life. Anxiety becomes a sleep-robber, headache-giver, and joy-squelcher. All we can think is, *Just get me out of here!* But we must remember who is anchoring our life. God's powerful grip secures us—even in the most difficult times. He comforts us with His loving presence that defies understanding. He provides wisdom to guide our steps through life's toughest challenges. We can rest assured that His support is steady, reliable, and motivated by His love for us.

Jesus, my Rock and Fortress, thank You that Your strength is made available to me. Steady me with Your love. Replace my anxiety with peace and joy, reflecting a life that's secured by the Almighty. Amen.

A Heart That Sings

I will sing of your strength, in the morning I will sing of your love;
for you are my fortress, my refuge in times of trouble. . . .
I sing praise to you. . .my loving God.
PSALM 59:16–17 NIV

Talk about trouble—David had a lion's share of it! Day in and day out, year after year, fueled by a king's jealousy, David was a wanted man: homeless, on the run, and accompanied by a bunch of lowlifes. Yet, amazingly, in Psalms we see that David's crying out to God turns into joyful music or praise. What an example he sets for us!

You, too, can be that real with God by telling Him your heart's burdens. Vent your hurts, disappointments, and struggles to Him. He can handle it. David didn't try to sound spiritual. He was genuine before the Lord. Once he cleared the air, his heart turned to thanksgiving and praise. He'd bring out the instruments, write a song or two, and regain his strength.

Playing God-focused music and joining in a song of praise can become a spirit booster. Humming along can help refocus a grumbling heart and brighten a dull day. Keep songs of praise and worship handy to maintain a cheerful heart.

Mighty Father, thank You for the wonder of music.
Help me to sing Your praises, to sing of Your
strength and love daily, for You are my refuge. Amen.

Shop Till You Drop!

She is energetic and strong, a hard worker.
She makes sure her dealings are profitable.
PROVERBS 31:17–18 NLT

Here's some great news for shoppers. Shopping is good for our health!

Shopping makes most women feel good. It's a mood booster because of a chemical in the body called dopamine. Dopamine has numerous roles, not the least of which includes feelings of pleasure. Just the anticipation of a good experience (like heading for that super sale at the mall) can cause a surge of dopamine.

Some researchers theorize that shopping has other benefits. The physical exercise of walking—and carrying bags full of bargains—has its reward in building strength and toning muscle. Top that off with doing all that mental calculating and price comparison. The result? A feeling of accomplishment for the shopper: full bags and a fully charged brain.

The Proverbs 31 woman possesses many qualities that some women feel they lack. Many of us have our hands full trying to juggle housework, a job outside the home, and post-graduate classes. We'd never think of tackling sewing or gardening—even if we owned a sewing machine and a plot of earth! But God looks to delight us where we are. He doesn't overlook the woman who works hard. God commends the woman who desires to do the best for herself and her family—including being a consummate bargain hunter.

Thank You, Lord, that You reward me for hard
work through the simple pleasures of life. Amen.

....

....

....

....

....

....

....

Unshakable Love

"For even if the mountains walk away and the hills fall to pieces,
my love won't walk away from you, my covenant commitment
of peace won't fall apart." The God who has compassion on you says so.
ISAIAH 54:10 MSG

We live in a scary world. Anxiety and fear can easily cloud our view of God and distort our perspective. If we're not careful, we can dissolve into frightened, anxious women who rarely take risks or initiate new adventures.

However, God doesn't want us to live isolated, dull lives. His Word encourages us to be bold, passionate, and faithful. Yikes, we think. I'm scared to go out in the city at night by myself. How can I venture out in a dangerous world without fear?

The answer is love. All through the scriptures, God assures us of His constant, comprehensive love for us. He promises in Isaiah that even if our world literally caves in, as it has for people who have endured natural disasters, He will never walk away.

Because of His compassion for His frail children, He has a commitment to give us peace. And if we take Him at His word, we will be filled with confidence and inner peace. That kind of peace comes from knowing that we are deeply, eternally cared for—whatever happens.

Lord, thank You for Your love and Your covenant commitment
to peace for me. Help me to take You at Your word.

....
....
....
....
....
....
....
....

Proverbs Wisdom for Life

*My son, if you accept my words and store up my commands within you. . .
then you will understand the fear of the Lord and find the knowledge of God.*
PROVERBS 2:1, 5 NIV

In an age of electronic communication, isn't it a joy to receive a letter in the mail? Letters are especially sweet when they come from someone who loves us. In the Bible, King Solomon wrote a wonderful letter to his sons. We call it the book of Proverbs, but at its core, this little gem is a heartfelt love letter from a father to his sons—not only from Solomon to his sons, but from God to us.

Proverbs contains an abundance of short and sweet sayings as relevant to us now as they were to Solomon's sons centuries ago. The wisdom of Proverbs can apply to every area of our lives. It addresses everything from relationships to our finances and our work habits.

"A righteous man is cautious in friendship" Proverbs 12:26 NIV.

"A greedy man brings trouble to his family" Proverbs 15:27 NIV.

"Commit to the Lord whatever you do, and your plans will succeed" Proverbs 16:3 NIV.

These aren't guarantees; they are timeless truths, guidelines for living, ways to increase your chances of success in life—biblical success: righteousness, integrity, honesty, wisdom that's yours for a lifetime.

*Father, thank You for the wisdom
found in the book of Proverbs. Amen.*

Standing Firm

I. . .didn't dodge their insults, faced them as they spit in my face.
And the Master, God, stays right there and helps me, so I'm not disgraced.
Therefore I set my face like flint, confident that I'll never regret this.
My champion is right here. Let's take our stand together!
ISAIAH 50:6–8 MSG

Sarah had faced resistance every step of the way. Regardless of her sacrifice and dedication for many months on the project, she repeatedly met opposition from others. From the beginning, she faced their cutting remarks and hostility. She had understood the challenge of going against the grain and had braced herself, knowing she needed to stand for what was right. But she was worn thin—frayed and tattered. A soul can only take so much on its own.

Isaiah reminds us that we are not alone in our battles—even when everyone is against us and we feel outnumbered and outmaneuvered. But remember, your champion, God, is right there, saying, *"I am not leaving you! We are sticking this out together. You can put your chin up confidently, knowing that I, the Sustainer, am on your side. Let's take our stand together!"*

Lord, boldly stand beside me. May the strength of Your arms gird me as I take a stand for You. Lift my chin today; give me confidence to face opposition, knowing You are right there with me. Amen.

Profitable Things in Life

For bodily exercise profiteth little: but godliness is profitable unto all things,
having promise of the life that now is, and of that which is to come.
1 TIMOTHY 4:8 KJV

Katrina wiped the sweat from her forehead and headed for the shower. As she passed her mirror she glanced at the reminder she had taped in the corner.

"Remember: physical exercise is good, but godliness is even better, and its effects are longer lasting." She smiled as she thought about the meaning. She'd always been conscientious about her health. She ate and slept properly and tried to exercise right. Physically she felt wonderful. She'd always thought about 1 Corinthians 6:19 and said that because her body was the temple of the Holy Spirit she needed to take care of it. Still, she felt a bit empty inside.

Then she came across 1 Timothy 4:8 and realized she'd missed the point almost completely. She discovered that while caring for her physical health was indeed being a good steward, it was more important to make sure she was spiritually healthy. As she began to feed more on God's Word and to exercise the things she learned, she began to feel satisfied and complete.

O Lord, I know I must take care of myself both physically and spiritually. Help me make sure my priorities are in the right order.

Perfect Peace

*You will keep in perfect peace him whose
mind is steadfast, because he trusts in you.*

ISAIAH 26:3 NIV

Peace: that inner sense that all is well, the calm assurance all is under control. The canvas of peace depicts a glassy sea and clear, blue skies.

Peace is something we all desire, yet few obtain. Why? We mistakenly think a different life scenario will quiet our hearts. But perfect peace is not contingent upon perfect circumstances. In fact, many times just the opposite is true. Perfect peace can be experienced in the most terrifying storms of life. How is that possible?

Perfect peace can only be found in the Prince of Peace, Jesus. He imparts peace to our souls. Regardless of the circumstances, when we completely surrender ourselves to the Lord, we experience His peace. It is unexplainable. It passes all understanding. The Lord has all things under control even when we lack spiritual eyes to see that truth. Faith enables us to believe that all is well even when our emotions scream the opposite.

Is your spirit at peace or is it stirred up? Jesus calmed the storm while in a boat with His terrified disciples. The Prince of Peace can calm the raging waters in your soul. Trustfully turn to Him. Receive His peace. He will bring you safely through.

Dear Lord, help me trust You regardless of my circumstances. Impart Your peace to my heart and give me the assurance that all is well. Amen.

Whispers of Deceit

Throw off your old sinful nature and your former way of life, which is corrupted by lust and deception. Instead, let the Spirit renew your thoughts and attitudes. Put on your new nature, created to be like God—truly righteous and holy.

EPHESIANS 4:22–24 NLT

Everywhere Marcia turns, she sees signs that she isn't good enough. "I'm less of a person because I'm overweight." "I'd feel better about myself if I had stylish clothes and I ditched this old clunker car."

The world's lies pull her away from God, sucking life out of her spiritual walk. The lies aren't always blatant. Most are subtle, cunning, and shrewd—lies of deception.

In Christ, we have a new mind-set—fresh thinking. We know we are loved and treasured. The very God who spoke the universe into existence loved us enough to leave heaven and live in this imperfect world so He could save us from eternity in the hell we so deserved. Talk about significance! The delusions of this world fall away in light of who He is and what He has done for love of us. Our daily intake of His Word secures us in those truths. The lies of the evil one become ineffective.

Christ, rid me of my old way of thinking. Put the new mind-set within me to see daily the lies I fall for. Help me to walk in rightness and holiness, reflecting You in all I am. Amen.

Learning to Trust

*"If we are thrown into the blazing furnace, the God we serve is able to
save us from it, and he will rescue us from your hand, O king. But even
if he does not, we want you to know, O king, that we will not serve your gods."*
DANIEL 3:17–18 NIV

The third chapter of Daniel tells a powerful story of Shadrach, Meshach, and Abednego, who refused to compromise their faith. Confident in their God, they make it clear that their beliefs do not depend upon Him saving their lives. Rather than setting up a provisional contract—"If God saves us, then we will not worship the idol"—the three men stand against the king regardless of the outcome.

Like these faithful men, we often cannot know that God will provide a way out of a trying situation. Cultural and worldly idols tempt us to forfeit our allegiance to an intangible Being and to instead put our faith in the tangible here-and-now.

This passage offers a challenge: to trust God unconditionally, whether He chooses to extend a rescuing hand or to remain silent. We cannot know the future or know what plan will best serve His greater purpose. We do know, however, that He is sovereign and that He calls us to trust Him. And He is pleased with that trust.

*Dear God, remind me of Your power and Your nearness.
Teach me to more fully trust You and Your plan for my life.
May I refuse to bow to the lesser gods of this world and
instead place my faith in You. Amen.*

Premier Place

My heart is steadfast, O God; I will sing and make music with all my soul.
Better is one day in your courts than a thousand elsewhere.
PSALM 108:1, 84:10 NIV

Goose bumps surface and tears pool in Paige's eyes. She watches the artistry of worship in song through sign language by a handful of ladies at the conference. She is beckoned into God's presence by witnessing their glorious expression of praise and adoration. There's an abandonment of self-consciousness, a freedom to experience the intangible presence of God unashamedly as they gesture. Their faces are aglow, uplifted, and exuberant. They are silently making music with all their souls. There is no other place they would rather be.

Your worship might not be as outwardly expressive, but just as desirable a place to be—in His presence. There is no better way to spend your time, no better place to be than connecting soul to soul with your Creator. Whether corporately or alone, whether through song, instrument, dance, prayer, artwork, written word—His presence energizes, strengthens, and restores our hearts. It brings joy, peace, and a feeling of completeness and contentedness. Why wouldn't we want to stay there? The psalmist knew this from experience. Do you?

Heavenly Father, I praise You as the Creator of all and realize that You created me to worship You. I want to experience Your presence today. Help me to connect soul to soul with You in a way that expresses my gratitude and awe of who You are. Amen.

Faithfulness and Obedience

*"O Lord, God of Israel, there is no God like you in all of
heaven and earth. You keep your covenant and show unfailing
love to all who walk before you in wholehearted devotion."*
2 CHRONICLES 6:14 NLT

Have you ever felt the panic that comes from overcommitting yourself? King Solomon and the Israelites found themselves in a similar situation. As they gathered together, God gave them detailed plans for building the temple. They must have felt seriously overcommitted.

After seven years of hard work, thousands of workmen, and unfathomable amounts of money, Solomon finally completed the temple. The priests carried the Ark of the Lord's Covenant into the inner room of the sanctuary, and suddenly, the presence of God appeared in the form of a cloud. The people were overjoyed, and Solomon led them in this prayer of thanksgiving and praise.

Sometimes, as God's people, we can be overwhelmed by the requests God makes of us. We may not be expected to build a temple, but God certainly asks us to obey Him in other ways. Thankfully, when we feel overcome with panic, we can rely on God's loving faithfulness to see us through our challenges. We simply must acknowledge God's power and eagerly obey His will.

*Dear Lord, truly You are the one, true God in all creation.
Thank You for Your faithfulness and unfailing love.
Teach me to eagerly obey Your will. Amen.*

Object of Faith

And as Moses lifted up the serpent in the wilderness,
even so must the Son of Man be lifted up, that whoever
believes in Him should not perish but have eternal life.

JOHN 3:14–15 NKJV

In Numbers 21, the children of Israel complained against Moses as he led them through the wilderness. God sent fiery serpents among them and many were bitten and died. The people came to Moses repenting, asking him to pray God would take away the serpents. Moses prayed for the people, but God didn't take away the serpents. Instead, He provided an object of faith, telling Moses to make a serpent and set it on a pole. Whenever someone was bitten, he was to look at the serpent and he would live.

When Nicodemus inquires of Jesus how a man receives eternal life, Jesus recalls this Old Testament image. Knowing He would be lifted up on a cross, the Lord Jesus points Nicodemus and us to faith in Him alone. We must repent of our sin and believe in the Son of God who died on the cross. Sin and its consequences are around us like serpents, but into the midst of our fallen world God has sent Jesus to save us. He is the object of our faith. The crucified and resurrected Christ is the answer. He is the truth, the way, and the life.

Father, fix my gaze on Your Son lifted up for me.

Continual Witness

And daily in the temple, and in every house,
they ceased not to teach and preach Jesus Christ.
ACTS 5:42 KJV

"Have a nice day," the cashier said, smiling at Autumn.

"Thank you—have a blessed day," Autumn replied. "Here, I'd like to give you something to read." She handed the woman a gospel tract and gathered her bags. Later, as she babysat her niece, she shared with the child God's glorious gift of salvation. The girl was young, but she could see that her aunt was sincere in the message she shared, and its truths began to sink in, so that one day in the not-so-distant future she would also accept Christ as Savior.

Autumn was so excited about her relationship with God and about how He had cleaned up her sinful life. She took His command to spread the gospel very seriously. She shared it at every opportunity God gave her, and she always prayed for those to whom she had witnessed. She never learned how many people she had reached, but she knew God would do His part by giving the increase.

How about you? How serious are you about sharing the Good News? It's a commitment we all need to make.

Wonderful Savior, it's a great gift You've given me.
How can I help but share it with others?

The Peace of Christ

"Peace I leave with you; my peace I give you. I do not give to you as the world gives.
Do not let your hearts be troubled and do not be afraid."
JOHN 14:27 NIV

Many people believe peace means nothing is going wrong in their life. But the Bible tells us peace is more than that.

Only Jesus can offer real peace. The true peace of Christ means experiencing a deep knowledge that no matter what happens or what goes wrong in your world, God is still in control. This is the type of peace that transcends all understanding.

Philippians 4:7 says this peace will guard our hearts and minds in Christ Jesus. We don't have to be afraid, and we don't have to worry. This verse tells us Jesus doesn't give to us as the world gives to us. When we receive something from someone here on earth, the gift usually doesn't last for long and it sometimes has strings attached. The Lord's gift of peace is eternal and available to all of us who call Him our Savior.

Ask the Lord for His presence during your times of trouble, and He will be faithful to you. He will comfort you and give you a peace that goes beyond anything you can understand.

Dear Jesus, thank You for leaving me Your peace that passes understanding. Help me not to be afraid in times of trouble, but to remember that You are always with me. Amen.

What's Your Fragrance?

*But thank God! He has made us his captives and continues to lead
us along in Christ's triumphal procession. Now he uses us to spread the
knowledge of Christ everywhere, like a sweet perfume. Our lives
are a Christ-like fragrance rising up to God.*
2 CORINTHIANS 2:14–15 NLT

It has been said the average human being can detect up to 10,000 different odors. Smells can evoke powerful images—the smell of mothballs can take us right back to when we were eight years old playing in Grandma's attic. The scent of pine can transport us to the ski vacation we took in college with friends.

As followers of Christ we have been given a unique fragrance. And whether we intend it to or not, our very presence in the lives of others always leaves a lingering scent. When we are kind to someone who doesn't deserve it, it smells wonderful. When we help a person in need, the fragrance lingers long after we've gone. Paul says regardless of what we do, our fragrance should always remind people of Christ.

As you go about your business today, what kind of fragrance will you take with you? Pause for a moment to ask God to help you be a sweet representative of Christ, leaving His delightful aroma lingering in the air behind you.

*Father, help me to touch, in some small way,
each person I meet today. Help me to leave
behind a fragrance that reminds them of Christ.*

....

....

....

....

....

....

....

Beauty Within

"Come now, let us reason together," says the Lord.
"Though your sins are like scarlet, they shall be as white as snow."
ISAIAH 1:18 NIV

Freshly fallen snow is a beautiful white blanket that covers the imperfections on the ground beneath it. But the truth is that snow is full of impurities. That flawless, white snow is made of dirty, cloud-formed particles that fall to earth. Still, those impure particles—the cloud's very rejects—form something pleasing and beautiful to the eye.

We, as children of God, are just like the snow. We are sinful rejects, dirty and of no good purpose on our own. But with the simple touch of God, we became as white as snow. We blanket the world around us with His beauty. Although we are sinners who fail, He looks at us the way we look at glistening snow—as a sign of awe and beauty. He doesn't see our impurities; He sees us perfectly clean.

Jesus, I know I am a sinner. Thank You for Your forgiveness that cleanses and purifies me so that I am pure and white as snow in Your eyes. Amen.

Spiritual Food

Meanwhile, the disciples were urging Jesus, "Rabbi, eat something."
But Jesus replied, "I have a kind of food you know nothing about."
"Did someone bring him food while we were gone?" the disciples asked
each other. Then Jesus explained: "My nourishment comes from
doing the will of God, who sent me, and from finishing his work."
JOHN 4:31–34 NLT

Jesus' purpose on earth was to do God's will. He walked on earth and willingly gave up His life to bring men and women into His heavenly kingdom.

Jesus' disciples were often confused and had difficulty comprehending the meaning behind His words. That's because Jesus emphasized spiritual reality, while they focused on the physical realm. He spoke of establishing a kingdom, and the disciples expected an earthly one. He met physical needs in order to convey spiritual truth.

Like the disciples, we also struggle to focus on spiritual reality. We try to satisfy our souls with physical substitutes. We crave nourishment to alleviate the gnawing hunger in our souls. Attempting to fill the void, we overeat, accumulate possessions, watch TV, or pursue pleasure. Yet we remain unsatisfied.

Try nourishing your soul with spiritual food. Draw close to God. Read His Word. Let Him speak to your heart. Seek to be in the center of God's will. Then you will be nourished, your soul will be satisfied, and your cup will overflow.

Dear Lord, bring nourishment to my soul by
helping me live in the center of Your will. Amen.

What Real Religion Is

Real religion, the kind that passes muster before God the Father,
is this: Reach out to the homeless and loveless in their plight,
and guard against corruption from the godless world.

JAMES 1:27 MSG

When Marjorie moved to a new town, she felt lonely—especially during the holidays. With her family far away, she longed to find someone—or something—to occupy her time during the Thanksgiving and Christmas seasons.

When she found a church to call home, Marjorie heard about their soup kitchen ministry and decided to volunteer. Along with several other people from the congregation, Marjorie prepared and served more than 200 meals to homeless and needy folks on Thanksgiving Day.

At first, Marjorie was nervous. But the camaraderie in the kitchen, the grateful faces of the people she served, and the joy in her heart as she served calmed her. In fact, she later signed up to volunteer weekly in the ministry. And instead of spending Christmas longing for her family, Marjorie decided to go back to the soup kitchen.

On Thanksgiving night, Marjorie's devotional reading centered on the passage in James 1 that talks about pure religion, the kind that reaches out to the homeless and lonely. She went to sleep with a smile on her face, feeling God's pleasure and His confirmation that she had honored Him.

Father God, forgive me for taking so much for granted.
May I honor You and act upon the blessings You've
given me by giving myself away to those in need.

Never Forgotten

The Lord will keep you from all harm—he will watch over your life;
the Lord will watch over your coming and going both now and forevermore.
PSALM 121:7–8 NIV

When we sit in a worship service or read the Bible in private study, it is easy to think about God. But often in the activity of our day, we forget about Him. Though His presence is always with us, we are unaware of it. We move through our days sometimes without a single thought of God, yet our heavenly Father never forgets about us. He cannot; we are His children, belonging to Him through Christ.

Our lives are like an ancient city contained within walls. In an ancient city, the gatekeeper's job was to make decisions about what went in and out of the city. God is the gatekeeper of our lives. He is always watching, always guarding, and ever vigilant in His care of us, even when we are least aware that He is doing so.

Proverbs 2:8 (NKJV) says, "He guards the paths of justice, and preserves the way of His saints." By sending His Son to save us and His Spirit to dwell in us, He has assured us that we are never forgotten and never alone.

Forgive me, Father, for how often I forget about You.
Help me remember that You are guarding and preserving
me and that nothing comes into my life without Your permission.

Live Forward

"In righteousness you will be established; you will be far from oppression,
for you will not fear; and from terror, for it will not come near you."
ISAIAH 54:14 NASB

Living in fear of your past mistakes is much like living in prison. Maybe you spend each day held captive by fear that someone will find out about your old life and the mistakes you made, or perhaps you are afraid you might succumb to the temptation of falling back into old habits.

Jesus came to offer you freedom from your old life—transforming it into something brand new. Through the gift of salvation, He has forgiven you, broken the chains of bondage, and given you a fresh start. While you and old friends may still carry the memories of past mistakes, these sins are not only forgiven but forever forgotten by the One who loves you most.

It's time to live forward. When you turn your face toward Him, you are no longer to look behind at where you used to be, but instead focus on the future He has planned just for you. Refuse to look back at what was, and embrace Jesus and the future He wants you to have. Start today.

Lord, thank You for forgiving me for my past mistakes.
Help me to forgive myself and let go of who I was so
I can become who You created me to be. Amen.

....
....
....
....
....
....
....
....
....

Skinnier Times

Keep your lives free from the love of money and be content with what you have,
because God has said, "Never will I leave you; never will I forsake you."
HEBREWS 13:5 NIV

It can seem like God has left, when you are bone-weary, working for meager earnings, giving all you've got, and the creditors are banging at the doors of your deficit account. You ask, "Where are you, God? You want me to be content? Look at everyone else. They drive their shiny new cars to get their nails done and fuss about mall crowds while buying their fancy designer purses. I just need to find time to get to Wal-Mart to catch the toilet paper sale!"

Life's richest lessons come from our hard times. It is there that we are stripped of our self-sufficiency. We can see life from a perspective we miss in cushy-comfort times when we feel less of a need to come to God in prayer. When we have need, we cry out to Him. In those times, He becomes our sufficiency, and we learn His resources are inexhaustible. His presence and comfort are irreplaceable. These lessons from skinnier times deepen our walk with Christ, bringing more contentment for what we have.

God, You've promised to never leave or forsake me. Help me to remember that in the sparse times You are there with me. I can be content because it all flows from Your hand. Amen.

Remember

*I am the Lord your God, who brought you
out of Egypt, out of the land of slavery.*
EXODUS 20:2 NIV

Just before God gave the Israelites the Ten Commandments, He reminded them that He had brought them out of slavery in Egypt. It is easy for us to read this verse and wonder why the Israelites needed reminding. After years and years of harsh treatment and manual labor in Egypt, wouldn't they always be grateful to the Lord for delivering them from slavery?

The truth is, we also forget. We forget the way God has provided in the past. We hit a trial in life and worry ourselves sick, not stopping to reflect on all the trials our Father has already brought us through.

Establish for yourself some reminders of God's blessings. Start a prayer journal where you can record your prayer requests and God's answers. Review the pages of your prayer journal when you face a hardship. Thank God for taking care of you in the past and ask Him to increase your faith. He wants you to trust that He will never leave you or forsake you.

Like the Israelites, we forget. God is faithful in all ways for all days. Remember that today. Think back to a time when you could not imagine a way out and God provided one.

You are faithful, Father. You have freed me from the gates of hell and given me an abundant life with the promise of eternity with You. Grow my faith. Help me to remember. Amen.

Dumped

"I have chosen you and have not rejected you."
ISAIAH 41:9 NIV

Children feel the stinging pain of rejection. Teens, according to experts, fear rejection by their peers even more than they fear death. As we go on to adulthood, the threat of being overlooked in the workplace or ignored by colleagues still wields power over us. Those who have been dumped by boyfriends or excluded by a girlfriend know what it's like to be put aside like garbage set out for trash pick-up.

Jesus knew full well what it was like to be rejected. Even the Old Testament foretold He would be "rejected by men" (Isaiah 53:3 NIV). Christ told His disciples He wasn't what the religious leaders wanted or thought He should be. As a result, He would be "rejected by the elders, chief priests and teachers of the law" (Luke 9:22 NIV). The Lord doesn't dump us when we don't measure up. And He doesn't choose us one minute only to reject us a week later. We need not fear being deserted by our loving Father. He doesn't accept or reject us based on any arbitrary standards. He loves us with an everlasting love (Jeremiah 31:3). By His own mercy and design, "he hath made us accepted in the beloved" (Ephesians 1:6 KJV).

Father, thank You that I don't need to fear Your rejection of me. Amen.

Straight Paths

Trust in the Lord with all your heart and lean not on your own understanding;
in all your ways acknowledge him, and he will make your paths straight.
PROVERBS 3:5–6 NIV

Our knowledge is limited. As hard as we try to figure things out, our wisdom is finite. We cannot see the future. We cannot grasp how today's events will affect tomorrow. We are not God. If we lean on our own understanding, we will invariably make wrong decisions that lead to dead-end roads.

God rarely reveals what tomorrow has in store. Instead, He chooses to light our path today so that we must trust Him for tomorrow. As we trust Him moment by moment, He shines light on our next step. He enables us to navigate one step at a time as He reveals pitfalls and prevents us from stumbling. His light helps us traverse the steepest mountains and deepest valleys—one step at a time.

Do you feel as though you've been going around and around in circles? Or perhaps you find yourself on a dead-end road. Cry out to Jesus, the Light of the World. He wants to lead you down a wonderful path for your life. Trust Him with all your heart. He will shine His light and show you the way. Acknowledge Him. He will make your paths straight.

Dear Lord, please make my paths straight
as I trust You with all my heart. Amen.

....
....
....
....
....
....
....
....
....

Memory Collector

"Each of you is to take up a stone on his shoulder. . .to serve as a sign among you. . . . These stones are to be a memorial to the people of Israel forever."
JOSHUA 4:5–7 NIV

Shortly after Cassie moved out of her parents' house, her mother presented her with a box. When Cassie opened it, she was surprised to discover a stash of memorabilia from her past. Photos, ticket stubs, ribbons, dried flowers; each held special significance to Cassie during her school years. Memories of people and events long forgotten came flooding back to her as she picked up each cherished item.

We often save items from special events as a way of preserving priceless memories. This is also an important biblical concept. In fact, God instructed the Israelites to do the same thing to remember His faithfulness to them.

Just as the Israelites built altars as a way of remembering God's provision and deliverance, we can do the same. Has God blessed you through a word of encouragement from a friend, a special provision in a time of need, or just the right scripture verse at just the right time? Consider finding a tangible way to remember these blessings. Make a treasure box for your spiritual milestones, just as you do for your physical milestones. Keeping these memories fresh is one way to find encouragement during times when we need it most.

Father, help me to look for tangible ways to remember Your faithfulness to me. Amen.

Merry Christmas!

"She will give birth to a son, and you are to give him the name Jesus, because he will save his people from their sins."
MATTHEW 1:21 NIV

The month of December is a wonderful time of year. It seems the whole world catches the Christmas spirit. Houses are decorated, trees are put up, and stores display aisles and aisles of holiday wares. Gifts are wrapped, cookies are baked, and Christmas cards are sent all over the world.

In the busyness of the holiday season, don't forget the true reason that we celebrate: God became man and lived among us so that He could save us from our sins. As you enjoy your holiday festivities and traditions, ask the Lord to show you ways you can hold the true meaning of Christmas in your heart and share that with everyone you come in contact with. Is there someone you know who has a need you can meet? Is there a lonely elderly person you can bless? Pray for ways to meet the needs around you and focus on why Jesus came to earth: to save all people from their sins.

Dear Jesus, happy birthday! Thank You for coming to save me from my sins and to save the world. Show me how I can share this great message of salvation with those around me. Amen.

Ponder the Acts of God

But Mary treasured up all these things
and pondered them in her heart.
LUKE 2:19 NIV

Mary was someone who pondered—are you?

The night Jesus was born, an angel appeared in the night sky and told the shepherds of the Savior's birth and where they could find Him. The shepherds hurried off to Bethlehem and found the baby Jesus lying in a manger. They worshipped Him, and then they began to spread the word about what the angel had said. The Gospel of Luke tells us everyone was amazed at the shepherds' message about the child. Luke also records that Mary treasured these things up and pondered them.

Mary was a thinker. She pondered the things she saw and heard at Jesus' birth. She knew He was a special child. She had never been sexually active, and yet she became pregnant with this baby. She believed God and submitted to His plan for her life, however absurd it must have seemed at the time.

As God reveals Himself to you, whether in big or small ways, ponder His presence in your life. Treasure up the acts of God that take place in and around you. Ponder them.

God, slow my pace. Carve out time in my hurried days for me to meditate on Your work in my life. Let me recognize Your hand in my life and never simply dismiss Your acts as happenstance.

Holding on to Hope

"In this world you will have trouble.
But take heart! I have overcome the world."
JOHN 16:33 NIV

Images on television sometimes convince us that evil triumphs over good. War. Hunger. Poverty. Domestic disputes. Random acts of violence. Drugs. The list goes on and on.

Seeing the world's brokenness can leave us discouraged. And we Christians do not find ourselves immune from that brokenness. Divorce, racism, and greed pervade our congregations as they do our communities. Some days it is hard to see the difference between how the world lives and how we live: in fear.

This should not be. Christ tells us to hold on to the hope we have in Him. He tells us to "take heart" because the evil has already been conquered, and He has already overcome the world. Do you live your life as though you trusted His words, or do you live in doubt?

Live your life as a statement of hope, not despair. Live like the victor, not the victim. Live with your eye on eternity, not the here and now. Daily remind yourself that you serve a powerful and gracious God, and decide to be used by Him to act as a messenger of grace and healing to the world's brokenness.

Lord, forgive me for growing discouraged and not placing
my full trust in You. May I learn to trust You better
and to live my life as a statement of hope.

Black and White

"Stop sinning and do what is right."
DANIEL 4:27 NLT

Differences in biblical interpretation have led to countless debates and church splits, not to mention the devastating effect they can have on our faith. At times it seems that attending church, reading our Bibles, and discussing issues with other Christians lead to more questions than answers. As we delve further into our studies, issues we once saw in black and white sometimes begin to turn murky shades of gray.

Daniel lived in a pagan land, full of temptation and threats to conform to the beliefs and practices of the Babylonians. He also saw and interpreted visions that were both bewildering and terrifying. But instead of succumbing to the confusion of these pressures and dreams, Daniel trusted in God and therefore was able to remain steadfast in his faith. Daniel still saw God's commands in black and white and delivered them as such to the king.

As Christians who struggle with issues that appear in shades of gray, we must remember Daniel's words. God's commands still give us clarity today: love God, love one another, stop sinning, and do what is right. We simply must look to God as Daniel did and trust in His words for guidance.

Dear Lord, thank You for Your Word. Please help me to resist the temptations of this world and to trust in You and Your Word for guidance. Amen.

Waiting with Joy

It is good to wait quietly for the salvation of the Lord.
LAMENTATIONS 3:26 NIV

Melissa sits by the phone, waiting for a call from her potential employer. Last week's interview went well, but she is nervous about her prospects. Will the company hire her? Or will she face rejection—again?

We've all waited—or are presently waiting—on a dream to be fulfilled. Some women long for a mate or a baby, while others pine for a dream job.

And while there's nothing wrong with wanting good things from life, we need to strike a balance between hoping for the future and living in the moment. It's difficult to find that middle ground, but it's also imperative if we're to live with joy in our current circumstances.

How do we live fully in the present? God's Word tells us to leave our cares at His feet, trusting that He knows best and will give us what we need when we need it.

Sure, we may have to wait longer than we think is necessary for certain dreams to come true. Still, we can rest in His care for us, confident that He knows us better than we know ourselves, and He is working out a perfect design for our lives.

Lord, forgive me for worrying about my future. I give You my dreams, and I ask for peace and patience as You work out Your plan for me.

Skeptics and Cynics

For ever since the world was created, people have seen the earth and sky.
Through everything God made, they can clearly see his invisible qualities—
his eternal power and divine nature. So they have no excuse for not knowing God.
ROMANS 1:20 NLT

You can see the love of Jesus in the eyes of a newborn baby. You can see the paintbrush of God in the colors of a sunset. It is awe inspiring to look at the handiwork of God and attempt to grasp His majesty and incredible creativity. For a Christian, it's impossible to see His creation and deny His existence.

There are skeptics and cynics, though. They love to question the possibility of a divine Creator. They have seemingly sound arguments based in logic and science. We can share testimonials, blessings, and miracles from our personal lives and from scripture. But these are often met with disbelief and tales of big bangs and evolution.

In order for a skeptic to be changed to a seeker, Jesus must grab his attention, often using His children to do that. Take time to really consider the miraculous works of God that prove His existence. Pray for wisdom and compelling words to lead cynics to the throne.

Father, help me to be a good witness of You and Your
miraculous wonders. Give me the words to convince even
the most hardened skeptic. Guide me to people, according
to Your will, so that I can make a difference. Amen.

Why Did Jesus Come?

*I have come into the world as a light, so that
no one who believes in me should stay in darkness.*

JOHN 12:46 NIV

New Year's Eve: Christmas is over, cookies have been eaten, stores have begun discounting holiday items, and you wonder why people go to all this trouble each year. New Year's Eve can be a depressing time for some, but it doesn't have to be! The lights are still up and a party is about to begin, so ask the Lord to speak to your heart tonight and remind you why we celebrate each year.

God's Word tells us Jesus came into the world as a light. He came to save us and keep us from eternal darkness.

As you ring in the New Year at midnight, remember that Jesus is the Light of the World and He lives inside of you. Seek out those around you who are having a hard time with the close of the year and pray for ways to share Christ's love with them. Be an encouragement to your friends at work and to all those around you.

Ask the Lord to show you how you can be a light in this dark world. God doesn't want anyone to stay in darkness. It is our job to share His light with them!

Dear Jesus, thank You for all the blessings You have given me this past year. Show me how to be a light and a blessing to others. Amen.

Scripture Index

Psalms

Proverbs

NEW TESTAMENT